MEETING THE KILLER OF CONSTABLE GEORGE HOWELL

Ray Matheson

Inspiring Publishers
P.O. Box 159, Calwell, ACT Australia 2905
Email: publishaspg@gmail.com
http://www.inspiringpublishers.com

 A catalogue record for this
book is available from the
NATIONAL LIBRARY OF AUSTRALIA
National Library of Australia

National Library of Australia The Prepublication Data Service

Author: Ray Matheson
Title: Meeting the Killer of Constable George Howell
Genre: Nonfiction

Paperback ISBN: 978-1-923250-14-7
ePub2 ISBN: 978-1-923250-15-4
PDF eBook: 978-1-923250-16-1

Cut off even in the blossoms of my sin – HAMLET

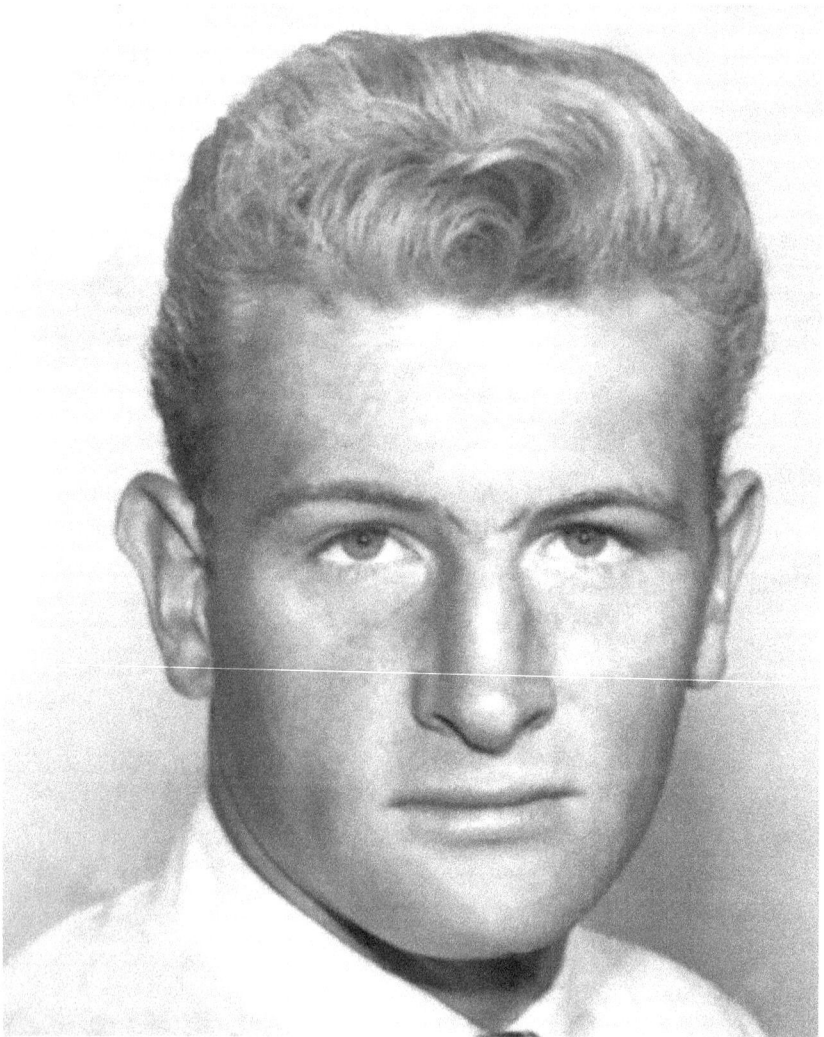

INDEX

1. GOING

They hanged a man in Adelaide on the day that we arrived. They were getting him ready for the drop as we came down the Adelaide hills. We were in a semi-trailer after hitching a ride and our driver told us about the hanging. He went on to say what the man had done.

'He killed those people up north . . . remember?'

Sure, we remembered. His victims were a woman, her daughter and a man, all murdered on a cattle station known as Sundown.

'That's right. So he hangs this morning at 8 o'clock,' and checking his watch he further announced, 'it won't be long now.'

As we made our descent, there was not one cloud in a winter sky and a tepid sun now and then flickered through the eucalypt. Down and down we weaved our way closer and closer to Adelaide. To hold the semi in check, our driver used the brakes and its lower gears. He loved to work those gears. There were fourteen in total and managed by two gear sticks, one on the stalk of the steering wheel and the other erect from the floor. On the approach to each bend, he inched forward on his seat and wedged the steering wheel with his knees. Then he toed the brakes, doubled the clutch and with a wide sweep of his arms slapped both gear sticks down through their gates, simultaneously. The engine responded with a roar that drowned the waves from the radio while he grinned like a fiend. Hand over hand turning the wheel he took us through the bend, then steering with his knees again, he swung his arms like a band leader and raised us into a higher gear. Relieved of its strain the engine gasped and as it adopted a steady drone music from the radio flooded back again.

We couldn't help but like our driver. He talked a lot, laughed a lot and sometimes joined the chorus of a song on the radio. He must have thought we were okay as he offered us drink not once but twice.

'Say, would you boys like another beer?'

'Sure,' we said, like we often took a beer or two before we had our breakfast.

He fished up a king-sized Coopers and levered off its cap under the lip of an ashtray sited on the dash. After taking a few swigs he passed the bottle to me. Life on the road had been kind to us and the going was good in that semi. Sitting in its cabin with a beer and roll your own, listening to Johnny Cash and Co do battle with the engine and watching the rush of bitumen and mile posts sailing by. In the warmth of that cab, amongst a haze of tobacco smoke and whiff of diesel fumes, we felt the pulse of the engine as it surged from grunt to growl. It was first class. Even better than first class. Money couldn't buy a trip half as good as this.

On the way down to Adelaide some of the hills went up and where an incline lay ahead rising from a dip, we hurtled down towards the dip gathering momentum for our upward haul. Through the dip, climbing, and soon as our impetus started to fade came again the famous two-handed change of gear. A magpie standing by the road raised one wing and waved us on. And on we went.

I wondered if we would see the city while we still had height, lying far below and gathered in a cluster, or would we meet an urban fringe without ever catching sight of its centre point. Around each bend, beyond each peak lay more of the same - the road ahead snaking through unmolested bush.

We were close to the city when the hour came. We were watching the road slip underneath the progress we were making when our driver alerted us. With a hand in the air and his eye on his watch he held our intent. 'Wait, wait for it,' and soon as the radio's beeping stopped he slammed his hand down hard onto the steering wheel.

'That's it. He's gone. He's a goner.'

Nobody spoke for a minute or so. There is something about a hanging. The image of a noose, the springing of a trap and a black-hooded body plummeting through it to end its fall with a jerk. That jerk snaps the neck and the man will dangle without a twitch as life seeps slowly from him. Just as the judge decreed, he will hang by the neck until he is dead. The doctor waits half an hour before he tests the pulse, by which time it's a certainty he won't be able to find it.

Those present will have seen a tidy execution. Not like the bad old days when hangings were done in public. Back then the hangman didn't know the rules for weights and measures. A rope too long could decapitate, ripping the head from its shoulders at the end of the fall. Or a rope too short failed to snap the victim's neck. As he kicked and thrashed while slowly choking to death, the crowd raised a shout.

'Pull his leg. Pull his leg. Pull his leg.'

If he continued to writhe while his leg was being pulled, the crowd took up another chant.

'Pull the other one. Pull the other one.'

With both legs being pulled, the victim would be dispatched. Pulling somebody's leg these days is the term for a joke. I was wondering how that came about when a question came from Ron.

'Where do they do the hanging?'

'Where do they do the hanging. I'll tell you where they do the hanging. Adelaide Gaol, that's where. They do the hanging in Adelaide Gaol.'

Who in the world would have thought that before the week was through, Ron and I would be locked inside that same Adelaide Gaol. That we would be in the same yard as where the hanged man had been. Who would have even considered it. We didn't. Nothing was further from our minds.

3

2. ADELAIDE

I was born in Adelaide; it had a claim on me and neither time nor travel could loosen the hold it had. An umbilical cord is cut at birth, but a bond to the birthplace remains intact. It stays secure, it stays strong. People go to war because of where they were born, prepared to kill and be killed. That's how strong the bond is. And it can stretch to great lengths, mine all the way to Melbourne where I was taken when three months old. I had not seen Adelaide since but I knew one day I would go back. The pull to my roots every now and then reared up and gave me another tug. It made me want to get to know the place where I was born. I had a need to know its streets. I wanted to feel a part of it. There was never any doubt, one day I would go back.

One thing I knew about Adelaide was its history. Unlike other cities to the east and west, Adelaide had never been a convict settlement. It was peopled by true pioneers who had to sail for three long months, three oceans and the Bight, before they reached Gulf St Vincent and the river Torrens. Six miles upstream they stepped ashore and cleared the land to make a place where they could build their dream. Word got back of what they found and more ambitious travellers packed their bags and followed on. The British Government was keen to populate the colony. Fares were subsidised. Those willing to relocate could travel cheap. They could live their lives under the sun where the land was free.

One ship after another sailed for the Southern Ocean.

Those early Adelaidians did not face the hardships of other colonies. There were no hangings or floggings, no chain gangs or prison terms; no pardons. Slave labour did not exist. There were no runaways or ticket men. Rules were made for society. Another church had to be built for every new establishment that served alcohol. They meant to keep a balance between their pleasure and their ideals. And they built a lot of churches.

It might have been another Eden in this fair and fertile land. The immigrants came with hope, they came with good intentions. But what they also brought with them were all the human weaknesses. There was drunkenness and theft, adultery and arson, battery and assault, rape and even worse. A stockade was erected to keep wrongdoers off the streets. As the population grew so too did the number of miscreants. The stockade could no longer cope. In 1841 Adelaide Gaol was built. The cost of it almost bankrupted the fledgling colony. The jail was too big, too grand. Stone carved gargoyles were shipped from London to adorn its walls. There were too many yards and too many cells. The job ran over budget and the builders were never fully paid. Its planners were abused. Citizens were up in arms. What were they thinking? What a waste of money. Infrastructure was required. The public wanted the money spent on improved services.

But the planners were right all along. By looking ahead they saw the need to cater for future growth. Even then their estimate fell short of what was required. By 1854, Adelaide Gaol was over-crowded and Yatala Labour Prison also had to be built.

3. ARRIVING

When the time came to quit Melbourne, and that time came with a rush, we had yet to agree on a destination. Ron had a yen for the tropics.

'Let's go to Queensland,' he said. 'Think of it, the sun on your back every day of the year and all that beach for thousands of miles.'

'Sounds good to me,' I said, 'but let's take a look at Adelaide first.'

'Adelaide!' Ron began.

In his opinion Adelaide lay in the wrong direction, and furthermore like Melbourne was still in the grip of winter. He wanted the sun. He wanted to head for the sun. That's what Ron wanted to do. This was my chance to see Adelaide and I was prepared to fight for it. I thought if we went west, we could take in Adelaide and then go north through the red centre. We would pass through the opal fields where everyone lives in caves. See the Alice and Olgas. Then up near the Top End turn east towards Mount Isa. We would get to Queensland just the same and see more of the country as we made our way.

It was a good plan and I put some fervour into proposing it. I expected an argument but Ron conceded right away.

'Alright, alright, keep your hair on. We'll go that way then. But we're not staying long in Adelaide.'

'No, no need. Get a feel of it and move on. About a week should do it.'

So we took the road to Bacchus Marsh and the Grampians beyond, out and away from the big smoke, all our bridges burnt.

We travelled light and by the thumb, nothing but time on our hands. We lingered a while in country towns that we passed through on the way. Big country towns with wide streets lined with veranda posts and small country towns - shop windows full of not much choice and where you had the feeling all days would be the same.

In one small town we had to stop as an old man stood in the middle of the road trying to light his pipe. The car we were in eased to a halt. Our driver sat and waited and watched. The old man hunched over his pipe with knees bent and back arched. One hand shielding his pipe held a box of matches. He couldn't raise much suck and all his puffs were empty. Our driver didn't blast his horn or shout out at him. He didn't even drum his fingers on the steering wheel. I looked at Ron and Ron looked at me, his eyebrows high and arched.

The old man tried another match.

By and by we were signalled by smoke that he was about to make a move. He transported the matches to trouser pocket and slapped his thigh to ensure they were properly housed. Then he began to take his feet to the opposite side of the road. Our driver didn't budge. He watched the old man reach the curb, step over it, mount the path and start to walk along it. Then he crept into action. He looked right and looked left, ran the back of his hand along the underside of his nose, checked the mirror, fumbled the gear stick into a slot, eased off the clutch, tip-toed on the accelerator and we trundled on our way.

We had rides in different makes of cars and trucks of various sizes. We passed through one-horse towns, no-horse towns and some towns just a string of shacks between two signs that named the place. Then out on the open road again where bird life changed to suit terrain. Eagle over hill, emu on the plain, and through the bush magpie and sulphur crested cockatoo. Galahs were out in the open too in uniforms of pink and grey. And once beside us a flying mass of swirling yellow and green. There must have been a hundred or more of budgerigars on the wing. When switching one way they were yellow and switching the other way green. Beside us they dipped and rose, zigged and zagged while shimmering all the time – yellow green – yellow green – yellow green. On rising higher they curved to the left, and zip, they were gone.

We saw sheep and cattle, horses and goats, pigs and kangaroo. An echidna hobbled beside the road humping a load of quills on its back. Mile after mile of grain stubble, hectares of vegetable green, here and there an orchard but mainly the country was grass – grass and dirt dotted with gums. We crossed rivers, creeks and railway lines, bridges big and small and eventually the border into South Australia.

We slept rough that night in a farmer's barn. A cold wind whistled through our sleep and a rooster had us wide awake well ahead of dawn. We were early on the road, the sun still crouching down below a far-off rim of land. We kicked frost from roadside grass and fists jammed in our pockets, jumped up and down, bouncing our heels on and off the surface of the road. Small pin points of light appeared. We watched as they drew closer, grew bigger, became multi-coloured, and a semi-trailer loomed out from a dingy half-light. It was lit up like a Christmas tree. On reaching us it yielded to the hitcher's rule of thumb. We ran to where it stopped, some twenty yards beyond the spot where we hailed it down. Getting a lift in that semi was our break of the day.

As I slid in beside the driver, he asked where we were headed and before I could say a word, Ron, with one leg inside the cab and the other hanging out, said, 'Queensland.'

'Queensland, eh. What part?'

'Surfers Paradise,' Ron said, hauling in his other leg.

'Say, where are you boys from?'

When I told him Melbourne he laughed and said we must be on some kind of a clockwise route. But he could take us through to Adelaide.

'Perfect,' I said.

And it was perfect. We were the company that he sought and he gave us wheels and entertainment. He even furnished us with beer. He took control and steered our talk through different fields of sport. Football had the most mileage in it. After a spell on athletics we returned to kicking a ball. We managed to get him onto bikes - three weeks on the Tour de France and six-day races on the track. We told him we'd seen Sid Patterson ride at the Essendon velodrome and how top sprinters came from Europe to challenge him. Then on a straight stretch of road, our driver swerved, ditched the bikes and steered us back to football. He said he was a Bulldog's fan because he came from Footscray.

At times he joined the chorus of a song on the radio. On hearing the start of Ghost Riders in the Sky, he saddled up with Burl Ives and rode the whole song through. He was really into it, slapping his hip as he galloped along. The miles just fell away. He took us right through to Adelaide and dropped us in its centre. With a wild salute and a blast of his horn he headed for the port, Patsy Cline in his ear and a Benzedrine glint in his eye.

It was a late June day in 1958. The day they hanged Raymond Bailey at the old Adelaide Gaol. That was the day Ron and I lobbed in Adelaide. The city I'd long waited to see. I never did manage to wander through all its city streets. In fact we didn't venture far from Rundell and King William. We didn't cross to the north side of the river Torrens. We didn't see the port or any of its beaches. We didn't take a ride on a bus or tram. We didn't see the railway station, but then we didn't seek it. We didn't see the Town Hall or the GPO. But we saw Police Headquarters and its lock-up too. We saw the courts, both high and low and we saw Adelaide Gaol. We got to see plenty of Adelaide Gaol.

Ron could have had a go at me. I half expected it. He didn't say a word. Not a peep. But I bet he wished we'd gone due north when we set off on our travels.

4. ARRESTED

The police knew where to find me and exactly when to come. They told me what had happened and named all the names. Someone had told them everything. I was last to be seen they said. The arrest was polite and quite professional. Handcuffs were not used. Once in their car the two cops talked as if I wasn't there, and I could tell that they were pleased with themselves. They had wrapped the whole case up in less than twenty-four hours.

At police headquarters, the bigger of the detectives was the one who took my statement. That's what he called it – a statement. If he said confession I would have been more wary. We sat either side of a table in a narrow room, a typewriter placed between us. The cop wound a sheet of foolscap into the machine's roller. He asked me only two questions.

'What's your full name?' and 'How do you spell it?'

Once my name was into print, he continued bashing the keys. He did the rest by himself, requiring no further assistance from me. With index fingers held high he dive-bombed the keys, each strike caused a spindly arm to leap from the machine's belly and smack an inked ribbon against the moving page. A pair of reels slowly turned to keep the ribbon moving and the foolscap was peppered on the move while being dragged along. Clack, clack, clackety clack. At the end of a line a bell rang and the cop grabbed a chrome lever and hurled the carriage sideways. It whizzed along on its rails and crashed into the buffers, whereupon the cop resumed divebombing the keys.

I stared out through the window at an abutting wall, a whole window-full of bricks, rusty red in colour and each brick surrounded by thin lines of mortar. The vertical lines were perfectly plumb on every second course. I could hear the typewriter clacking, the ding of a bell and whir of the carriage whizzing along on its rails. Then silence. The cop was leaning forward, examining the page. A finger tapping his chin. Forehead deeply creased. Then he lunged to turn down the page and resumed bashing the keys. When finished, he reefed the foolscap out of the roller and handed it to me with a pen. If I knew how much trouble I was in I would have refused to sign it.

That's the trouble with trouble – knowing when it is serious.

The room had a door at both ends. It was a room for going through. We went through it. Next came the finger prints. Each finger was rolled onto an inked plate and rolled again into a box on a pre-printed page. From there I faced a camera mounted on three legs. I realised at the camera's flash how I had been done - nailed good and proper. No wonder they get the statement first before the prints and photographs.

Dusk was getting ready to pounce as we left the building. Twenty yards ahead, the lock-up's bars were backlit by a weak internal light. The detective loped along on my left while on my right the cop's short legs stepped busily. A cool breeze had been introduced to the evening air.

Darkness was falling from the sky, killing colour everywhere.

At the lock-up the cop unlocked a gate, pulled it open and stepped aside. Not a word was spoken. As soon as I passed through the gate it clanged shut behind me. Down the passage before me, a row of cell doors were running along its left side. I wasn't too concerned. Things like this had a way of working themselves out. They always had done in the past. Nothing bad had ever happened. And to tell the truth I was curious to see what the lockup was like.

5. LOCKUP

The first cell door lay open. Through it lay a square shaped room with bench seats running around its walls. It might have been a waiting room at a bus or railway station. Men were sprawled on the benches, whereas Huckle and Ron were standing in the middle of the room. Ron welcomed me with a shrug, while Huckle offered a weak grin. After scanning the men on the benches, I said, 'where are Baker and King?'

'They must be somewhere else. King is only sixteen, you know.'

'How would I know? I could hardly see him in the dark.'

'It was him that gave us up.'

'King didn't know where Ron and I lived.'

'He fingered me and Baker and Baker knew where you lived.'

Possible, I let it go. We chatted before we left the cell to take a walk in the corridor. The other cell doors, all empty, were standing open. The last door was a toilet - its door closed. After doing a few lengths, a chill coming through the open bars persuaded us to return to the cell. Our cellmates wore shabby clothes and looked to be either drunks or tramps. Three of them were asleep. We stood rather than sit in spaces between the other occupants. A new arrival at the door attracted our attention. We watched him walk across the cell and sit on the bench. His worried eyes peered out from a narrow pinched face. His three-piece suit fitted him well. I took him to be an accountant caught cooking the books. Yet there was about him an air of innocence.

Maybe half an hour later, the next incomer arrived. The type of guy you'd expect to meet in a police lock-up. His face, his stance, his manner – all shifty. He flicked his eyes around the cell before entering it, and made a bee line for the three piece suit.

'Have you got a spare smoke, Jack?'

Three-piece didn't smoke. He hit on Huckle next.

'Come on Jack, give a man a smoke.'

Ron cut in to say we were short ourselves.

'What about you, Jack. You'll give us one won't cha?'

I offered him my stub, and snatching it he sucked it down to its cork tip. He did a round of the drunks and tramps and then sat down, smokeless.

The blankets came in late. Two cops handed them around. Mine had a frayed hem and cigarette holes were burnt through it. I tried not to think about the blanket's history. As we stood with our blankets draped around us in the manner of capes, a voice boomed from the doorway.

'Who's been naughty boys then?'

The figure marching towards us swung his arms up to shoulder height. His shirt lay open across his chest, one sleeve rolled and the other flapping. On reaching us he declared:

'My name's Bulla.'

We shook his offered hand in turn and introduced ourselves. He had no interest in what we were called.

'I broke the record tonight boys. It took five coppers to bring me in. Five!' and he laughed the laugh of a man who had been but no longer was fighting drunk. A few odd teeth were visible inside his mouth. Though slightly built, the muscle on his upper arm bulged from under the rolled sleeve. The vein running over it was almost pencil thick. A puffiness lay beneath one eye and the raised lump on his forehead looked as if it might throb.

'I landed some good ones on those coppers. They'll be waiting for me when I get out. You can betcha life on that,' and he laughed at the prospect of it.

'Have you got a spare smoke, Jack?'

Bulla turned and said, 'don't call me that.'

'Don't worry about it. That's what I call everyone . . . Jack.'

WHACK. The punch was as quick as a switch blade sprung from the clasp of a knife. It cracked into the man's face and knocked him back on his heels. He tottered but managed to keep his balance. He opened his mouth to say something, then shut it without saying a word and slunk off like a man who really needed a smoke.

Looking down at his hand as it unfolded a fist, Bulla explained, 'I told him not to call me that,'

I realised Jack was too close to Jacky, Joliffe's cartoon aborigine and the butt of every joke. Bulla was Jacky to no man. A point he was keen to establish.

I slept poorly, in trying to keep the blanket clear of my face and the wooden bench was uncomfortable against either hip. The drunks settled down like a litter of pups and slept through the night. I had expected them to snore.

After a breakfast of beans, we were herded into the passage, where Detectives formed two ranks along the corridor. When each man's name was called, he walked between the ranks to the gate and made his return. With eyes narrowed and jutted chins, the cops scanned each passing face. Ford was the name of three-piece suit. As he stepped to the head of the line, one of the cops said:

'Back again. Can't keep away from it can you,' and what the cop said next meant Ford was a homosexual.

When I did my stint, I thought the cops were wasting their time in memorising my face. As soon as we were out of here, Ron and I would be back on the road. Bulla's name was Adrian Rigney. When called he swaggered between the ranks with both hands in his pockets, swaying his shoulders and elbows with every step he took. He kept close to one side and ogled each face on passing it. At the end of the catwalk he paused - one, two, three, and swivelling on the ball of a foot he stepped across to the other rank. On making his return, he took slow deliberate strides, thrusting his face towards each cop on passing him. He left in his wake tightened lips and hard stares. One cop breathed heavily and reddened dangerously. Bulla looked very pleased with himself when he reached the rest of us standing by the toilet.

6. GREEN DOOR

Handcuffed in pairs, we walked from the lock-up to the court. Just a short distance. Ron, Huckle and I were raced through the proceedings, in and out as quick as you like.

'Held on remand,' said the judge. Bail not getting a mention.

There were fewer of us in the Black Maria than in the lock-up overnight. One of the drunks was asleep already. Dead to the world before we set off. During the journey, Bulla lolled in his seat jiggling an outstretched boot. His attempts to whistle were thwarted by an absence of so many teeth. Not that Bulla seemed to mind. Ford the three-piece suit sat with hands between his knees. Huckle stared vacantly and Ron had something on his mind. I felt fine. I thought this would be a short episode and we would soon be back on the road.

The man who called everyone Jack then began to speak.

'They lock the wrong people up, they do. They really do. I shouldn't be here. The idiot who owned the car, he's the one that should be here. I had no intention of taking that car - none. I was on my way to the shops to buy some cigarettes and there was this car, its doors unlocked and key in the ignition. I mean what kind of idiot leaves a car like that. What did fool think would happen? It was begging to be taken that car. So I took it. I was only reacting to human nature. Anyone could have taken that car, anyone. Just my luck it happened to be me. I don't know, I don't know,' and he shook his head from side to side to shake off any further blame.

Adelaide jail sat on the fringe of the city proper. We were there within minutes. The Black Maria stopped and reversed towards a

16

pair of green gates. As we passed between the gates the man who called everyone Jack, said:

'Now I know what's behind the green door.'

A burst of laughter broke out. 'What's behind the green door' was the chorus of a current hit song. Our laughing woke the sleeping drunk. Once inside the sallyport, we trooped from the Black Maria where we were told to strip. Our clothes were bagged and tagged. Then one by one we were ushered through a glass fronted shower booth. The first man through emerged gasping. Steam rose from his body. He entered the booth lily white and came out a blotched pink. Detainees rushed through the booth, looking scalded and startled. I tried to look nonchalant when braving the steaming water. Bulla, when called, sauntered into the deluge and stopped midway to face the glass, and raising each arm in turn, he scrubbed their pits with an imaginary bar of soap. On making his exit, steam rising from his body made it look as if he was smouldering. We used towels dropped at our feet and put on prison uniforms. Everything was second hand – white moleskin trousers, blue denim shirts and black felt jackets. Boots and socks were second hand and slouch hat too. I yanked up my pants commando style as underpants were not supplied. Once everyone was dressed, we were led through the inner gates. Coming into jail felt like my first day at high school. I didn't know what to expect next.

7. ADELAIDE GAOL

The space through the inner gates was shaped like a semi-circle. Six solid gates were placed around a far distant wall, where to the right a bell hung from a bracket attached to the wall. A knot at the end of its clanger's rope was shaped like a monkey's fist. The leading warder crossed a path and veered left to stop by the first gate, and raising a bunch of keys from his belt he selected a long-shanked specimen and inserted it into the lock. A second warder called three names from a list held in his hand.

'In here,' the first warder said, pushing the gate open. Ron and Huckle passed him to go through the gate. As I tried to join them, Bulla barred my way and when I skirted wider, he leaned towards me and slapped my shoulder.

'See you later,' he said.

The gate slammed shut as soon as I passed through it. The three of us were standing at the sharp end of a long triangular yard. A three-tiered cellblock stood on the right, close to the bottom wall. Prisoners were scattered throughout the yard mainly at its lower end. To our left an indigenous boy stood on one leg, his other leg cocked with its boot sole planted against the wall. His thumbs were hooked through belt loops and a handmade cigarette dangled from his lips. He gave us a wink as we passed by. Further into the yard, two men on their feet were watching a game of chess being played on the ground below them. Neither the watchers nor the players paid us any heed us as we passed. All four were Mediterranean types, Italians I presumed.

Opposite the cellblock, prisoners sprawled on the ground were listening to a warder address them from where he sat on a

18

stool. The warder struggled up to his feet and hobbled forward to meet us, a big bull of a man, his huge head sagging forward, chin close to his chest. Rocking from side to side with every step he took, his legs were bowed as if they had been buckled by his body weight. Short of breath on reaching us, he offered a warm smile. A genuine smile that cracked his face into a myriad of lines.

'You can call me Sarge,' he said.

He showed us which cells to take. Ron's cell was next to mine on the lower level, while Huckle's lay on the landing above.

'That one there, see,' pointing as he added, 'third in from the left.'

As he returned to his stool, I crossed to my cell and entered it. The mattress on a metal framed bed was only a few inches deep. Nonetheless a mattrass. The cotton sheets and pillowslip were neat and clean. Both blankets were in good order. I sat on the bed, plumped up and down. A corner shelf inside the door acted as a table and resting on it were a knife, fork and spoon, an aluminium mug, safety razor, a small mirror, a bible and two small wooden tubs. One tub contained salt and the other a white powder that I spat from my tongue when I tasted it. A stool was parked under the shelf.

Sarge's voice was rumbling outside as I scanned the rest of the cell. A slop bucket stood in the corner at the foot of the bed. It and its lid were painted red. A rope knotted through two lugs acted as its handle. Beside the bucket, newspaper squares took the place of toilet tissue. Across from the bed, an enamel bowl on the floor had a towel and soap nestled in it. Next to the bowl was a water jug made of tin and painted red.

I waited for Ron at the door of his cell and together we ventured into the yard. Inmates gathered round Sarge suddenly burst out laughing. Leaning against the wall behind him, the warder took a leisurely pull on his cigarette.

We wandered up to the chess group and watched their game for a while. They played at an amazing speed for such a convoluted game. Pluck and plonk the pieces went from here to there whizz bang. Each player seemed determined to make the fastest moves. A bishop zipped across the board to land on a suicidal square. Black declined to take the piece and shored up his defence instead. Ron and I moved on.

The indigenous boy watched our approach. On reaching him we fell into an easy conversation. Jim Brodie had a laid-back manner, and though raised on a mission, he was just as streetwise as any city kid. I asked how come he was smoking.

'Ain't you got your backy yet?'

'Where do you get it from,' Ron asked.

'They give it to you, man.'

'Do you have to buy it?'

'Hell, no. It's on the house.'

He offered us a roll-up and said we could pay him back later. I asked him about the white powder I found inside my cell.

'I know one of them is salt. What's the other one?'

'That's whiting, man.'

'What's it for?'

'To clean your knife and fork – and your teeth.'

'I haven't got a toothbrush.'

'No one got a toothbrush,' and raising a finger he said, 'but everyone got one of these.'

By the gleam of his teeth I reckoned the whiting must do a decent job. While we were chatting the gate swung open and a younger warder entered the yard. He strode briskly past us.

'Time for lunch,' Jim said, 'now we get locked up.'

All inmates were mobile and heading for their cells. Once inside my cell, the young warder shut the door, opened its hatch and moved on. I could hear cell doors slamming shut before he took to the steps. Before long, an aluminium dish landed on my hatch flap. I brought in the dish and removed its lid. Hot food for lunch, a pleasant surprise – a large sausage-roll and mashed potato. A yell at my hatch told me to put my mug on the flap.

Which I did. An inmate tilted an urn and filled the mug with tea. The warder on his return from above slammed my hatch flap shut.

My teeth had not been cleaned since the previous day, and having finished my lunch, I used the whiting from its tub. Horrible! Like rubbing chalk dust over my teeth. I rinsed my mouth from the water jug and spat into the bucket. Surely there must be a better way. I added water to salt and whiting held in the palm of my hand and rubbed the resulting paste over my teeth and gums. Much better. Apart from adding taste, the salt gave a cutting edge while the whiting prevented the salt from being too abrasive.

Having nothing to smoke, I took off my boots and lay on the bed. A poor night's sleep in the lock-up had caught up on me. Daylight through bars above my door shone onto my face. It didn't bother me at all. Nothing could keep me awake.

8. NUMBER ONE YARD

As the days and weeks passed, life became a fixed routine in number one yard. Ron and I played chess before we moved across the yard to watch the experts play. Not Italians as I assumed but Yugoslavians. They changed places after each game, a watcher replacing the loser. We copied their openings when we played, and also picked up other tips. A concealed check is ingenious if you can engineer it. Our chess improved day by day.

We talked with fellow inmates, mainly Jim Dalton the indigenous boy. Huckle by now avoided us and mooched around the yard alone. We spent at least two sessions each day listening to Sarge's stories. This big old bull of a man was a supreme story teller. All of his stories were based in Yatala - the state penitentiary. On nearing retirement, he had been moved to Adelaide Gaol to act as a keeper for first-time offenders.

Sarge was midway through a story when we joined his group. He paused to draw on his cigarette and then resumed talking. Every word came out of his mouth in its own puff of smoke. His listeners were intent, their eyes fixed on him. They were stretched on the ground, sat with crossed legs or bent forward hugging their knees. All were captivated. Sarge paused and leaning forward, lowered his voice to a whisper. His audience sat entranced. Suddenly he sprang back, and throwing up his hands, boomed out a turn of events that nobody had foreseen. The boys fell about laughing. Sarge looked puzzled at their guffaws and looked to the sky to give them time to settle down again.

'Now there was this other fella . . .'

22

A new character came on the scene. A common trend with Sarge. In the process of building his story a new character could emerge. The new person brought about a twist that affected what had gone before. The boys burst out laughing again and this time Sarge joined them, barking like an old sea lion. The gist of the story was lost on me as I watched his performance. His rheumy eyes peering out in a benevolent gaze. Young thugs sprawled at his feet were spellbound. His timing was impeccable. He knew when to pause for effect, when to raise his voice and when to lower its tone. He knew how to heighten expectancy by slowing down his speech and when approaching a critical point his words came out in a rush. I knew the climax was coming when he dashed to the punch line. On reaching it, he hurled his cigarette to the ground and mashed it with his boot. Uproar. The boys threw back their heads and hooted. On settling down they looked at each other with smiling faces. Not Henry, who continued to laugh as if he would never stop.

'Put a sock in it, Henry.'

'Shut your gob you mug.'

A bunch of knuckles into his back persuaded Henry to shut his trap.

Meanwhile Sarge had fetched a packet from his tunic pocket. He tweaked out a fresh cigarette, lit it and inhaled before he started another story from his vast repertoire. He related his stories all day long, going from one to the next and never short of an audience. He used the present to relive his past and ignored the future, eking out his days as if they would go on for forever.

We were locked in our cells in the afternoon and the evening meal, came early. After the meal Ron and I set up chess boards on our corner shelves. Then standing on our stools, we called moves to each other through bars above our doors. That's how it was. That's what we did. Being on remand was not exactly unpleasant. And jail was good for my chess game. It was getting better all the time.

9. FOUR CORNERS

They came through the gate like two stars who had just won the game for a grateful team. Lurching forward, they bounced their shoulders against each other while swinging their arms and kicking their feet out in front of them. Waggling their heads and laughing. Grimshaw and Dutchy burst into the yard, yapping and whooping as they swaggered deeper into our midst. Most newcomers were quiet at first and took a few days to find their feet. Not these two. Brash and cock a hoop, they charged from the gate and stormed into the yard. Grimshaw swivelled his head around and leered at felons as he passed.

'Me and Dutchy have been on a spree,' he shouted to one and all.

Strutting along beside him the Dutchman puffed out his chest and nodded his agreement. Sarge hauled himself up from his stool and eyed the pair's approach. No smile to greet them. No introduction. He pointed to the cells they should take, both on the top landing. Grimshaw sprinted towards the steps and shouted over his shoulder: 'I'll beat ya.' Dutchy refused to take up the challenge and bracing his shoulders thrust out his chest and marched towards the cellblock.

We should have known what to expect. Ron and I were talking to a young Italian kid. He spoke with a broad Australian accent though his English was poor. He thought money meant hands. I was trying to explain to him the rules of Aussie football.

'I don't understand.'

'But you talk so good,' Ron said.

'No, I don't understand.'

That's when Grimshaw barged in.

'I reckon I hold the record for knocking off cars in this state,' and turning to Dutchy he said, 'how many cars have we swiped, Dutchy?'

'Aw gee, I dunno, plenty.'

'Yeah, plenty, and before I met Dutchy I knocked off tons by meself.'

Hooking a thumb at the Italian kid, I said, 'he doesn't know what you're talking about and we're not interested.'

Grimshaw ignored what I said and launched into a lecture of how to hotwire a car.

'You put your hand behind the dash and jam a ball of silver paper between the ignition wires. That's all there is to it.'

I told him again we didn't want to know. He took no offence and wandered off, Dutchy trotting behind him. Huckle spread the word of how the pair had met. Dutchy was a sailor and jumped ship in Adelaide. He met Grimshaw in a pub where they found they shared an interest in stealing cars and burglary. That's what Grimshaw told Hanson. I had my own ideas. I reckoned Grimshaw had led the big Dutchman astray. Everybody soon learned to keep clear of Grimshaw. Not an easy thing to do in a small yard. He caught me unawares one day and told me about a shoe box they found in a stolen car. Inside the box was a hundred and fifty pounds, equivalent to three hundred dollars. Ron heard the amount was two hundred pounds. Value of the money increased with each telling of the tale. Another time I heard him tell an inmate he had cornered:

'I burnt off the cops didn't I Dutchy? Their car was more powerful but I done them on the corners.'

Later there were two cops' cars. A pimply boy with sticking up hair said he heard a motorbike was also in the chase.

I caught Dutchy alone one day and asked him where he had been at sea. All over it seemed - through the Suez and Panama canals, round the Cape of Good Hope and up the Persian Gulf.

He'd done the Americas, Japan and also Shanghai. I asked him what these places were like. He summed up a port in a few words. I thought he would be more excited about his worldwide travels.

'Where's the best place you've been? The best port.'

Dutchy pondered. Stroked his chin. He said err and ahh a few times while giving the matter serious thought. Finally he said, 'Montevideo. Yah, Montevideo.'

'What was so good about it?'

'Oh, the bars, the honky-tonks, the girls – everything really.'

'Where is it?'

'South America.'

'Which country?'

Dutchy paused and crumpled his brow.

'Argentina, I think it's in Argentina.'

I was about to ask him why he didn't jump ship in Montevideo, but Grimshaw arrived and wormed his way between us. He slapped Dutchy on the back.

'Hey Dutchy, what about that Ford we rolled out by Port Augusta?'

'Yah. Jeeze, weren't we lucky?'

'How many times did it roll? Three times or was it four?'

I left them to it. Over by the cellblock, a bunch of young larrikins was making a loud racket. Shouts of protest rose from the ruck followed by cheers and hoots of laughter. A loud claim was met with sneers of ridicule and a further comment brought on an outburst of cheering. I wandered over to check it out. As I arrived a thickset kid with bad teeth yelled at the top of his voice:

'It's the best pub in town. I'm tellin youse.'

'Nooooooo!' rang out a chorus.

The names of different pubs were thrown into the heated debate. None that I knew. None where Ron and I had drunk. Jeers and laughter met head on. Names of other pubs were called into the chaos. Everyone had an opinion. Everybody yelling. Conflicting points of view clashed in the overall uproar. No bad feelings were shown in the heated debate, just a good-natured battle of differing opinions.

'We go all the time' – 'it's a dump' – 'don't we Johnno?' – 'wouldn't catch me there dead' – 'you should try (name misheard)' – 'nah, used to be good once, not now' – 'anyway, the best pubs are out of the city.'

In a brief lull, a fat lad with a crew cut yelled:

'What do ya reckon's the best beach?'

Off they went again with the names of different beaches tossed into the ring. Huckle was in the thick of it, him being a local. Some place called Glenelg met with general approval. Everywhere else was up for debate. Two boys who liked the same pub were at odds over a beach. Somebody said a certain beach was a good place to pick up girls. The ruckus swung from beaches to where you could pick up a girl. Certain street corners, dance halls, different parks and by the river. From there they raced from the city to different towns in the state. Who had been where? Which was the best? Who had travelled the most? Grimshaw suddenly by me, yelled that he'd been everywhere - all over the state and across the border. He was shouted down, the same as everybody else. It was mad. I couldn't help but smile. Grimshaw nudged me.

'You don't know Adelaide well, do you?'

'Not really.'

'Did you know Adelaide has got four corners?'

I gave him a so what look.

'No, listen. Adelaide has got four corners. Right. The hospital is in the first corner, Adelaide jail in the second, the asylum is in the third and the cemetery in the fourth. And do you know what they say?'

I didn't give him any sign I was interested.

'They say, what they say is, if a man is born in the first corner, and before he's buried in the last, if he's spent some time in the other two he has led an interesting life.'

'That's what they say, is it?'

'Yep, that's what they say.'

The ring of truth in what he said was disconcerting. No hint of exaggeration. Not a trace of a lie. There was no reason to doubt him. It made me think. I was born in the first corner and less than a week back in town I had made it to the second - halfway to the cemetery. I had no wish to complete the loop. And wouldn't. As soon as we were out of here Ron and I would be back on the road. Or so I thought.

10. COURT

On unlocking my door in the morning the warder told me to go to the gate. Ron had been told the same thing. Huckle also joined us at the apex of the yard. Once all cells were unlocked, the warder opened the gate and led us through the circle to the sallyport. We were given our own clothes to wear and removed our uniforms. So nice to tug up my y-fronts, slide my arms through nylon sleeves and pull on cotton socks. My slip-on shoes were comfortable after wearing second-hand boots.

Only the three of us in the Black Maria as it breeched the gates. H.M. GAOL ADELAIDE was chiseled into the arch that curved above the gates. During the trip Huckle's eyes never moved from the rear window. Even in a weak sun, chrome shone on the bumper bars of the cars trailing behind us. On their hub caps too. Into the city proper we sped.

The court appointed a lawyer to act for Ron and me. He drew us in a lottery. Over six feet tall, young and cocksure, he asked us few questions and offered zero advice. He was itching to get into court, though one thing he said pleased me.

'Don't worry, I'll get you off on a good behaviour bond.'

Huckle's parents had hired a separate lawyer for their son. Once proceedings were under way the prosecution called a witness. The person entering the witness box gave his name and took the oath.

'I understand,' said the prosecutor, 'you are commonly known as Dognuts.'

'Yes,' Dognuts said, and from there he mumbled answers to questions put to him.

The Judge interrupted to say, 'speak up Mr Donuts, we can't hear what you are saying.'

'It's not Donuts, sir,' explained a clerk of the court, 'it's Dognuts.'

'Dognuts is it? My, my, what a peculiar name.'

Tittering broke out in the court and the judge beamed a happy smile. It was good to see the judge in a happy mood. The case moved on swimmingly. Dognuts was asked another question by the prosecutor.

'Can you see the perpetrators here at present in court?'

Dognuts ran his eyes across the three of us. He looked puzzled and blankly stared. He expected to see King, the only person he knew involved in the incident. King was not here. He and Baker were being tried in a juvenile court. As far as this court was concerned King and Baker did not exist.

After staring at us, Dognuts answered, 'no.'

The prosecution's witness was suddenly a dud. Useless to the case. There was no other evidence linking us to the crime. I might have walked free from the court right there and then. It's a pity I signed that statement and entered a guilty plea. At high school, I used to admit wrongdoing if I thought another student would name me as the culprit. I confessed immediately. The headmaster said he found it strange that I always admitted my guilt. On other occasions when merely a suspect and with no witnesses, I said I didn't do it and the headmaster believed me. A good ruse at school but a bad idea when dealing with the police and a court.

Huckle's lawyer, an elderly man, then clambered to his feet and asked Dognuts a few tame questions. Then he sat down. Our lawyer rose to his feet, stood on his toes to further extend his considerable height, rocked back onto his heels, steadied himself and ripped into Dognuts. It was wonderful stuff.

'And you – YOU have YOU been in trouble with the police?'

Dognuts shuffled in the box. 'Yes.'

'So you have a criminal record?'

'Yes.'

'What was the offence?'

'Receiving.'

'Receiving what exactly?'

'A pair of pyjamas.'

I burst out laughing. I didn't mean to, it just happened. Our lawyer stooped and hissed in my ear.

'Stop that! Stop it. Do that again and I'll walk out on you.'

I didn't think he could he do that. The court had appointed him. It was his job. Now flustered he carried on but he had completely lost the plot. His fumbled words came out as if he had forgotten his lines. His questioning lost its thrust. His attack fizzled out and after rambling for a while he let the witness off the hook. Dognuts was allowed to escape and fled from the box. The judge from there on conducted the case in a steely resolve. No more quips to entertain the court. Strictly down to business in a brisk and formal manner. Nothing of any importance emerged from then on. The court was adjourned. Our case was fated to drag on and we were returned to Adelaide Gaol.

11. TIGERS

When Henry left his usual spot sitting at Sarge's feet, a lanky hooligan stretched out his legs and occupied the empty space. Henry, on returning from his toilet break saw his place had gone and plonked down next to Ron, bumping him in the process. Ron shoved Henry away and gave him a swift mouthful.

'Keep away from me you sick creep.'

Henry started to cry. He didn't just sob, he bawled. Tears streamed down his cheeks. He cried as if in physical pain. Sarge interrupted his story and tried to placate him.

'Go on Henry, go to your cell and calm yourself down.'

Henry did not let up. He continued to sit there howling.

'Go on son. Go to your cell for a while. You'll feel better after that.'

Henry bumbled up to his feet and sobbed his way across to his cell. All of us glad to see him go. No one felt sorry for him. There was something wrong with Henry. He didn't understand that he had done a terrible thing. Sorry for himself now sobbing across the yard. Did he ever cry for the little girl whose life he tried to ruin? When the courts were done with Henry he'd end up in the asylum, where he rightly belonged. Sarge returned to his story once Henry had gone. It concerned a hard man from the bad old days. A man who refused to settle down in jail. He bucked against the system and was nothing but trouble. He did spells in solitary and time in separate confinement. When disobeying orders, several warders were needed to bundle him into his cell.

'I thought we'd never get rid of him,' Sarge growled, 'extra time was added to his original sentence and he took a beating every time he confronted us. He wouldn't learn. He was a glutton for punishment.'

Sarge raised his cigarette, took a long drag of it and breathing out smoke added, 'I thought we were stuck with him forever,' and dropping the shortened fag to the ground he squished it with his boot. Out came the packet, another fag and the lighter from his trousers. Once lit he drew on the cigarette and exhaled. Then he carried on with his story while stowing the lighter away.

'Well, we had a riot, and you can guess who was there at the head of it.'

Sarge broke off to cough and coughed again. He tried to clear his throat. This brought on a volley of coughs more violent than before. His eyes began to water and his body heaved. Loud eruptions burst from his throat. He slumped forward, lowering his head close to his knees before jerking upright again. When he slumped again, a string of saliva could be seen hanging from his bottom lip. The saliva snagged on a button and snapped when he jerked upright. A dribble of it remained on his chin. The coughing did not let up. His eyes bulged - his face turned purple. Explosive sounds coming from him were horrible. His mouth hung open as he heaved, his face all contorted. He rocked about on the stool so much it seemed he might fall off. Suddenly he straightened up, shook his great head, roared like a lion, and doubling over gasped between deep rasping croaks. The attack showed no sign of letting up. The cigarette fell from his fingers - a tailor-made cigarette, barely used. Nobody picked it up. Everybody was looking at Sarge, a man under siege.

His blood pressure and his poisoned lungs in a race to finish him off.

He pulled a handkerchief from his pocket and clamped it to his mouth. His coughing became muffled. Became less violent. Grew weaker. Stopped. He sat very still, breathing in and out through his nose. Slowly he sat upright and offered a weak smile. Then he daubed his eyes, wiped his mouth and cleared the dribble off his chin. He had won through. To celebrate his victory, he drew a packet from his tunic, plucked a slim white trophy, stuck it between his lips and put it to the flame. Though dazed he had not forgotten his story. But its structure had been shot. His words came out in a mumble as if he had lost his bearings. He spoke like a man in a trance.

'Yes, he was in the thick of it. He had to be. But he was brought down. . . I brought him down. . .' Sarge raised a clenched fist and smacked its heel into the palm of his other hand as if clutching a baton.

'I laid him out. I cracked his skull. He lay on the wing for three days until the riot was quelled.'

A distant gaze in his eyes now. The boy in front of me turned around with his forehead creased, his mouth open. We had never heard a story like this before. All the listeners were restless. Concerned looks were being exchanged. Sarge remained unaware, lost in recalling an incident from long ago.

'When released he was quiet . . . a very quiet man. We never saw him again.'

Then he said it. This is what he said. He said:

'We tamed tigers up at Yatala. Yes sir, we tamed tigers.'

He raised his head from where it sagged and firming his jaw peered at a distant past through his rheumy eyes. Each blue iris lay submerged in a shallow red rimmed pool. I saw him then. I saw him as he used to be – an enforcer, a brute. His massive head held aloft by a bull-like neck. Broad across his back. Legs like pillars of stone. When he swung a truncheon there would be real force behind it. I wondered how many skulls he cracked as a younger man. I only knew Sarge as an old man. In that regard I was lucky.

12. COURT AGAIN

We were off to court again. After six weeks on remand the novelty of jail was beginning to wear off. Maybe now we would make some progress. I was eager to get on with my life. Back in the Black Maria and driving to the city, Huckle's eyes stayed fixed on the rear window. He seldom spoke these days. Kept himself to himself. Not the braggart he used to be. Ron had something on his mind. I felt fine – I thought we might be getting somewhere at last.

Into the heart of the city we drove, into its buzz and bustle. People milled on the pavements - traffic pushed its way through. The Paddy Wagon swung off the road and pulled into a yard – a courtyard for the court. An escort led Ron and I into a small room. Our lawyer already there practically ignored us. He gave us the impression that we were a hindrance to the case. That he'd make a better job of it if we were not involved.

Once in court he rose to his feet, gripped the wings of his gown and in a loud voice called my father! The last person I expected to see. I watched in shock as he rose and walked briskly to the box. My father was a company man who dragged his family from city to city in order to climb the corporate ladder. Mind your fingers on the rungs when he climbs over the top of you. Not only ambitious but also deadly efficient. Composed now in the witness box, hand on the bible and taking the oath. Smart business suit, trimmed moustache, clear eyed and confident. Then in an assertive voice he began to lie through his teeth all on my behalf. He said things like, 'completely out of character' and 'never been in trouble before'. Blatant lies made credible by their polished delivery. If I didn't know myself I would have believed every word. No wonder he's good at business. Calm and relaxed in facing the court, a model citizen - respectable and honest. He didn't look at me, not once. Not when striding to the box and not when inside it.

When aged six or seven, my father grabbed me around the neck, lifted me off the floor and pinned me to the wall. He then shook me by the neck as he shouted into my face. One of his thumbnails broke the skin and left a red mark. Next day I saw him looking at it.

'You did that,' I said, pointing a finger at the mark on the front of my neck.

'I did not. I did not,' he said in a trembling voice.

At that moment, I believe the incident frightened him more than it had frightened me.

On completing his testimony he walked past me with eyes to the front. I knew he had not come by choice. My mother had nagged him to come. Taking time off his precious job would have been a wrench. It was his life, what he lived for - entertaining clients with a generous expense account. Though by nature he was a frugal man. The cost of this trip would come from his pocket. He must have flown from Sydney, by car or train would take too long. And if he stayed overnight, well, that didn't bear thinking about. Paying for a hotel as well as incurring travelling costs would have wounded him.

I wondered why the lawyer contacted my parents. Did he think that would help the case. A different reason then occurred to me. To clip them for a fee. Legal aid did not exist. He was not getting paid for this job. He drew it in a lottery. That's why he contacted them – to raise a bill. No wonder my father refused to look at me.

I spotted Huckle's parents in court - country people, humble people, looking uncomfortable in the court. They didn't go into the box and left their lawyer to speak for them. Judging by his performance, I'd say they got him cheap. An old man, a country hick out of place in a city court. Though something he said stuck with me. Huckle had been a clean-cut youth until his brother was killed in an accident. The brother he looked up to. Huckle went off the rails after his brother's death.

I expected more details of the case to emerge at this hearing. That didn't happen. The witness Dognuts did not appear. Apart from pleas for lenience, there were only character references. As with other trips to court the session ended abruptly. We were handcuffed, led from the court and returned to Adelaide jail.

13. CONVICTED

Once in the sallyport, we changed into prison uniforms. A warder led us into the circle and turning right he stopped at gate number four. Not the gate we left by earlier that morning.

'Why are we changing yards?'

'Now you're convicted, that's why.'

Nothing was said in court about us being convicted. It would have been nice to be informed. The warder did not reach for his keys but raised a hand with its fingers bent and examined his nails. Then buffed them on the front of his jacket. After a brisk polishing he lowered his hand and looked to the sky. Just stood there staring into space. It was time for another question.

'Why are we waiting?'

'You want to eat don't you,' he snapped.

So we waited. The jail was deadly quiet. All inmates were locked in their cells for the midday break. Silence hung in the air. And then a prisoner appeared from beyond the circle, holding a stack of lidded dishes in his outstretched hands. I knew this man. I knew him from somewhere, but couldn't figure where that was. Middle aged with a robust build, he carried himself well. His ruddy face marked him as an outdoor type. A farmer perhaps, or labourer. Huckle relieved him of the top dish and Ron accepted the second. I looked him in the eye when I took the last dish. In meeting my gaze he showed no sign of recognition. Just blankly stared at me. And empty handed he turned around to retrace his steps, straight backed - head held high.

The warder hoisted the chain on his belt, selected a key and opened the gate. On following him into the yard I surveyed its layout. Another triangular yard, bigger than Number One. Bigger because it was wider. There were two cell blocks - one either side of the yard. Both were two tiered structures with arches on the bottom level to support the landings above them. The warder pointed at me and said, 'come with me,' and ordered the others to wait where they were.

I followed him to the left-hand block and mounted a flight of sandstone steps. A deep groove was worn into each yellow slab. Halfway along the landing he stopped by an opened door. As soon as I entered the cell he slammed the door shut. Its layout was the same as my previous cell - same furniture, same fixtures. I placed my dish on the corner shelf and removed its lid. I could have eaten twice as much as was in that dish. Potato mash, peas and a pork sausage. Normally a chunk of bread, but not that day. I drew the stool from under the shelf and lowered myself onto it. When polishing the fork on my shirt tail, I realised who the prisoner was - the man who gave me my meal. No wonder I couldn't place him. He had changed so much. He was a drunk from the lock-up. The same drunk who was asleep when we arrived in jail. That human wreck had blossomed into a robust figure, exuding health and strength - a remarkable change in him over six weeks. Incredible. Being here so long, I presumed he'd been here before. A repeat offender. A drunk who spent his life by going in and out of jail. After recovering in jail, he would be released to go through the same cycle again. It must be the pattern of his life. Without these spells in jail he might well be dead. Jail was helping to keep him alive. Jail was actually good for him. Not for a minute did I think the same might apply to me. That thought never entered my head.

14. FOUR YARD

As soon as I woke I knew that something was out of place but I couldn't work out what it was. Everything seemed in order. My clothes were folded on top of the stool, everything else where it should be. Yet an unsettled feeling continued to linger with me. Then it registered with me – the bell. When it rang in the circle its peal came from the wrong direction. Of course, I had been moved to another cell in a different yard. A brighter cell too. Daylight flooded through the bars fixed above my door. When my hatch was opened, I peered at the other cellblock lying across the yard. Above it was the sky. All I saw from my previous cell was a high brick wall. It's nice in the morning to see the sky. A cell on the upper landing feels less cut off from the world.

After breakfast my door was unlocked and stepping from my cell and seeing other prisoners were standing by their doors, I did the same. Cells were being unlocked in the opposite block. On completing his task, the warder strode along its landing and descended the stairs, and joining his colleague in the yard he raised a whistle to his lips and blew it. Men left their doors from both cellblocks and poured into the yard. Inmates greeted each other and lines of men abreast of each other began walking lengths of the yard. A few of the prisoners wore their own clothes instead of a prison uniform. Ron emerged from under an arch and I crossed the yard to join him. Together we made for the bottom wall and turned to walk beside it. A guy aged about thirty fell in to stroll beside us.

'You're new, ain't you,' and jerking back his head he flicked away the hair that hung over one of his eyes.

I said we were new in this yard but had been in Number One.

'First timer's yard, huh,' and turning to me, he added, 'was you in there long?'

'We came inside just after Raymond Bailey was hanged.'

'He was here Bailey, in this yard. I talked to him, talked to him a lot. He said he didn't do it but I'm not sure about that. I reckon he panicked and shot the sheila's after he shot the man.'

Another jerk flicked back the slick of fallen hair. He was walking almost backwards, facing us as he walked and talked.

'If he hadn't panicked and shot the sheilas he might not've hanged. Don't panic, eh? Whatever happens, don't panic.'

We were now walking beside my cellblock.

'There are two killers in here now,' and stopping he placed a hand on my arm. 'There's one of them there, see,' and he pointed at a prisoner standing alone in the yard. The prisoner had both hands tucked into his jacket pockets.

'That's Kitchen. He shot a man. See him facing us, that skinny bloke?'

I could see him. Kitchen's face was chalky white. His eyes were sunken deep into a pair of purplish sockets. The fact that Raymond Bailey hanged probably got in the way of his sleep.

'Now where's the other one?' Slick said, turning to scan the yard.

I kept my eyes on Kitchen, standing with his shoulders hunched, a man marooned - isolated. His eyes like the vacant windows of a deserted house.

'There he is - the Greek,' said Slick, pointing this time to a chubby figure who in the company of two other men was doubled up with laughter. 'Dunno who he killed, but acts like he's glad he done it.'

I gauged the Greek to be in his mid-twenties. His swarthy features were creased with mirth as he continued to chuckle.

'Look at him. He's like that all the time.'

Slick nudged me as a man walked past, an old man, stooped forward from the waist as he puttered along. His arms dangling in front of him like those of a rag doll.

'That's Ted. He's loopy,' said Slick, touching the side of his head. 'As soon as he gets out he breaks into a house, finds the liquor cabinet and drinks himself stupid. Then he flakes out on a couch. Silly old bugger. He's lucky no one has brained with a cricket bat.'

Ted puttered further on, moving as if in a trance.

'That suit he's wearing – didja see it? Must be forty years old that suit. It'll last him a life time. He only gets to wear it one day out of jail. He can wear it now coz he's on remand.' Flick went the forelock. 'He don't have to wear no uniform not till he's found guilty. It's his right. Gives him a chance to wear his suit. Might as well, eh, let him get some wear out of it?'

Slick pointed out different men and told us what they had done.

'See him? The tall geezer, second from this side.' A line of men had walked past going towards the gate. 'He just got four years. He'll go up to Yatala on the next escort.'

We were standing just below my cell. Pointing at other prisoners, Slick related details of what they had done. The greasy slick of hair fell down to cover an eye again. A toss of his head flicked it away.

'Look at that Greek. I can't work him out . . . always laughing and messing around. All killers come into this yard even if they're first timers. Kitchen has been here before. I don't know about the Greek.'

Plain to see it annoyed Slick in knowing so little about the Greek. The information he gave us came without a single prompt. We didn't ask for it. He offered it willingly and completely free of charge. And then at last and far too late Slick named his price.

'What are youse in for, anyway?'

I borrowed a line that Bulla used when we were in the lock-up.

'Oh, you know, we've been naughty boys.'

He thought what I said was an opening line, thought there was more to come. His mouth was hanging open as he looked at me. The grin I formed let him know I had nothing more to add. His mouth clamped shut as both his eyes narrowed down to slits. I looked at Ron, nodded towards the gate and moved on.

'See you later,' I heard Ron say and on catching up with me he was grinning too. On passing the gate Ron said, 'I wonder what he'll say about us.'

'Don't worry, he'll make up some story.'

15. GREEK INCIDENT

The Greek killer was seldom seen without a smile on his face. An infectious smile that prompted others to smile along with him. Or laugh out loud. He was a happy chap. Not an energetic type, I never saw him walk the yard. His usual spot was by the wall close to the gate. As Ron and I were passing, we heard laughter coming from inmates in his company. We stopped to see what was happening. The Greek was sitting on the ground with one leg outstretched and the other bent with its foot resting on top of the opposite thigh.

'See, it's easy.'

A man on the ground beside him said: 'Yeah, that bit is easy.'

'Now you do the same with the other leg,' and the Greek lifted his straightened leg and bending it placed its foot on top of the folded leg. Sitting like a grinning Buddha, he said, 'come on, you do it. You try.'

The man sitting beside him tried to do the same.

'Hooaahh, that hurt,' he said, rolling onto his back. 'His knees must be made of rubber.'

'From here you can do this,' and the Greek rocked back then forwards again and raised onto his knees. Balancing on his folded legs, he extended his arms to either side like wings of an aeroplane. 'Now, watch – watch.' And swinging his body from side to side he waddled along on his knees, laughing. Laughing as if he didn't have a single care in the world.

A few days later, while standing outside my cellblock, I watched men walking lengths of the yard. Nobody walked alone that day, not even Ted. They walked in groups abreast of each other between the gate and bottom wall. I identified men by the manner in which they walked. There are so many ways to swing a leg. No two men walked the same. Ted shuffled along in his own unique style. Others I knew by various means, by lean of their body, length of their stride, the angle of their head, or by what their arms were doing. Shoulders could be braced, slumped, or roll in time with each stride. I knew men not by name but by how they walked.

While idly watching, I noticed the Greek crossing the yard and coming in my direction. He moved at a brisk pace which drew my attention to him. A grimace was fixed on his face. On coming up behind a man he raised an arm above his head and then plunged it down. A glint of metal flashed in his hand as it struck the other man's back. The victim lurched forward - open mouthed. On regaining his balance, he spun around to face the Greek. I expected to see blood and a weapon sticking out of his back. There was no blood, no sign of a weapon. The victim's jacket was unmarked. Two men grabbed the Greek and one of them twisted his arm. I heard a dull clunk as something dropped from the Greek's hand. I rushed towards the incident and joined a swirl of activity. The Greek squirmed while being held. The weapon lay on the ground – a fork, its shaft bent and all of its prongs doubled over and skewed. Made of a soft alloy, the fork could stab nothing firmer than a pork sausage.

The victim, a stocky character with black sideburns, verbally abused the Greek. He called him an idiot. Called him worse.

Inmates were drawn to the scene and on rushing in they asked what had happened. The Greek managed to wriggle free and rushed away.

'What happened – he stabbed him – who – the Greek – who did he stab – him - he looks alright - it was a fork - where's the Greek – gone – get the fork before a screw sees it - what happened?'

Warders failed to see how the melee started and the crowd quickly dispersed. The incident was a talking point for the next few days. Men spoke of the revenge they expected to see. The man with black sideburns was taking his time to retaliate. He and the Greek avoided each other. After a week it became clear that there would be no reprisal. The victim of the attack spent more time alone. He withdrew into himself. The Greek returned to his happy self. He kidded around, smiled and laughed and continued to do his yoga trick. Though when he laughed nobody chose to laugh along with him. His laugh was no longer infectious.

16. REG MAGEE

Reg Magee came through the gate as if he owned the place. Striding like an athlete he sliced through the yard with head held high and his eyes aimed directly ahead. His shoulders rolling in time with each deliberate stride. Confidence oozed from him. Six foot tall in a pale blue suit and soft felt hat of a matching shade. Blond hair on the back of his head contrasted against his out of season tan. He cut a dash. Men watched him stalk through the yard. He drew the eye. He looked the part.

Like Errol Flynn back in Oz after his time in Hollywood.

He was placed in the cell next to mine. Four times a day I watched him standing at the door of his cell, self-contained and aloof.

He was popular with certain men who chose to walk beside him when doing their lengths. They hustled along beside him hanging on his every word. The same men tacked onto his line day after day. Not me. Not when as a neighbour he chose to ignore me. I didn't want to be another hanger-on. There were other lines I could join. Plenty of lines to choose from – the strollers, the brisk walkers or those that dawdled along.

Men in the line I joined that day were discussing a crim named Chicko.

'I was in Pentridge with him,' said a voice three places along from me.

'I knew him out west,' said a deep voice near the far end. 'He stirred up things out there. The cops told him to get out of Perth and never come back. Do you know Chicko?'

'Never met him,' said a new voice, 'but I've heard a lot about him.'

Another offered, 'He's in Sydney now, driving a taxi.'

'Nooo,' said deep voice. 'Can't be. Chicko driving a taxi. I can't believe it.'

'Yep,' said the man in the know. 'More than a year now. He married a sheila and gave it away. He reckons from now on he'll be treading the straight and narrow.'

'Chicko driving a taxi. I can't believe it.'

'Neither can I,' said the bloke next to me. 'What would his passengers think if they knew who was at the wheel?'

'He was here. He did time in Yatala about four years ago.'

I didn't catch who said that as we turned near the gate. The original speaker went on to say, 'they reckon Yatala's a bad jail.'

'It is.'

'Can't be as bad as Boggo Road,' offered another.

'Believe me, it is.'

A few paces passed in silence before the next comment.

'Worst jail I've been in is Gladstone. As soon as you come inside, the screws kick you across the circle and throw you into a yard. That's just to let you know how it's gunner be.'

No one made a response. To keep the conversation going I said, 'So Gladstone has got a circle, like here?'

The man next to me replied, 'All the old jails have got a circle. You know why don't you?'

He was tall, my neighbour; six-three at least. When I said I didn't know he carried on to tell me.

'When these old jails were built, motor vehicles weren't invented. People came into jail in a bullock wagon. Now, when a bullock wagon was between gates it couldn't go out backwards could it? So when everyone was put in their yards the bullocks came through the inner gates, walked around the circle and went out through both sets of gates.'

'So the whole design of the jail was to allow the bullocks to leave the sallyport.'

'You've got it.'

I did get it. Not only for the bullocks, but by catering for their exit I saw how it improved the function of the jail. Yards placed around the circle meant all cellblocks were a similar distance from the inner gates. That is clever and an efficient usage of space. I could picture the jail's design from a birds' eye view. Or mapped out on a blueprint. All neat and functional. Allowing for the bullocks helped create an effective design. Hard to see how it could be improved. The structure of the jail was perfect for its use.

It may seem strange when in jail to learn of and appreciate the logic behind its design. But like they say, jail is not a college but it can be an education. And it's true. All kinds of lessons can be learned during penal servitude.

17. CLERK OF THE COURT

After the midday break, a warder on unlocking my door instructed me to go to the gate. There's someone to see you he said. From the bottom of the sandstone steps I made my way to the neck of the yard and waited. Arriving a few minutes later, the warder unlocked the gate and led me across the circle. He stopped at a door just to the left of the inner gates, knocked, pushed the door open and ushered me through it. He remained outside. Inside the room, a man wearing civilian clothes was sitting behind a desk, looking at an opened file laid out before him. He did not look up as I entered. I approached the desk and gazed at a bald patch on top of his head. Whispery growth around the patch indicated that his baldness was going to spread. I cleared my throat. He did not look up. Then drawing a chair back from the desk I lowered myself onto it.

'Yes, you can sit.'

A fly buzzed by window as it bounced itself against the frosted glass panes. Bars visible through the glass were blurred images. My eyes returned from the fly to stare at the bald patch. Lifting up his head, he presented a lifeless face, as bland as a blank mask.

'My name is Mister whatever-it-was and I am a clerk of the court. I've been instructed to compile a pre-sentencing report,' and glancing at the file before him, he said, 'you know Mister Johnston.'

'No.'

'Mister Johnston,' he repeated. 'You do know Mister Johnston.'

'Don't think so.'

'Are you sure you don't know a Mister Johnston?'

I looked him square in the eye. 'I - don't - know – any - Mister – Johnston.'

Back went his eyes to read the top sheet on the desk.

'Hhmm, you do know Mrs Moore?'

'Ah yes . . . I know Mrs Moore.'

'Who was Mrs Moore?'

'My probation officer.'

'She was, wasn't she?' And reading again: 'Breaking and entering. How old were you then? Thirteen, yes thirteen.'

'It wasn't as bad as it sounds.'

'Doesn't sound very good though, does it?'

I held my tongue, held my composure. I met his gaze. He didn't deserve to get the answer he was determined to extract. Our eyes were locked. Time trickled by. Tick tock would go a clock if one had been in the room. Silence. Even the fly had gone quiet. After a spell it dawned on him a reply would not be forthcoming. The bland expression on his face didn't alter, didn't change.

'So now you know who Mister Johnston is?'

'No I don't'

'No?'

'No.'

'He was your Sunday School teacher.'

Oh him. So that's what he was called. I couldn't stand the man and the feeling between us was mutual. I hated Sunday school and he hated me being there. It was my father who forced me to go.

'He said in his opinion, you were an uncontrollable child.'

Just what I would expect him to say. He would enjoy getting that entered in an official report. To get back at me. A man full of Christian spite. Once I kickstarted his motorbike. Only fooling around, I didn't expect it to start but its engine roared into life. I must have been eleven years old. Vibrations of the bike caused me to lose my grip and the bike fell onto the road with its throttle jammed wide open. Its engine screamed like a fighter plane coming in for the kill. The racket it made brought two men running from the church.

Another time in church, I released a jam tin full of crickets. They hopped off in all directions. Chaos erupted at the end of the prayer. Ladies jumped up onto pews holding their dresses high while men dashed around and stamped on all of God's little creatures, squashing them to death. They made a real mess on the polished wooden floor. Those sleek black insects when squashed squirt out different colours - green and yellow mainly with small blobs of red. I didn't try to explain the empty jam tin. Even then I was not expelled, either from the church or the Sunday school. There was no escape, not for another year or so.

The clerk of the court sifted through papers in his file.

'In Sydney you used a gymnasium in . . . in Falcon Street.'

I don't why he mentioned the gym. Nobody there would have complained about me. Was I supposed to be impressed by his detective work? And then he referred to a neighbour living close to my parents. He would have to find him, wouldn't he. I don't know how he managed that.

I wondered why the clerk of the court needed to make this visit. He learned nothing new. He had this information already. It was in his file. Did he make the visit just to get a day out of court. Or had he come simply to gloat? During our time together the expression on his face didn't change. It remained fixed, like a cardboard cut-out. His voice never wavered from the same dull tone. His eyes were dull and lifeless. There was nothing distinctive about him. He was anonymous, nondescript and easy to disregard. A minor jumped up official full of his own importance. I knew in the future if I looked back I would have no idea what he looked like. Mister putty face, utterly forgettable. His name had gone already, gone completely even before I had left the room.

18. SPRING

June and July were gone and now August had passed by too. On being unlocked in the morning, Reg Magee stepped from his cell, strode to the edge of the landing and thrust both arms towards the sky. Then drawing in a deep breath, he exhaled, and declared, 'what a glorious morning, the first day of spring.'

On turning to face me he said, 'I'm off to court this morning and I won't be coming back. They haven't got a thing on me.' He returned to stand by the door of his cell. 'I'll be at the races this afternoon and what a fabulous day for it. Nothing beats a day at the turf. The sport of kings. My God, I love it.'

He had been my neighbour for more than a week and never uttered a single word. Now on this his last day, he was in the mood to elaborate.

'Do you know, the only jail I've ever done is three months. Three months for a pint of milk. Isn't that ridiculous. I was coming home one morning and lifted a pint from a doorstep. A cop had been following me and pinched me on the spot. Three months for a pint of milk. That's how bad they wanted me. If anyone tells you there's no collusion between the police and judiciary - don't believe them.'

Looking at the sky, he took another deep breath, then smiled.

'They're desperate to get me again, but they won't be having me today and that's a racing certainty. They haven't got a thing on me.'

Turning to face me again, he looked me up and down.

'You're not from round here are you?'

'No, Sydney.'

'Ahh, Sydney. I spent a year there once – in San Souci. Do you know it?'

'Can't say I do. Where is it?'

'What! You're from Sydney and you don't know where San Souci is. Eastern suburbs, that's where, close to Botany Bay.'

'I lived on the north shore and was only there for two years.'

'Sydney was good for me. I had a nice lady friend and we lived a good life. We didn't want for anything. I didn't do any thieving all the time I was there. Lived entirely off gambling. Don't know why I left. Maybe I'll go back. I might do that.'

Reg asked me what charge I was on. When I told him he said it was a bad blue. 'The lawyer said he will get me off on a good behaviour bond.'

'No, you won't get a bond for that. You'll have to do time.'

I chose to ignore what he said. A lawyer would know better than him, surely. Besides, I preferred to believe what the lawyer said.

A whistle blew from down below. Prisoners on the landing started to file towards the steps. On the turn and over his shoulder, Reg Magee conveyed to me his parting advice.

'Take a tip from me. Always work by yourself and never take anything but money.'

Then he skipped down the steps and made for the gate. Head held high, loose limbed, his back ramrod straight. Immaculate in his powder blue suit and matching soft felt hat. A splash of colour slicing through a sea of monochrome uniforms. Men watched him go, they always did, like members of the cast in awe of the movie's star. On reaching the gate he stood erect - calm and self-satisfied. Waiting for his ride to court and expected freedom. A warder duly arrived, opened the gate and Reg Magee stepped out from his brief internment. True to his word he did not return.

My next appearance in court was due. It could be me leaving soon without having to return. Two months in jail was long enough for what I did. I felt confident that the court will agree.

19. SENTENCED

'Two and a half years,' the judge said, 'hard labour.'

I heard the words but somehow felt they weren't meant for me. Or was it as they whizzed past I didn't catch their meaning. My mind was elsewhere at the time, wishing the rest of me was elsewhere with it. But a threat in the air dragged me back to where my feet were planted. The court sat in a hush, as still as a photograph. All those solemn silent faces looking in our direction. Slowly . . . slowly . . . I turned to Ron. He looked as if he had just been shot. His mouth agape, eyes bulging in alarm. As soon as I realised he'd been hit I was struck by the ricochet. Two and a half years. Christ Almighty! How could this be happening? And suddenly a bad dream in the glare of broad daylight. I came to court expecting to walk. Our lawyer said he would get us off on a good behaviour bond. I needed to believe and I believed in him. What he promised turned out to be nothing but worthless hope. Reality came with a jolt and as it juddered through me it switched off all my senses. I went numb. I lost touch with what was happening. I have no memory of being taken down. I don't know if I walked stiff limbed trudging like a zombie, or if I stumbled with shoulders stooped like a broken man. I would like to think I made my way with long deliberate strides, while holding my pride up high. That is what I prefer to think.

I found myself on a bench seat, elbows on my knees and head held in my hands. I ran my eyes around the floor and looked to the wall on either side. I was in a tiny naked cell - no slop bucket, no water jug, not even a bible. I raised my head to face the door a short space in front of me. A door with a peephole but no hatch.

I leaned back against the wall and let my gaze climb the door. Just below the ceiling, a light bulb glowed from inside a heavy glass dome. The dome was secured by a metal grid. Even the light was held behind bars. Like a moth I was drawn to the light while going around and around in my head was the term – two and a half years, two and a half years. It seemed an inordinate length of time. I tried to measure it. What had I been doing two and a half years ago? Back I went and further back and there I was as thin as a stick and not yet needing to shave; regularly. What had happened since then? Whoosh! A stampede through my memory. A mighty rush of images flashed across my mind – people, places and events - a whole host of incidents. Too many to contemplate. Too many to recall. And now for that same length of time I will be locked in jail. I felt overwhelmed. Crushed.

At eighteen it felt as if my whole life had gone down the drain.

I tried not to think about what lay ahead of me. I didn't want to dwell on all the things I would miss. Thinking only depressed me. I had to stop it – wipe my mind clean. I felt tired, weary - exhausted. As if I had over-exerted myself. I let my neck go slack. Let my head droop. I allowed my shoulders to slump. Closed my eyes. Before long I started to drift and felt myself floating away, leaving all my troubles behind. I drifted off into a void, a vast expanse of nothingness. My mind completely blank as if in the deepest sleep I had ever known. I have no idea how long I remained in that state.

20. REDDA LEWIS

A loud bang startled me. Another bang and then another - BANG. Cell doors were being opened and slammed against the wall. I knew in an instant where I was and what was happening. As a key turned in the lock of my door, I rubbed both eyes with the heels of my hands and rose to my feet. Bang went my door as it thumped against the outside passage wall. I stepped out of the cell. Across the way Ron stood in a slump. Next in line was Huckle. Big mouth Huckle, tough guy Huckle, there he was now - little boy lost. As mastermind he had drawn three years. Further along was old Ted, his dead fish eyes unblinking, wide open and opaque. The man on my left had his body braced to contain a seething rage. His lips were clamped shut as he breathed heavily through his nose– in and out, in and out. A policeman stepped between us and shackled our wrists together. As the cuffs were ratcheted tighter, my co-joined turned to me with fury blazing in his eyes. He grimaced to bare his teeth and a strip of gold on the top row glistened dangerously. His anger seemed about to explode. I couldn't stand to look at him and averted my eyes.

There were six of us to be sentenced that day. We came in pairs from Adelaide jail and in pairs we were to return. We were led along a corridor, around corners and through doors, then out through a gate into a yard. Two by two we stepped into the back of a Black Maria. Its engine revved and we leapt forward, swerving through a gate to merge with traffic on a busy street. All eyes inside the Black Maria were drawn to its rear window. People out there were on the move. Pedestrians and motorists. Everybody had somewhere to go, people to see, things to do, a normal life to lead.

A normal life never looked so good. I would've given anything to be out there and living it. People out there could choose what they did, today, tomorrow and for the rest of their lives. If only they realized. Options were open to them. They could do anything they wanted to do. The only thing holding them back was their own constraint. They had choice. Inside the Black Maria, we had no choice at all.

Silence all around me. Stunned faces. An overall air of despondency permeated the air. Huckle looked ill. Ron was staring at broken dreams. There had been other trips from court but never before a trip like this.

'What did you get?'

The question came from my neighbour. Redda Lewis was his name. Due to his broken nose, I took him for an ex-fighter. Most ex-fighters have gentle eyes, all their aggression left in the ring when they quit the game. Not so with Redda Lewis. His ice blue eyes resembled those of a hired assassin. And yet they held no menace when I turned to face him. The tone of his voice was friendly too. I told him my sentence.

'I'll be glad to see you go, means I'll be halfway through mine.'

'Five years?'

'Five years, yeah, for GBH. A mug at a party kept needling me. I told him to back off. I said I'd do him if he didn't quit. He wouldn't listen. He wouldn't be told. He kept it up. So the mug got what he was asking for and I get five years.'

The words were spat from lips drawn back against his bared teeth. There was that strip of gold again, flashing ominously.

'The judge had it in for me. I defended myself, and every time I had the jury coming a bit my way, he jumped in to lend a hand to the prosecution. He said, and this is the judge I'm talking about, not the prosecutor, he said the mug's injuries were so bad, they must've been done by the boot. If not by the boot - a bottle.'

The wrist shackled to mine leapt up and brandished a fist. My hand got yanked up with it.

'I've never had to use the boot or a bottle in my life.'

His eyes demanded I believe. He then relaxed and both of our hands lowered into the gap between us. He had no more to say. Silence resumed. None of the others had uttered a word. We arrived back at Adelaide Gaol. With a crunch of gears the Black Maria reversed into the sallyport. Once in the yard we were locked in our cells for the midday meal.

In the afternoon I stood in the yard, my back against the wall. Men were walking the yard, doing their lengths. Only vaguely aware of them, I paid little attention. I had never felt so low, so empty. And leaning against the wall, I realised someone was approaching me. Getting closer. I widened my eyes to focus and saw it was Redda. He came right up to me and stood very close, though his eyes were looking over my shoulder at something on the wall. When he spoke his voice was husky and not very distinct. He should first have cleared his throat.

'When you get out of here . . . go home. Go home to your mother.'

The last thing I expected to hear coming from Redda Lewis. He didn't look comfortable. His eyes were avoiding mine. I didn't know what to say. How should I respond? I had no intention of going back there. My father and I did not get on. I left home because of him, but I shouldn't reject Redda's s advice, not when he made the effort to come and give it to me. My throat went dry. I was stuck for words. His eyes met mine for a second, then switched back to the wall. He looked more uncomfortable now than when he first arrived. I wished he hadn't come. I'm sure he wished he hadn't come. I couldn't break the silence between us. I felt awkward. Struck dumb. After an age Redda felt the need to speak again.

'It's too late for me,' he said, in the same husky voice, 'this is my thirty-second offence.'

Thirty-two offences! What could I say to that? Nothing seemed appropriate. I should have said something next. It was my turn to speak. My mind had gone blank. I stood like a dummy. I was desperate to speak, desperate to say something but my brain refused to function. We were locked together in mutual embarrassment. The silence between us was killing me. Redda deserved some kind of response. I wasn't able to give it. He had said his piece. My turn now to speak. Words wouldn't come. I hated what was happening. My lack of reaction must have seemed like disrespect.

Suddenly Redda spun around, turned on his heel and walked away. I watched him go. I had let him down and felt bad about it. I wanted to call him back to say, hang on a minute, give me a chance to think. Let me think what I want to say. I wanted him to know how grateful I was. I should have thanked him for the advice. That's the least I should have done. But it was too late. He'd gone. And so was my chance to say anything. I was annoyed with myself.

Then it struck me. My misery had gone. I was no longer feeling sorry for myself. Concerned at letting Redda down made me forget how low I had been. He had done me a huge favour. Not how he intended, but that's beside the point. His visit and what he said snapped me out of my misery.

I watched him tag onto a line of six or seven men. He picked up the pace and scurried along. It's a shame I couldn't find a way to show my gratitude. I owed him. Maybe one day I would let him know. Relieved at feeling better, I vowed to never let myself sink into those depths again. Self-pity is a disgusting weakness. The minute I felt it coming on I would ward it off. That was my firm resolve.

21. CHANCE

It came again in my cell at night; a feeling of deep despair. I lay awake in knotted sheets staring at the dark. Though weak and exhausted, sleep refused to come. I felt stunned - pole axed. The sentence hit me hard because I didn't see it coming. It should have been obvious. As time passed, Huckle and Ron became quiet in expecting the worst. I remained cheerful. Not for a minute did I reflect on the unacceptable. I ignored Reg Magee when he said I would have to do time, and when the clerk of court referred to his presentencing report its meaning did not register with me. I held onto the belief that freedom was within reach.

Maybe jail had always been on the cards for me. When aged four I knocked on doors collecting food for war orphans. The big kids told me what to say.

'The orphans like tinned peaches, Misses.'

Irish stew and that kind of stuff we dumped in rubbish bins. Johnny Crocker carried a tin opener in his pocket. We sat by the aerodrome fence, eating tinned peaches, fruit salad and pineapple rings. When all the fruit was gone, we slurped syrup from the cans. What fun. I waited in the afternoons for the big kids to come home from school. They taught me how to shoplift. Once the shopkeeper's back was turned, grab chocolates off the counter. I loved the thrill of it. Getting what I wanted for nothing. From there I became a petty thief – an opportunist. I beat the law of the land time and time again. Another law brought me down - the law of chance, the law of probabilities. Nobody wins all the time. Not at everything. Even the great and the good get caught one way or another. Every sequence has to end. No one can throw a head on every toss of the coin and the longer the sequence the closer its end.

Men in the yard spend their lives going from one jail to the next. I had better things to do with my life. I had to change. Would change. Vital that I did. I couldn't go through this again. I knew I would have to work for everything I wanted to get. That's fine. I wasn't lazy. Work didn't bother me. Where I might struggle is dealing with authority. I had always kicked against it. Other people manage. They tolerate being told what to do. It can't be difficult. I could learn. Adapt. Or better still, find a way to work for myself. That had to be my long-term goal.

Having made these resolutions, I thought I'd be able to sleep. Not a chance. A dread of Yatala kept me awake. What would it do to me? What would I be like at the end of it? The night dragged on.

22. ARMED ESCORT

I am leaving Adelaide Gaol – goodbye, goodbye. There I go, out between the bottle green gates, slipping under the sandstone arch. Goodbye. I'm off on a one-way trip to Yatala Labour Prison, me and other convicts in the back of a Black Maria. Roughly a dozen of us. I am not in the mood to take a proper count. Silence reigns. Sombre moods amongst us. Knitted brows. Glum expressions. Everyone lost in their own thoughts. I can hear the whir of tyres on the road and rumble of our engine. This shouldn't be happening to me. But it is.

We are being escorted by armed police like very important people. But there are no crowds beside the road watching us go by. Not that I care to check. I have no wish to look at the world I am being taken from.

Everyone dressed in civvy clothes. Ted in his old-fashioned suit, all I've seen him wear. Redda is also wearing a suit which is creased and long overdue for a trip to the cleaners. The brim of his hat tugged down low. Ron and Huckle are here, also Grimshaw and Dutchy who were sentenced during the same week. Grimshaw's jeans and jacket are scruffy. He looked better dressed in a prison uniform. Dutchy's outfit is foreign. Buttoned flaps cover the breast pockets of a tweed jacket. It might look smart where he comes from. When stripped, Dutchy's chest bore a memento from his seafaring past. A fully rigged ship cut through waves just above his navel. The top of its main mast reached his neck and unfurled sails spread across the width of his chest. He took a deep breath to get more wind behind his sails, then twitched a few muscles to make the canvas flutter. The best tattoo in Adelaide Gaol was shipping out.

63

I thought I'd remember everything that happened in Adelaide Gaol. Later, I discovered there were gaps were in my memory. I could only remember Sarge as being our warder in number One yard. That can't be right. Over six weeks, he must have been relieved on weekends, yet I could can only remember Sarge as being our keeper. And when a warder was stabbed to death by the river Torrens, Ron said we knew the man that did it. His eastern European name meant nothing to me.

'You must remember him. You played him at chess.'

'Did I? Are you sure?'

'You played him more than once.'

'Was he one of the Yugoslavs?'

'Not in One Yard, in Number Four.'

'There wasn't chess in Four Yard.'

'Come on, think about it. It was a remand yard wasn't it? There had to be chess.'

And thinking hard I could recall chess being played under the arches of Ron's cellblock. And really concentrating, I could see myself sitting there studying pieces on a board. But not an opponent. I couldn't form a mental picture of anyone I played against.

Inside the Black Maria, Ted begins to hum. A half-smile on his face. He is going home. And Grimshaw is also wearing a grin. It doesn't seem right that he got six months, considering the number of jobs he did. Not when my sentence is five times longer. His judge must have been in a really good mood.

Grimshaw's grin turns to a leer as he addresses Dutchy.

'I'd say we got a good deal. Six months for six grand's worth of stuff. A month for every grand. Pretty good I reckon. Can't complain about that. And we'll be out for Christmas.'

'Will we,' the Dutchman says.

'Sure we will. Six months commutes down to four and we've done a month already.'

'That counts, does it?'

'Of course it counts. And Yatala ain't that bad, I've been there before,' and Grimshaw looks around to see if what he said made a good impression. The first thing his eyes meet is a poisonous glare coming from Redda Lewis. He dips his head and stares at his desert boots. They fascinate him. He can't drag his eyes away from his scuffed footwear. Nobody else has said a word. The rest of the trip is made in silence.

23. YATALA

Yatala is a serious place and I was aware of its seriousness as soon as I stepped from the Black Maria. Warders stomped around in their boots barking orders and acting tough in bossing us around. Once the handcuffs were removed we were jostled into a line.

'Get over there - there, not here. Move yourself.'

We were told to strip and stand before them naked. Always the first step in establishing control. An older man watched proceedings from a raised doorstep. He wore a grey civilian suit. A black band encircled the crown of his grey felt hat. Arms folded across his chest as he surveyed the new intake. This was my first sighting of the prison governor.

Uniforms dumped at our feet were the same as in Adelaide jail – white moleskin trousers, blue denim shirt and black felt jacket. The slouch hat was identical too.

'Don't put that on yet,' a warder shouted.

Dutchy removed his hat.

An elderly prisoner stood alone beside a wooden chair. He held a pair of scissors and a cloth was draped over one arm. The first man on the chair had clumps chopped off his head. They tumbled down onto the cloth tucked around his neck while lighter tufts fluttered out and sprinkled to the floor. Clippers then ran from his neck up to the top of his head. The barber's eyes seemed unaware of what his hands were doing as if the clippers were working of their own accord. His face had a yellowish tinge like newspaper left too long in the sun. I looked from the barber to old Ted further along the line. A fine pair of examples of what too much jail does to a man.

Once shorn we marched through the inner gates. The vast size of Yatala came as a shock. Acres of asphalt lay before us. Off to the right a long high wall was dotted with tiny barred windows and further ahead lay another high windowed wall. The open space and huge cellblocks dwarfed the size of Adelaide Gaol.

We were lined up before a warder, whose jacket and pockets were fastened by shiny silver buttons. Silver braid adorned his cap and epaulets. A man judging by his build very fond of the knife and fork. His rubbery lips protruded from a pair of fleshy jowls. After clearing his throat, he began dictating prison rules. He paraphrased certain rules and added riders to others.

'Do I make myself clear? Is that understood? Bear this in mind. Do this at your peril. Under no circumstances will you . . . '

In love with the sound of his own voice. Lessor warders standing behind him tried to retain the menace they earlier showed in the sallyport. Glancing over my shoulder, I saw an armed guard on top of a tower. The rifle slung over his back pointed at the sky - a Lee Enfield 303.The induction lecture droned on. And on. At last it came to an end.

Prisoners were led away, going in different directions. A warder led me across the square. We turned right at a low complex and passed a diamond wire fence. Beyond the fenced yard, we entered a T shaped cellblock. One wing lay to the right, one to the left and the third directly ahead. We turned right and then stopped halfway along the wing.

'This is your cell, A Bottom 13. You'll come here when you've picked up your lunch.'

The cell looked bigger than I expected. Almost spacious. Then it dawned on me, it had no bed inside it.

'You'll leave your cell like this every morning, blankets and pillow on top of the hammock.'

The lumpy shelf was a hammock, rolled and strapped to the wall with bedding stacked on top of it.

'Come on!' The warder was striding along the wing.

I followed. We passed a flight of steps climbing to higher levels, and then beyond the middle wing we reached another gate. Through it we entered a small space that fed two yards. I was ushered into the yard on the left. Ron was there already and together we inspected the yard. An open-ended shed backed against an iron fence. Chicken wire ran along its front from waist height up to its roof. Inside it a canvas water bag hung from a rafter. From the shed we ventured down the yard to reach a brick outhouse. Inside it were a toilet, a hand basin and a tap. I yanked the toilet's chain to check if its cistern flushed. It did.

Two sides of the yard were lined by wire fences, another by galvanised iron and a cellblock's brick wall formed the fourth side. A wide walkway ran between the wire fences and perimeter wall. In the corner of the wall, another armed guard gazed down from the top of a tower.

Huckle, Grimshaw and Dutchy arrived and began exploring the yard. Grimshaw's interest suggested he hadn't been here before. Huckle, meanwhile, moped around alone. An hour or so elapsed before other prisoners arrived. They filed in through the gate and ignoring the new arrivals talked amongst themselves. All were young. After twenty minutes or so, a warder opened the gate and a line formed as prisoners then filed through it. Once through the cellblock we passed the yard I had seen earlier, then empty and now full. This was number One yard, reserved for habitual criminals. The low structure beyond it, I now saw was the kitchen. I accepted my lunch through a hatch from a pair of hands. I was first to arrive on my wing. On reaching my cell, I placed my dish on the corner shelf. Between it and the hammock, a pair of earphones hung from a socket. Apart from the hammock and earphones, fixtures and fittings were the same as in Adelaide Gaol.

The ring of feet on metal steps echoed throughout the wing as boots clomped on cast iron steps up to higher levels. More prisoners were arriving. I stood at my door and watched them come, watched them pass. No one paid me any attention. On placing meals inside their cells, they re-emerged and began talking to each other. A man appeared in the doorway of the opposite cell. I didn't see him arrive. Different to the others, he was bright eyed and alert, cleanly shaven. The skin on his face looked as if it had been daubed with lotion. His uniform was immaculate – jacket neatly buttoned, trousers pristine white and a bright sheen on his shoes. The crown of his hat was flat-topped and its brim as flat as a vinyl disc. Apart from its colour it looked like a tango dancer's hat. He switched his glance from me to address the prisoner on my left. Paddy, he called him. The two neighbours engaged in a friendly conversation. The man on my left, an unassuming type, looked like a middle-aged bachelor or somebody's favourite uncle. Though different types, Paddy and Tommy became involved in a lively discussion, like neighbours at the end of the day gossiping over a garden fence.

'Stand by your doors,' boomed a voice from the top of the wing. In the ensuing lull, Paddy noticed me and smiled. He asked if I'd like a newspaper. Yes, I said. He ducked into his cell and emerged with a folded paper. I took a step towards him and stretched out a hand to take it. He lowered the paper, preventing me from taking it.

'Boss,' he called to a warder, higher up the wing, and raised the paper above his head as if hailing a taxi. The warder approached and accepted the paper.

'For this boy,' Paddy said.

The warder checked my cell's number and slashed the paper's front page with a crayon. After writing something on it, he gave the paper to me. A column of cancelled cell numbers ran down the front page. My cell number, AB13, appeared at the foot of the list. I remembered the senior warder saying that trafficking was an offence. Extra time in jail was served if caught giving something to another prisoner. Anything passed between inmates had to go via a warder. Even a newspaper it seemed.

Men moved into their cells as warders bore down on them. I did likewise. As my door slammed shut, my hatch flap dropped open. When all the doors were shut, an order rang out from the vestibule.

'Stand by your doors.'

Down the wing came warders again, taking a count as they flipped each hatch flap shut. Numbers of the count were called, from our wing and above. I sat on my stool and unfolded the paper. Though two weeks old, it was all news to me. I hadn't seen a paper in months. Its front page, grubby and creased, had apart from cell numbers, columns blanked out by printer's ink. I laid the paper aside and removed the lid from my dish. Food was much the same as in Adelaide jail, but conditions here were harsher. At least I had a friendly neighbour in Paddy living next door. Something to be grateful for.

24. TAILORSHOP

On climbing cast iron steps, I could hear the din of sewing machines as I neared the top of the wing. The warder reached a barred gate that he unlocked and opened. Ron and I bypassed him to enter the tailorshop. A warder showed us where to sit and explained what we had to do. My seat was second from the end of a long narrow bench. Ron sat on my right. I soon got the hang of the job. Pressing a pedal under the bench brought my machine to life, and I pushed two pieces of moleskin forward to be stitched together. Machines along the bench fired and stalled and fired again making a racket sounding like bursts of machine gun fire. The overall noise was deafening. Ron and I were the only boys working at the bench. All the other tailors were men. We spent the morning sewing and making moleskin trousers. At the end of the shift we clanked down steps, passing the workshops used by the tinsmiths and cobblers. On reaching A Division we were body searched. Then through its foyer we were counted into our yard. We fetched out our tobacco bags and were rolling cigarettes when someone approached us. His receding hairline made him look too old for this yard.

'I hear you'll be with us for a while,' he said on reaching us. 'My name's Vern. I saw you in the tailorshop.'

We introduced ourselves.

'I've been here seven years.' Vern said, ' If I knew what it was going to be like I would've topped myself. It's been so long now I might as well see it through. They'll have to let me go some day.'

His sad blue eyes were a contrast to a strong jawline and powerful neck.

'How long are you doing?' I asked.

'I'm on the key.'

'What does that mean?'

'Governor's pleasure, they can keep me here for as long as they like. I haven't got a fixed sentence.' Vern shifted his feet and folded his arms. 'I didn't do myself any favours when I first came in. I told them they'd never tame me. That was a mistake, but I wanted them to know they couldn't grind me down. I did solitary a few times and months in separate. That will count against me.'

Behind Vern I could see more inmates coming through the gate. These were outside workers, jostling each other as they swaggered deeper into the yard.

'I copped it sweet,' Vern said. 'Took everything they threw at me. And then I tried to escape. I didn't plan it. One day I'd had enough and just went for it. Back then the brickyard had no fence, just rolls of barbed wire. I hurdled the wire and kept running. A screw shot me from up there,' and Vern pointed at the tower in the perimeter wall.

'I didn't know I had been hit till I stumbled in a ditch. I put out my arms to save the fall and this arm collapsed.'

Vern removed his jacket and rolled up his left shirt sleeve. He raised the arm and turned it round to show a wide jagged scar, running from wrist to elbow.

'I can't bend this finger, see.'

His little finger stuck straight out like how certain ladies prefer to hold a cup of tea.

'The screw who shot me said he was sorry. Said he aimed for my legs, so I said to him, yeah, right, that's why where you hit me is exactly level with the middle of my back.'

Vern was about to roll down his sleeve when Dutchy came up behind him.

'Jeeze, how did that happen?'

Vern turned to study the Dutchman. 'How long are you here for?'

'Less than three months,' said Dutchy, grinning. 'I'll be out by Christmas.'

Vern turned his back to Dutchy, rolled down his sleeve and began threading his arm into the jacket.

'I gave them good reason to keep me here longer. Not smart, but there you go.'

Grimshaw arrived and barged between Dutchy and Vern. 'I'm with Dutchy,' he announced.

Before he could say another word, I chipped in. 'You'll know Grimshaw, Vern, he said he's been here before.'

Vern gave him a hard look. 'He's never been here before.'

Grimshaw showed a flicker of panic, before recovering.

'I . . . I was here under a different name . . . and in a different yard,' and turning to leave, he stopped, beckoned Dutchy to join him and together they wandered off.

Vern watched them go. 'He's never been here before. I know the type. I've seen'em come and I've seen'em go. In here for a sleep and when he gets out he'll tell all his mates that he's done hard time. Jerk!'

Vern began to tell us about the a pair of tailorshop warders - both decent men, he said. A call came from the gate and we tacked onto the line of prisoners going into the cellblock. On walking behind Vern, I noted the number on his back – twenty-seven. Numbers must have been scrapped not that long ago and started again from number one. I had seen numbers two and three working in the tailor shop My number was 936. That's who I was, 936. That's how warders addressed me, 'nine - three - six.'

25. MURPHY

There was always the clatter of sewing machines in the tailorshop, a racket that lasted all day long. I paused in my work amongst the din and watched men crouching over the bench busy at their sewing. Rattling of the sewing machines made the bench vibrate which caused the cotton reels to jiggle around on their posts. Moleskin trousers were being made at my end of the bench, while further along denim shirts were being put together. A little guy sitting opposite me noticed I was sitting idle and he stopped sewing too. Squinting through his glasses he said, 'So, you're only eighteen.'

I nodded. The lenses of his glasses, that were enclosed in wire frames were milk bottle thick.

'Eighteen,' he repeated, shaking his head from side to side. 'I was twenty-two before I stole anything,' and he leaned in closer across the bench to further elaborate. 'I was standing in a crowded bar when I noticed a ten bob note on the floor. I put my foot on it right away. A crowd of blokes beside me were talking as they drank. I kept my foot on the money as I sipped from my glass. Just taking my time. I got more excited as time passed. I was thinking to myself – I'm going to get away with this. It felt great. I was desperate for these blokes to move, to finish their beer and leave. But they got in another round and seemed in the mood to stay for a decent session. So I bent down, put my glass on the floor and pretended to tie a shoe lace and scooped up the ten bob note when rising to my feet.

'I was nervous when I stood up but nobody noticed anything. When I knew I was in the clear, that feeling, that thrill, that's what I try to get back all the time.'

A funny little bloke. I'm not convinced that what he did would be classed as proper theft. It's what a little kid might do, older people too. Just then Murphy started to speak. He was sitting on my left at the end of the bench. I hadn't realised until then that he'd been listening too.

'I used to be scared of jail,' he said, looking at me aside from an upright stance on his chair. 'I thought I'd end up in jail one day and it frightened me. Then up in New Guinea during the war they put me in the stockade. That fixed it. I was never scared of jail again. Nothing scary about it. I got to sleep in a bunk every night. My feet were always dry. I had three regular meals every day and there weren't any mozzies - or not many. I was comfortable and safe. Not like in the jungle. It was dangerous out there. If the Japs didn't kill you the jungle probably would. There were snakes, crocodiles and Christ knows what else. That stockade was the best thing that ever happened to me. Lost my fear of jail, I'm telling you,' and after a pause he went on to add, 'In fact, I've been in and out ever since.'

He then began to laugh in a high pitched giggle and his strange gleaming eyes took on a brighter shine. I turned to my lengths of moleskin, held them firmly together and slamming my foot on the pedal, pushed them towards the needle.

After lunch in my cell and back in the tailorshop. Murphy made a quick return to New Guinea.

'Snipers held us up once,' he said, when our machines were at rest. 'They had us pinned down for almost a week. Finally they surrendered. We starved them out I reckon. They came up the track in single file. The nip in front waved a white rag tied to a stick. We watched them from both sides of the track as they walked between us. One of the Japs had his foot blown off, his foot and the bottom part of a leg. He hobbled along on one leg and this other bloody stump.

'The bloke next to me said – look at that animal. Look at him will ya. He's the kind of fanatic we have to fight against. He raised the butt to his shoulder and when he pulled the trigger, a whole volley of shots rang out from both sides of the track. That Jap went down with more lead in him than there is on church roof.'

Murphy's eyes began to widen, became brighter, and his speech came at a faster rate.

'Later, the rest of them died. That's the problem with jungle warfare. If you take any prisoners there's nowhere to put them.'

'But you had a stockade,' I reminded him.

'The stockade! That wasn't for them. That was for the likes of us.'

He started to giggle, his mouth wide open and his chin bouncing up and down. His eyes took on a frenzied stare, grew bigger, and shone as if electrically charged. I had to look away. A pair of trousers lay beneath my needle's shoe. I got the needle going, guided the crutch around in an arc and raced down the inside leg. Murphy was still giggling as I locked off at the cuff.

26. SLOP OUT

Prisoners were standing at their doors before the evening lock up. Men chatted to each other all along the wing. Snippets of small talk passed between one convict and another. Gruff exchanges rose above the buzz of idle gossip. Casual banter carried on all along the wing, except for Tommy and Paddy who were engaged in an earnest conversation. Each expressed an opinion without trying to influence the other. There were no interruptions, no pauses, just a constant flow of dialogue. Tommy flicked his eyes my way and saw me gawping at him. He quickly looked away, but Paddy having seen the glance turned around to face me.

'How are you settling in?' he said, and to my muttered reply he added, 'do you like jam?'

When I answered yes, he said he wasn't keen on jam and ducked into his cell. He then emerged with a tin of jam held behind his back.

On thrusting the tin towards me, he said, 'quick, take it,' and he shook the tin in urgency, urging me to grab it. He was no longer facing me but looking further up the wing to where a warder stood.

I grabbed the tin, fully aware that this exchange broke prison rules. I hustled the jam into my cell and on my return found Tommy and Paddy had resumed their conversation. The order came to enter our cells. When the final count was done and hatch flaps were slammed shut, I examined Paddy's gift - a tin of jam three parts full, apricot in flavour.

The brand of the jam was IXL, very clever – I excel.

The senior warder in his lecture said we had to wait six months before we could buy from the shop. As a new prisoner, I

77

shouldn't have jam in my cell. I decided to eat all of the jam and return the tin to Paddy next morning. That night I heaped jam on my bread and wolfed it down. And taking spoon-fulls from the tin I shovelled them into my mouth. In the morning I mixed the rest of the jam in with my porridge - delicious. Breakfast fit for a king.

When my door was unlocked in the morning I stepped outside to find Paddy. He wasn't there, but remained inside his cell. Two warders, after unlocking the doors now stood on the wing, casting their eyes up and down. Prisoners emerging from their cells were ready for the slop out. Everyone holding their bucket by its rope handle. Still no Paddy. I had my bucket in one hand and jam tin in the other, held behind my back. Paddy still had not appeared. At last he sauntered out of his cell and started to talk to Tommy. My 'ppssst – ppsssts' went unnoticed. A warder looked my way, forcing me to keep quiet. The order came to move out. I ducked into my cell, removed the bucket's lid, dropped the tin into it and returned to the wing. We were on the march. I swivelled the bucket around by twisting its rope handle, hoping the tin would sink. As we marched out through the portal I sloshed the bucket around. On turning beyond B wing we met empty handed inmates coming towards us. Greetings and comments flowed between the two passing lines. I walked on tight lipped, swirling and shaking my bucket. Down we trooped between Five Yard and the stone wall. On reaching the corner where an armed guard towered above, I marched towards Four Yard. The latrine gang came into view. As I shuffled forward, closer to the cesspit, bucket lids clanged when slung onto a heap. Next came the splashes of slops as they were hurled into the cesspit. A warder, standing midway between the lids and cesspit supervised the process. I switched the bucket to the hand furthest from the warder. On nearing the heap of lids, I removed mine and saw with alarm the jam tin floating on top of the slops. The warder was bound to see it. On passing him I kept my eyes to the front. Another step, another step closer and I arrived at the head of the line. My bucket was taken. As I turned I heard the splash of my slops. I prayed the tin would sink, fearing that it wouldn't. And waited to hear my number called. Desperate to flee from the scene, I wanted to push the inmate's back who walked ahead of me. He continued to amble. Splash went the next bucketful. No shout from the warder yet. I was no longer last in the line of empty-handed prisoners. Another step from the cesspit, holding my breath and listening for the next splash to come. It came. It seemed I was in the clear.

On reaching the square, I gave a sigh of relief and had a big smile on my face as I joined the tailorshop gang.

27. SHOWERS

The weekly showers were done on a Saturday morning and my wing, A Bottom was first to be called. Directly from slop out, I returned to the cellblock and from a makeshift table picked up the bundle of clothes with 936 showing on the back of my brand-new shirt. I proceeded onto C wing and dropped my towel and change of clothes in front of a vacant booth. As a former cell, the booth's door had been removed and its window bricked in. Plumbing had been installed. Once stripped I ventured into the booth and turned on both taps. Water pelted down from a large showerhead, gushing at mains pressure. On stepping into the torrent, it felt as if hundreds of red-hot needles were striking me. Skin on my back and shoulders tingled from the needling. My first shower in months. I had no shower in Adelaide Gaol apart from the day I arrived. For two months I washed in cold water, splashing myself from an enamel dish placed on top of a stool. What a difference. This was wonderful. I felt enlivened - revitalized. And tilting back my neck, I welcomed the deluge onto my face. Heaven. The soap was the same type my mother used to rub on stained clothes. Awful stuff to lather. But here in the heat and steam, great dollops of suds were produced. I covered myself with slithery foam and nudged the hot tap further on. Clouds of steam filled the booth. I raised my arms and turned around, bent forward and turned from side to side. Then turned the hot tap further on. I could have stayed in there for hours. If the screws knew the pleasure it gave I would've been hauled out long ago.

I took a peep from the doorway and saw that men were drying themselves. Reluctantly I joined them. A babble of happy voices rang out along the wing. Everyone in a good mood, physically cleansed and mentally stimulated. Plenty of tattoos on display – panthers, eagles and naked women were common images. Lots of self-made tattoos too, that were made obvious by their needle pricks being spaced apart. LOVE and HATE on the knuckles, also the Saint, a stick figure with a halo hovering over its head. The Saint could be seen on arms and legs, on the front and sides of bodies and one prisoner's neck.

'Look at me,' called a burly figure as he came tripping down the wing, up on his toes and his outstretched hands fluttering like the wings of a little bird. 'Look at me, look at me, thirteen stone of big bouncing girl.'

A shout came from up the wing. 'Get out of it Mary, you're nothing but a hairy arsed boy.'

Mary stopped and standing knock-kneed, flapped an open hand in the air. 'Don't be horrid. Ouooo, don't be horrid.'

A warder then got involved. 'Get back here Mary or I'll put you on a charge.'

On making his return, Mary swung his hips from side to side as he sashayed past cat calls and hoots of laughter. When he had gone, I watched a well-built man towelling himself with vigour. Middle aged with a muscular build and not a tattoo on him. Turning to his neighbour and said, 'I don't waste my time in jail. I take the opportunity to educate myself.' I was surprised by the pride he showed in educating himself. He didn't look the type. I had a problem with education. I hated school with a passion and couldn't get out of it quick enough. My lasting impression of school was, 'sit still, shut up and listen.' It amazed me when my parents agreed that I could leave. I think at fourteen, they had given up on me. But educating yourself. That was a different concept. Learning what you wanted to know rather than having to memorise what a teacher dictated. I could see the sense in that.

A shout came echoing down the wing.

'Hey Janawouski what's that tattoo on your dick? It looks like a spider.'

'It might look like a spider now. When I get a hard on it's the Saint.'

Ah, that Saint, he certainly gets himself around.

Men by now were dressing. Some had brought clean socks with them. Mine were in my cell. I wouldn't forget to bring them on the following week. My uniform was brand new. Thrusting each leg through new moleskin felt luxurious, as did threading my arms into virgin denim sleeves. The warder in charge urged men on and seeing most were ready, gave the order to march out. I laced my boots and scurried along to join the line snaking into the foyer. Once back in my yard I felt like a new man. At last there was something to to look forward to in Yatala - the Saturday morning shower.

28. SHORTY

Saturday. A lovely spring morning. I had been showered unlike others in the yard. Shorty and I were leaning against the galvanised iron fence. I fetched out my tobacco bag and started to draw its strings apart.

'Put that away. Here, try one of these,' and Shorty offered me his tobacco tin. 'Those bags are no good. Boob weed is dry when you get it and by the end of the week it's like straw.'

'Thanks. What's this black stuff in your weed? Looks like mouse dirt.'

'Pipe tobacco, it comes in flakes. You grind it up and mix it with the boob weed. Go on, roll one. We call it grouse and we use the tobacco flakes for gambling.'

'And this thing,' I said, flicking a dark object that looked like a strip of leather.

'Potato peel. It helps keep the tobacco moist. A bloke on my wing works in the kitchen.'

I rolled a smoke, lit and drew on it. After months of boob weed, the grouse was sensational. Smooth on the throat, aromatic and had a real kick in it. I couldn't thank Shorty enough. He waved my thanks away and said he would give me his tin before being released. He was due to go out after Christmas. Sprawling there in the sun, refreshed by the shower and smoking grouse perked me up no end. Made me feel glad to be alive.

Over by the lean-to, Vern was talking to a boy due to go out next week. He and his friends had done four years for Robbery with Violence. They were also birched. I didn't know people in this state could get flogged. I asked one of them if it hurt. He didn't answer, just looked at me. I know, it was a stupid question. Vern would miss these boys. He liked to mix only with inmates doing a lengthy sentence.

'I guess Vern killed somebody, huh?'

'Yeah, he did. An old prospector, out by Iron Knob. Dunno why he killed him. He was on the run from reform school. He hid the body, came back to Adelaide and joined the army. Volunteers were needed for the Korean War. He put up his age and was sent to a training camp. It could have been the perfect murder. Nobody knew the prospector was dead. No one reported him missing and even if his body was found Vern would've been in Korea. Nothing to tie Vern to it.'

'How did he get caught?'

'He had nightmares. He confessed to the MP's and they told the cops. The cops took him out to Iron Knob to show where he hid the body.'

'Does his jail hard, Vern, doesn't he?'

Shorty agreed. I said I would hate to do the time that Vern had done. Shorty then astounded me. He reckoned he had been inside for as long as Vern. Shorty was only nineteen. How come, I asked?

'I started stealing cars when I was nine years old. Me and a friend did it together. One of us worked the pedals while the other steered and changed gears. We were always fighting. It wasn't much fun on the pedals. You couldn't see where you were going,' and Shorty paused to take a drag on his roll-up. 'So, putting it all together, I've done seven years I reckon. Yeah, seven years easy. I can't seem to stay outside for long. This time I'm really gunner try.'

I wondered if Shorty had been with a girl but didn't like to ask. And Vern, I thought about Vern. He killed a man and then confessed because of a guilty conscience. Yet he showed no sign of guilt on coming into Yatala. Getting sentenced made him forget about his guilty conscience. He told the screws they'd never tame him. Then tried to escape and was shot. He went through a phase of regretting he hadn't killed himself. Now subdued, you might say tamed, he was doing his jail hard.

Shorty's wing was called from the gate to go for its shower. Once standing, Shorty held up his tobacco tin and said, 'I'll leave you this before I go out.'

'Thanks,' I said, as Shorty joined two others in hastening to the gate. It was lovely lazing there in the sun, feeling clean and refreshed, wearing brand new clothes and smoking a roll-up made from Shorty's grouse.

29. COMEDIANS

Metal steps of the stairway rang to the stamp of prisoners' feet. Up, up, climbed heavy boots tied with leather laces. Up went pairs of kiddy-style shoes fastened with buckle and strap. Up from the bottom of A Division, up past the middle level, up to the top landing. Warders stationed at different levels watched the convicts pass – the jail's whole population, except for those locked in their cells after being pinched. On reaching the upper level, inmates filed along the landing above the shower block. Two warders counted the prisoners through a heavy cell like door. Once inside the hall, two rows of forms were split by an aisle running along its full length. The forms were being filled from the back. By the time I entered the hall it was roughly half full. On a platform at the front an unrolled screen hung from a stand, its base shaped like a pyramid. Once all prisoners were inside every form was occupied.

The flick of a switch cast the hall into semi-darkness. The curtains, made of a thin material, failed to stop daylight from filtering through them. A film projector hit the screen with its V shaped beam and a hush of expectancy settled throughout the hall. All eyes were focused on the screen. Perfect stillness in the room. The title of the film appeared followed by the names of its two protagonists. Men around me went mad. Whoops and hollers were accompanied by heels hammering on the floor. I liked Laurel and Hardy but we hadn't seen them yet. Only their names. When they appeared on the screen mayhem erupted throughout the hall. Men were clapping and cheering, nudging their neighbours and slapping their backs. Not one word of dialogue had been spoken yet. At the first quip in the film, the uproar rose to new heights. A man in the row ahead of me threw himself back with such force that he nearly fell off the form. All around the hall men were going crazy. As the film progressed, antics from my inmates became more bizarre. I spotted across the aisle, a tough looking geezer from my wing. He was almost in a state of collapse. Tears streaming down his face. I looked at the men around me, behaving like little kids at a Saturday matinee.

Beside me Ron had a chuckle, which was good to see. He had not been sleeping well. A neighbour informed him that the last man in his cell had hanged himself. Something Ron did not need to know. He said during the night, shadows in his cell formed gloomy images. His neighbour said he knew the suicide was coming. The man always looked depressed. It wasn't a big surprise when he strung himself up.

Behaviour all around the hall distracted me from watching the film. It amazed me to see all these men letting themselves go. A sudden eruption broke out – an explosion of laughter. I've no idea what brought that on. Men were rocking backwards and forwards, slapping their thighs and howling. I couldn't see on the screen what prompted the outburst.

When Laurel removed his hat and scratched the top of his head, the man on my right rose from his seat and shaking with laughter, pointed a finger at the screen while looking over his shoulder, making sure that everyone saw what Laurel was doing.

Over by the door, a warder sitting on a chair quietly watched the film. Every now and then he smiled. As you would expect. He and I plus maybe Ron were the only people in the room that hadn't lost their senses. I switched from viewing the audience to concentrate on the film. The the pair of comedians had worked their act into a perfect art. Hardy raised his necktie and twiddled it with his fingers. Nobody in real life does anything like that. It amused by being ridiculous. The man on my left had gone hoarse. He leaned forward and gasped, shaking his head from side to side.

The lights came on at the end of the movie. Men were smiling at each other and making comments like – 'how about when Laurel did this,' and 'I loved the part when Hardy did that.' All were happy and content. Everybody satisfied. When a warder gave the order to leave, men at the front rose from the forms and filed towards the door. A pair of warders counted them out. On pouring onto C wing, prisoners turned onto A, and clattered down the iron steps, chuckling and commenting on the film as they descended noisily. At the foot of the stairs men dispersed and returned to their yards.

Movies were shown in that hall every Saturday afternoon. Apart from comedies, there were westerns, war films, dramas and love stories. No films about cops and robbers. No film noir. Nothing that involved crime. It was months before I saw the next Laurel and Hardy film. I enjoyed it very much and laughed at the antics of the two comedians. And I didn't notice anything strange in my fellow inmates' behaviour.

30. SKEETER

On entering the tailorshop toilet, I put my back to the wall and slid down it to sit on the floor. Then fetched out my tobacco bag. Curley Wade, sitting beside the doorway, finished telling a story as I peeled a cigarette paper from its packet. The yarn delighted Skeeter, who seated on the dunny pan let out a series of high-pitched squeals that came out like - 'hee-hee-hee-hee-hee.'

Curley went on to say, 'another time, I went into a security firm to do a robbery. The woman in charge was a stunner. Not only gorgeous but classy. She dressed like a model and talked with a posh voice, not the kind that gets on your nerves. It sounded natural on her, and well, I liked it. I decided to abort the robbery and started talking to her. We went out together. Then I moved in with her. She furnished her apartment like she dressed herself – tasteful, you know, stylish. It suited me just fine,' and Curley flashed an impish grin.

'Everything was great for a while till she discovered how I earned a living. She asked me to leave. If it was up to me I would have stuck with her. Those hoity toity dames can really let themselves go.'

Curley's smile put a dent into both cheeks. Twinkle, twinkle went his eyes.

'Ah well, hi ho, it's back to work we go,' and Curley scrambled up to his feet and swaggered out of the room.

Skeeter was not amused by the second story. Not the kind of story he liked. And Ted, sitting across from me, remained straight faced. His expression hadn't changed since I entered the room. I finished rolling my cigarette and was putting a match to it when Skeeter started his rant. It poured out of him in a high nasal whine.

'This is the worst jail I've been in. The food here is disgusting. Pigswill, that's what it is, pigswill. Treat us like mushrooms here they do, feed us on shit and keep us in the dark.'

Ted did not agree with him.

'The food's alright. I like it.'

'What,' screeched Skeeter, 'you dopey old twat, you don't know any better. That's your problem.'

'What about last night. That steak and kidney pie was lovely.'

'Steak,' Skeeter shrieked, 'that wasn't steak. Chipped bone and gristle, that's what that was. What the butcher chops off. Shoulda been on the floor. Shouda been on the floor with the rest of the scraps. Struth, you wouldn't know what real steak tastes like. You're out of touch with the real world.'

Ted's face coloured. He started breathing heavily.

'I know what steak tastes like.'

'You oughta get out and see the world. See the kind of food you get in these other jails. You've got no idea. The food here is rubbish.'

Ted said he liked it, and Skeeter said he liked it was because he was a dopey old coot.

'I'm telling ya, if they dished up food like this in Pentridge or Long Bay there'd be a riot. And that's a fact. Nobody would stand for it. It's mugs like you that let them get away with it. Treat us like mushrooms here they do, feed us on shit and keep us in the dark.'

Ted was getting himself upset. His bottom lip started to quiver.

'Just you wait till Christmas. Christmas dinners here are great. There're as good as you can get anywhere.'

'Don't talk to me about Christmas. I was here last Christmas. Average, that's what Christmas dinner was – fair to crap.'

Ted looked as if he might cry.

'Cake. They give us cake, don't they?'

'That stodge. Call that cake, do ya?'

Skeeter was rolling a smoke and getting himself so worked up that strands of tobacco were spilling out and sprinkling over his knees.

'This is the worst jail I've been in, he squealed. I'm never coming back to this state, never,' and he jammed his makings into his tin, slammed on its lid and jumped to his feet. On striding to the door, he looked down at Ted.

'It's only mugs like you that let them get away with it,' and Skeeter was gone.

Though I didn't know at the time, I had just witnessed a rare event – Skeeter leaving the toilet of his own choice. The next time I saw him leave was prompted by Mister Conner. Ted was gazing at the floor in the space between us. When he looked up his eyes were moist. 'They give us cake, don't they? I like the cake they give us. You like cake . . . don't you?'

'Yes Ted, I like cake. I like it when we get it.'

We sat in silence for a while. Me smoking, while Ted continued to stare at something on the floor between us. Whatever it was had captured all of his attention.

31. LUGAL

I was getting to know boys in our yard; where they came from and also the kind of lives they led. John McCreery surprised me by saying he used oxyacetylene to cut a hole in a safe.

'I didn't think you could cut through the door of a safe.'

'Not through the door. I go through the back or one of its sides.'

'Oh.'

And I learned that a quiet English boy had beaten up little kids. Not only beat them but tortured them too. I wanted nothing to do with him. I also stayed clear of the quarrymen. Grimshaw and Dutchy had joined their gang. The quarry gang was welcome to them. I kept my distance. The Greek killer, having come up from Adelaide Gaol, shuffled around the yard in a subdued mood. He hadn't done his yoga trick and I hadn't heard him laugh once. That's what getting sentenced does. It knocks all the fun out of a man.

I mainly hung around with Shorty, Lugal, Geppy and Phillip. They did their jail easy and I hoped by being with them I would start to feel the same as they did.

'The first six months are the worst,' Phillip said to me.

He thought that would make me feel better. It didn't. Did I have to feel as low as I did for a whole six months. Still, I enjoyed being in the company of the four boys.

Lugal said, 'the screws put bromide in our tea to stop us thinking about sex.'

Phillip said they weren't giving him enough. He was at it every night, him and Madam Five Fingers.

'That's normal,' Shorty informed him.

Phillip came from Melbourne. The other three grew up together in the local reform school. Perhaps that's why they did jail easy. Reform school got them ready for it. Shorty mentioned a lad unknown to me. 'A pity Jammy's in solitary. He missed a good movie today. Best flick we've had for months. He's still got three days to go, hasn't he?'

Geppy ignored the question by posing one of his own. 'Always seven days ain't it? Never two or three days, always seven.'

'They can give you fourteen if they like. Seven in, seven out and back in for the other seven.'

Geppy snapped back at Shorty, 'that's what I said, seven days. It's always seven days.'

'Tell you one thing though, by the seventh day that bread tastes as good as Christmas cake.'

Geppy glared at Shorty. 'Christmas cake! Dunno what kind of bread you got. Mine tasted like bread - stale bread. That's what I got, stale bread every day and never enough water.'

The sun was out and bouncing off the fence's corrugations. Ron and Phillip were facing the fence. Phillip narrowed his eyes as they switched from speaker to speaker, while Ron's hat was dipped low to shield the sun's reflections. I was facing the lean-to. Grimshaw and Dutchy were in there with a listener trapped between them.

'One thing about reform school, there was no solitary,' and after a short ponder, Lugal added, 'and another good thing, it was easy to abscond. Can't do that here. Look what happened to Vern.'

Geppy said they took off plenty of times. Lugal agreed. We sure did, he said. They both laughed as they reminisced and told us some of the things they did when on the run. Geppy had the most to say and Lugal nodded as he repeated, 'yeah, yeah, we did, didn't we?'

Once they blew a safe. They stole gelignite from a quarry and put three sticks of it under the safe just like in the comics. After lighting the fuses, they sheltered behind a desk turned onto its side.

'Jeeze we were lucky. The door of the safe got blown off and smashed a hole through the wall.'

'Right above our heads,' Lugal interjected. 'Any lower and it would've killed us. Ain't that right, Geppy?'

'Yeah, it would've.'

And then they were fighting each other to finish off the tale. Geppy gave way to Lugal.

'And the money. The room was full of money, up in the air, floating down, money flying everywhere.'

And Geppy shrieked, 'some of it was on fire.'

'Didn't get much though, did we?'

'Nah, grabbed a handful of notes and got to hell out of there.'

Geppy said Lugal absconded more times than anybody else. Geppy would have gone with him if he knew Lugal was going. Lugal said he took off whenever he got the chance.

'I remember one time, I busted out and was hitching a ride. An old couple picked me up and I told them I'd just absconded. Don't know why I told them, but I did. They said I could go home with them. So I went. They lived on a farm and said I could stay for as long as I liked.

'The man showed me how to drive a tractor. I thought he only wanted me there so I could work for them. That wasn't true. I didn't have to work, not if I didn't feel like it. I could read books all day, or take out his twenty-two and shoot rabbits. They were nice people – good to me. The lady asked what I liked to eat. She'd cook whatever I wanted. Name it, she said. But her cooking was fine. Good tucker. They took me into the town, gave me money and bought me clothes. Couldn't do enough for me.'

I was watching a bird as I listened, a starling on top of the wall. The first bird I had seen in Yatala. There's nothing for birds to do in jail – there are no trees, no plants or grass, no dirt or any worms. I had never seen a bird fly over the top of Yatala. Birds gave Yatala a wide berth. This starling was looking down at us through the diamond wire fence. I wondered what a bird thinks when looking at humans in a cage.

'The man had a shotgun too. He said I could take it out, plus a box of cartridges. But I liked the twenty-two. I got pretty good at hitting a tin from a long way off. He let me drive their car too. He must've known I was too young to have a licence. I could take the car out by myself. They couldn't do enough for me. They were real nice people.'

Lugal had our attention now. Nobody interrupted. Not even Geppy. Though I guessed he had heard the story before.

'They had no kids. One day the lady told me they didn't have no family. No relations. Nobody. When they died there was no one to leave the farm to. If I stayed with them it could be mine. They'd leave it to me in their will.'

Lugal paused, drew in a breath and slowly let it out.

'I didn't want to steal from them but I couldn't live a life like that. I had to get away. One night I loaded the car and took off. I dumped the car at Port Lincoln.'

He shrugged and paused, 'I think about them sometimes . . . they were nice people. They were really good to me.'

Sitting crossed legged, Phillip sat with his head lowered to avoid the glare from the iron fence. He was flicking a leather bootlace.

'I wonder who'll get the farm,' he said.

32. MALARIA

Murphy was not the talkative type, and he never interacted with his inmates. He didn't talk to the prisoners sitting opposite him. Nor did visit the toilet where crims gathered for a smoke and to have a natter. When passing One Yard, I often saw him close to the fence standing alone. Basically, he was shy. But he often talked to me, probably as he thought of me as just being a kid. All he talked about was the war, about his time in New Guinea fighting the Japanese. Sitting straight backed in his chair, he sewed by straightening out his arms to push two lengths of moleskin towards the needle's shoe. He was tall, long in body and long in neck. His thick crinkly hair stood upright like a crop of grain. It was hard to tell where his scalp stopped and roots of his hair began.

He asked if I'd seen malaria. I told him I had. A kid in primary school got bashed and his father came into the schoolyard and threatened to beat the kid that did it. A real scary man, shivering as if he was very cold and his skin was sweaty and yellowish.

'A teacher said he acted like that because he had malaria.'

'Yeah, you've seen it. Horrible disease, horrible. He would have been in New Guinea fighting against the Japs. Plenty of our blokes got it. And it keeps coming back. A man thinks he's clear of it and back it comes again. It brought some good men down. But here's the thing, none of our mob got it. Not one of us. Malaria was rife except for our mob. We stayed clear of it. That was down to our Colonel. He was a clever bloke, our Colonel. He told us when we washed not to use any soap. He reckoned the mozzies only went for clean and fresh skin. That's what he worked out. He must've been right coz none of us got it. A decent fella too. Come to think of it, most officers up there were decent fellers.'

The little bloke opposite me had stopped sewing. I could see that he had tuned into what Murphy was saying.

'Not all of them, though. On the way up there, one officer on the ship was a pig of a man. Shouting orders all over the place. Full of himself. He put a soldier in the brig. Imagine that, putting a man in the brig when he's going to fight for his country. All he'd done was get drunk. We steered clear of him. He would've been a nightmare in a war zone. The kind of bloke who would send you out on a suicide mission.'

Murphy paused and his eyes took on a brighter gleam.

'Yeah, he was a wrongun. Nobody wanted to be with him when we reached New Guinea. As it happened he didn't make it.'

Staring at me, Murphy's eyes grew bigger, turned brighter and took on a luminous glow. His voice raised to a higher pitch.

'He went over the ship's side before we got to Moresby.'

Then he started to cackle with his jaw becoming unhinged. Eyes shining like beacons. His cackling became shriller as his eyes took on a brighter glow. I couldn't stand to look at him. Firing up my machine, I pushed two pieces of moleskin towards their intended union. The little bloke across from me started sewing too. His head was down. He was going at it.

33. CROOKED COPS

'Crooked cops, they should be shot and burnt,' and Skeeter's voice rose to a screech as he became more incensed. 'They're everywhere, the force is lousy with them. I've come across them in every state. Unfair competition, that's what they are. They rob the public as well as us and they'll say anything to get a pinch.'

Sitting on the toilet, he squirmed in agitation. 'I've been fitted up twice. It's a joke. Last time, I did eighteen months for a bust in Toorak. I was nowhere near the place. I was miles away doing a bookie's house over in Pascoe Vale. What chance has a man got, eh, what chance has he got when a cop stands up in court and tells a pack of lies? Crooked cops, God strike a light, they should be exterminated.'

Across the room from me, Harold was sitting beside a bloke with very thin lips. I was trying not to stare at his mouth. Skeeter sat shaking his head, his face screwed up in disgust. At that moment Ray Cullen strode into the toilet.

'Crooked cops, Ray, that's what we're on about. Aren't they the bane of our lives?

Ray squatted and sat on his heels across the room from Skeeter. I didn't know Ray's name when I heard him say he educated himself. Busy now rolling a smoke, his tobacco tin balanced on on top of a flexed thigh. All our eyes were on him. Nobody said a word. Skeeter's mouth hung open as he waited for a response. With the roll-up completed and lit, lid clamped on his tin, Ray took a leisurely drag, exhaled, and began to speak.

'I used to deal with a certain Sydney detective. I paid him to bury all the charges against me. The paperwork just vanished. Details of the pinch simply disappeared.'

Ray's voice had a commanding tone. Everyone listened. All of us watching him.

'Trouble was, the price kept going up. It started as a fair deal - a decent portion of the take. Then he wanted half of it. I didn't mind financing his standard of living, till greed got the better of him. On one particular job he wanted the full whack. All of it. I said I wouldn't pay it. He said there were lots of palms to grease, all that kind of rubbish.'

He paused to work his tin and matches into a trouser pocket. 'I said I wouldn't pay it. I'd take my chances in court. He said if I did that he would lay it on thick. He would make sure I went down. He did lay it on thick, saying how serious the job was and he tried to link it to other cases. The judge said he was making unsubstantial claims. Claims not supported by evidence. The judge threw the case out. I walked. The detective didn't know I got to the judge. He was cheaper too.'

Puckering up his thin lips the bloke across from me let out a whistle. Skeeter's weasel eyes were darting around in his head.

'On another occasion,' Ray went on to say, 'I blew a tank in an office above a Greek restaurant. This was in Melbourne at the bottom of Swanson Street. I didn't do this job with Tommy. Chook Todd was my lookout man. He waited in a telephone box just outside the restaurant and would ring if there was a problem. An unmarked car drove past and one of the cops recognised Chook. He wondered why Chook was in the box and not making a call. They drove around the block, pulled up and nabbed Chook before he could give me a ring.

'I blew the tank no problem and walked out the door with a bag full of money, straight into the arms of the law. Eight grand was in that bag. Things were not looking good. Then would you believe, the owner of the restaurant refused to press charges. He said the money was mine. Said he was holding it for me and lost the key to the safe. He arranged for me to blow it at night. So I walked from that job too,' and Ray took another drag on his cigarette.

'I asked the cops for my eight grand. I said I won it at the races. The cops said to forget it. The money had gone towards the Police Benevolent Fund, more like into their pockets.'

After that we sat for a while. A bit of small talk passed around before Ray finished his smoke and went back to work. I put a query to the bloke sitting across from me. Honestly, his lips were as thin as pencil lines.

'When Ray said Tommy wasn't with him on that job, would that be Tommy Godfrey?'

'Sure was. Ray and Tommy came in together. They're doing the key. They have to wait seven years before they ask for parole. They were fitted up too. Ray said they weren't even in this state when the job was done . . . yeah, I know, shocking. And it gets worse. A Sydney detective paid them a visit and said they'll be plucked at the gate when they get out of here and taken back to Sydney. Ray said they did that job and the cop's got evidence.'

We sat in silence for a while. Everyone in their own thoughts. Even Skeeter. I was thinking of Ray and Tommy. How they got on with their jail without seeming concerned. Spending that long in jail would have crushed me.

34. ABDUL

Redda Lewis, crouching low, scuttled along beside the bench and bobbing up he fired a shot from a finger of his right hand. I turned to look where Redda had aimed and there was Abdul returning fire from his barrelled fingers. His thumb upright and cocked while taking aim at Redda. On firing at each other, loud explosive noises came from the back of their throats.

'Gotcha,' Redda yelled.

'Nah, ya missed,' and Abdul let go three rapid shots.

Redda ducked. Now Abdul crouched and scooted towards where I was sitting. He was giggling like a little kid. I could see the top of Redda's head as he beat a hasty retreat on the other side of the bench. Good move Redda. Abdul paused in the space between Murphy and me, popped up and ran his eyes along the full length of the bench, and seeing no sign of Redda, sneaked past Murphy to round the bench and squint towards the toilet. Redda had gone. Abdul dithered, his gun still raised and cocked, as he pondered which side of the bench to take. Then he dashed past the little bloke sitting across from me.

When the gunmen had gone Ron and I grinned at each other. The little bloke in wire-framed specs shook his head and tut-tutted. Murphy sewed on regardless as if he had not seen anything. Except he did. Who knows what Murphy thought, him being a gunman himself.

It was good to see Redda easing himself into his five-year lagging. First time I'd seen his playful side. It suited him. His look of glee helped offset the hardened features of his face. The knob of knitted bone on his nose became less noticeable. He should smile more often. Abdul, on the other hand was always in a happy mood, often waggling his eyebrows as he smiled and showed off a huge gold tooth.

Abdul's name was not Abdul. Not his real name. Nobody knew what his real name was and Abdul wasn't saying.

'What would be the point? Nothing would change. I'd still get called Abdul. Besides, I've grown attached to the moniker.'

As the White Australia Policy was still in force, one might wonder how Abdul managed to get into the country. One suggestion was he descended from an Afghan camel driver who came to work on the telegraph line from Adelaide up to Darwin. News to me, Abdul said. Though one day in the toilet, a bank robber claimed it was Abdul who had started the rumour. Whatever his heritage, it was plain to see his ancestors were familiar with camels. If wearing a turban or fez, Abdul would look the real McCoy.

Despite not knowing his origins, Abdul impressed his fellow inmates.

'That Abdul, how does he get away with it?'

'Beats me.'

It beat everyone. And Abdul did not care to reveal. He shrugged, ducked the question and smiled. Flashed his golden nugget. Abdul did not work for the government. He didn't make prison uniforms. That wasn't for him. He didn't sit at a sewing machine making trousers or shirts. Nor did he make denim bags for tobacco and sugar rations. Abdul did his own thing. He worked at the top of the shop beyond the WC sitting on a highbacked chair at a private bench. Getting on with his project, or rather, watching the warder (Mister Conner's colleague) working on the project. Abdul supervised. He was supposed to be taking instruction on how to become a tailor. And I guess he was, apart from going to the toilet for a smoke or sloping off with Redda Lewis playing cops and robbers.

Abdul was having a suit made. A tailor-made suit to fit himself. The governor must have known about it. That's what nobody understood – the governor allowing a privilege. Unheard of. The governor took delight in removing privileges, not granting them.

Abdul had had the cloth sent in which must have been wrapped when it arrived. Everybody doubted that the governor ever saw it. Its broad bands of charcoal and cream were typical gangster material. The suit was at an early stage. All that existed so far was the foundation for its jacket, made from a stiff material similar to hessian. Pleats were tugged and tucked to fit Abdul's body shape and held in place by cotton stitches going in all directions. The scarlet cloth at its back may have been silk. No sleeves were yet attached but thick pads were stitched on top of both shoulders. Its lapels were wide at the top and tapered to a narrow finish below waist height. The jacket when finished was going to be a double-breasted garment. The bolt of fabric sat on the bench. Crims came to admire it and smoothing their hands over it nodded their approval.

Abdul would slip on the garment and strut around showing it off. One hand propped on his hip, the other held at the back of his neck. His gold tooth glittering and his eyebrows twitching up and down. The warder, delighted at the interest shown in the craft of tailoring, beckoned Abdul to join him and added another stitch, then ran his hand from Abdul's armpit down over his hip.

Ahh, that Abdul, inmates said, shaking their heads as they returned from their latest viewing. Nobody knew how he got permission to have his suit made and Abdul had no intention of letting anyone know.

35. PINCHED

The congregation fiddled and stretched. Feet shuffled and mouths yawned. Coughs rang out from various sections of the church hall. Elbows were lowered to rest on knees, heads dipped and yawns were stifled. And the priest droned on. I felt the need to fidget, drew in my legs then stretched them out and squirmed around on the seat. And the priest soldiered on. A loud sigh was heard to drift from the back of the hall. The sermon showed no sign of ending. On and on it went. A warder sitting by the door had both eyes closed. Chin resting on his chest. The tone of the priest's voice lacked any variance. It remained at the same level, a long monotonous drone pouring from his mouth, as if he wanted the congregation to go into a trance.

My eyes were fixed on the warder. He had begun to slump in his chair. He leant forward, further and further, his head lowered close to his knees. Then all of a sudden he sprang back and sat bolt upright. His eyelids popped open. No doubt the priest was a decent chap, true to his faith and well-meaning towards his fellow man. It's a pity he had to be such a bore.

The Catholics didn't suffer like this. Shorty said their priest was a hoot. Irish, Witt by name and witty by nature. His sermons had the Micks in fits. Between Hail Mary's and their chants he entertained the left footers. They bounced back into the yard, lively and refreshed after paying their dues to their religious belief. Lucky old them.

I thought I recognised the voice coming from behind.

'If I ever come back here, I'll be an atheist. I'd rather be in my peter than sit through this.'

'Me too,' added another voice and a few muffled grunts confirmed further agreement.

The warder's head drooped again. His eyes were shut. Falling forward in his chair, falling, falling. Damn, he jerked upright again. I willed him to fall asleep. Imagine if he started to snore. That would send the priest a message.

At last the sermon ended. It came to an abrupt halt. No summing up, nothing to link together all the rambling strands running through his sermon. He just stopped. The warder sat up popeyed.

The priest displayed a kindly smile. 'We will now sing a hymn,' and he declared its number.

The congregation showed its relief in getting to its feet. Necks were stretched, feet shuffled and men shook their shoulders loose. Throats were cleared as hymn book pages were being leafed through. When the Priest began to sing, he revealed that he could indeed vary the tone of his voice. I'm not sure what the hymn was called but its chorus consisted of 'Crown him, crown him,' repeated several times. At the second airing of the chorus the voice from behind said, 'with a beer bottle,' and the whole row behind me burst out sniggering.

I was sure I knew that voice and turned to see Redda Lewis with a smirk on his face. When I turned to face the front the warder was storming down the aisle with me fixed in his sights. On reaching my form he leaned in and hissed:

'936, you're pinched.'

Back in the yard I related what had happened in church. The boys fell about laughing.

'Wait till you meet the magistrate. Haaa!' was Geppy's retort. And Lugal added: 'When it's your turn to speak watch him adjust his hearing aid,' and Shorty cut in with, 'that's him switching it off.'

Didn't they laugh? They thought it was hilarious. I failed to see its funny side. I said the screw couldn't prove I said anything.

My back was turned to him. That really cracked them up. Talk about a scream.

'Save your breath,' Shorty said, 'that Magistrate's been coming here for ten years at least and he's never acquitted anyone. Not once, not ever.'

And Geppy again: 'He'll be half cut anyway. The Governor butters him up for lunch and tops him up with gin. Take a good look at his eyes, they'll be squiffy I bet.'

Phillip said I was lucky. The screw could have sloughed me up. I could be locked in my cell now without any smokes or anything. They delighted in telling me the punishment that I would receive. Loss of remission, no tobacco for two weeks, no library book or earphones and locked in my cell for two weekends. No movies or recreation.

'I wish I hadn't recognised Redda Lewis's voice.'

Other boys beside the fence had been listening. One of them, not long inside and a Melbournite, chipped in at that stage.

'Redda Lewis, he's a well-known gunman.'

'I don't think so,' I said.

'I'm tellen ya, he's a gunman, he's well known for it.'

I dismissed what he said with a shake of my head. I thought he had Redda confused with some other bloke. Redda said he had never used the boot or a bottle in a fight. Why would he need to carry a gun. The boy didn't like me doubting his word, and getting riled, he said:

'And I'll tell ya something else, he was married to the Black Widow. At least six of her boyfriends are dead. Either shot or stabbed. And Redda's been shot. He's been shot a couple of times.'

I looked at the boy and didn't reply. What he said didn't fit with the Redda I knew. The boy having said his piece snorted and turned his head away.

On the following Wednesday afternoon I fronted the magistrate, a thin bent old man with a pouch of flesh hanging beneath his chin. Cords of skin ran from his nose to either side of his mouth. I couldn't tell if his eyes were squiffy. They might have been. He did have gadgets in his ears to assist his hearing. He and the Governor faced me from across a desk. Babcock stood to my left at the end of the desk. The warder, on my right, stated the charge against me. I denied it. I said I didn't say anything. All I did was turn around to look behind me.

The magistrate asked the warder if he was certain it was me who disrupted the service.

'Absolutely, I saw his lips moving.'

He could only see the back of my head and apart from that my lips were not doing anything. For some unknown reason I then tried to be clever.

'Of course my lips were moving. I was singing the hymn.'

The warder trumped my lie with a better one. 'I can tell the difference between somebody singing a hymn and making a smart remark.'

As predicted in the yard the magistrate found me guilty. The boys were also right about the penalties. I lost two day's remission and all privileges for two weeks. The Governor sat with lips pressed into a pout. His gaze never left my face. He didn't utter a word. When dismissed, the warder marched me back to my cell. He confiscated my matches and tobacco. My hammock, blankets and stool were put outside on the wing. He removed my library book, my earphones and slammed the door shut on leaving.

I stared at the emptiness of my cell, at the walls that were green to waist height and stretched from there in a muddy cream to reach the ceiling and cover it. This is where I would spend the next two weekends. Not a happy prospect. In the future I would get used to it.

36. SLOUGHED UP

There was nothing to do inside my cell. I walked lengths of it, did press-ups and shadow boxed. I recalled hearing Shorty say that he played handball with a ball made of newspaper. He hit the ball against the wall and kept it in play. Worth a go. I damped the edges of paper and fashioned a ball. Being too light it failed to bounce so I added more paper to it, which on hitting the wall began to unravel. Starting again, I used more water, really dampening it. This ball hit the wall with a splat and dropped like a stone. That was the end of handball. More press ups, walking and shadow boxing. Voices from number one yard drifted in through my window. If I had my stool I could stand on it and watch what was happening out there.

My lunch arrived at hatch after prisoners were locked in their cells. No hot drink that day. I had to make do with water. Trying to take a nap didn't work as I wasn't tired enough. After the midday break, inmates returned to their yards, and on coming back to A Division they climbed the stairs to watch the Saturday movie. When they clanked back down the cast iron steps, I was occupied in solving jigsaw puzzles. I tore three sheets of newspaper into tiny pieces, mixed them together and then reassembled each sheet. By now my nerves were smarting for want of nicotine.

When inmates were locked in their cells for the night a warder allowed me to fetch in my things from outside on the wing - not the library book and not the earphones. While eating the evening meal, I noticed the bible beside my dish and recalled both Shorty and Geppy having claimed to have read it from cover to cover. Why not do the same? I unrolled my hammock and strapped it to the wall. Made up my bed and crawling between the sheets, I started reading the bible. I intended to reach EXODUS prior to lights out, but I found the bible hard going. A slog. At times I lost my place and going back to the top of the page I realised halfway down it I had read the page already. Sometimes you read but don't absorb the meaning of the words. I quit half way through GENESIS. But I was determined to finish it no matter how long it took. Time was something I had plenty of. Having found a project to keep me occupied, sleep came easily.

37. THE PILOT

The Governor stood at a suitable distance from the morning assembly, allowing him to view all the gangs as they were being organized by his officers. A small man, slightly built, he watched the count being done with arms folded across his chest and lips pressed firmly together. Babock, the chief warder, jotted the numbers into a book as each gang was counted. Prisoners and warders waited for him to reconcile his total with the jail's population. Some could be pinched and locked in their cells, others in solitary and separate confinement. Someone could be in hospital. It happened. He knew those figures already. On reaching a balance he gave the order for prisoners to march to work.

The gangs departed from the square in prearranged order. Quarrymen left in advance of the brickyard gang and skirted around the east side of B Division. Cobblers preceded tinsmiths and tailors in marching around the cellblock's west side. Kitchen hands and laundrymen, cleaners and odd job men were escorted to their places of work and the sole library assistant proceeded to where the books were kept. The locations of library and laundry remained unknown to me.

The inmate walking beside me that day might have been a stand-over man. A tough looking guy, solidly built with hawkish eyes that gave the impression of never having flinched.

'You might not believe this,' he said, 'last night I slept a solid fourteen hours.' He paused to reconsider before carrying on, 'yes, that's what it was fourteen hours. Don't you think that's remarkable?'

It was and I told him so.

We stopped and waited at the portal of B Division. Tinsmiths were not yet secured inside their workshop. Once they were confined, a warder shouted from above and we began climbing the stairs. On passing through the gate, the whir of a drive shaft could be heard coming from under the bench. Once seated on their chairs, tailors stamped on their pedals and leather belts tightened between their machines and cogs placed at intervals along the drive shaft. A host of needles burst into life.

Murphy wasted no time in taking me back to the jungle. He leaned across to catch my ear before making a single stitch.

'Once we brought a plane down with small arms fire. We blazed away at it as it flew overhead. No one expected to bring it down. Blow me down if we didn't. It went into a spin with smoke pouring out of its tail just like in the movies. We all cheered. Everyone reckoned it was their shot that brought it down. The pilot bailed out. We watched his chute open and fired at him as he floated down. Funny that. We hit a plane going at speed but couldn't hit the pilot. You could tell he wasn't hit because his elbows stuck out as he held the cords of his chute. But I reckon his chute got perforated.'

Murphy's eyes were brightening. They were always bright and scary, but now took on a brighter glow. His eyes were not natural. No one is born with eyes like that. Something happened to Murphy to switch his eyes on and now he couldn't switch them off.

'We watched him come down in the jungle. The Colonel sent two men to find him and bring him back. They had a hell of a job. They had to go in a straight line to keep their bearing and used their bayonets as machetes. They waded through a creek and chopped through thick bamboo. It took them ages to get to him. Anyway, they found him, up a tree hanging from his chute. They got him down. One of the blokes shinned up the tree and cut him loose. The Jap didn't have far to fall. There was nothing wrong with him but he refused to walk. Spud, he was one of the blokes,

Spud said they hauled him onto his feet and his legs buckled. More than once. Every time they propped him up he collapsed again. They slapped him around a bit and poked him with their bayonets but he refused to walk.'

Murphy's eyes were glittering. Shining directly at mine.

'So they tied his hands and feet together, then stuck a branch between them and carried him like a pig on a spit. Spud said it was murder. Bad enough getting to him but humping him back through the creek and bamboo was much worse. And the Jap wriggled all the way. It took them ages to get back to camp. They looked shattered when they arrived.

'The cook saw them coming. He shouted they've got one, and ducking into his tent, he came out with a pistol and ran across and shot the Jap in the head. There was hell on about that. Spud and his mate had to be stopped from bashing the cook and the Colonel went berserk.'

'I'm not surprised, shooting a man when he's strung up like that.'

'No, it wasn't the shooting. That wasn't it. The Colonel wanted to question him first. That was the thing. He didn't mind the killing. He was gunner get shot anyway. When the Colonel said our prisoners were inconvenient we knew what we had to do. No, it wasn't the killing. He should've been questioned first.'

Then came the giggling. It spurted out of Murphy like he would never stop. His glowing eyes wide-open in focusing on mine. I had to look away and return to my sewing. Even with my machine going at full pelt, I could hear him giggling.

38. PADDY

Tommy was sick of me gawping at him which I could understand. Whenever he glanced at my hatch, he would see me ogling him and with a look of annoyance, he turned and resumed talking to Paddy. It didn't have to be like that. If at the start I said something like, 'morning Tommy, how the hell are you today,' we might have got on together like a house on fire. But I had lost my pluck on coming into Yatala and I had a problem in getting it back.

In the yard I was one of the boys but on the wing I was timid.

Most inmates on my wing were held in number one yard. Hardened criminals as my mother would say. The only friendly face was Paddy's. Having him as a neighbour helped lift my spirits. I liked to listen to him and Tommy talk. That's why my eyes were fixed on Tommy's hatch. Tommy had plenty of time for the unassuming Paddy. Different types that got on well together.

Paddy's door was locked one morning. He didn't appear for slop out. I didn't say anything to Tommy, not then, but at noon when Paddy's door was still locked I asked what happened to him. I thought he must have been pinched.

'He's been released.'

A rude shock. I don't know how I missed hearing about that. I would have liked to say goodbye and wish him all the best. He helped me to get through my early days in Yatala.

The next man in Paddy's cell was a surly character. A man of few words. A face like stone. He gave me one look and dismissed me, making me feel more isolated. Tommy didn't think much of our new neighbour. That became obvious. They talked, after a fashion. Tommy made the effort. He opened with a subject that Stoneface killed with a blunt, 'yeah, right.'

From there on, Tommy talked to the prisoner on the left of Stoneface. Life went on as before. In the tailorshop, Murphy related incidents from his time in New Guinea. In the toilet I listened to crims tell stories of what they had done in the past. I lazed in the yard during weekends. I listened to earphones in my cell, read the library book and plodded through the bible. Then came the bombshell. It shook me to the core. I could scarcely believe it. But it was true. The grapevine went into overdrive and whipped the news around the jail – into every workplace, through the five yards and onto every wing.

Paddy was dead.

Back in Melbourne, he answered a knock on his door and said hello to a shotgun. It said goodbye to him, twice, once through each barrel. I heard it first in the tailorshop and then again in the yard. None of the boys in the yard knew Paddy but they aware he'd been released recently from Yatala. Now he was dead. Why would someone kill Paddy? That's what puzzled me. He was a likeable guy. Friendly. Not the type to cross anyone. Not a snitch - I was sure of that. I doubted a woman would be involved. It had me beat. I couldn't understand it.

Before our hatches were shut that evening, I heard Stoneface say:

'Did you hear about Paddy?'

Tommy Godfrey answered him with three curt words.

'Painters and Dockers.'

End of conversation.

I knew Painters and Dockers was a corrupt union. I thought it only arranged jobs and provided alibis. I didn't know it had people killed. That became common knowledge by the time the union was disbanded. It was held responsible for more than fifty murders. Paddy was an early victim. I never learned what he did to warrant being killed. Tommy knew, I felt sure of that, but I didn't care to ask. Tommy struck me as a man who knew what was going on. I am not so sure about that now. I later learned his wife had a baby with a younger man. She gave the child for adoption just prior to Tommy's release.

39. SUNDAYS

Shorty suggested I go with him to the Catholic Church. I agreed. Why not? A small chance of me getting pinched. Screws would hardly know I had come to the wrong church. Father Witt was the draw for me. I was keen to see if he could live up to his reputation. Besides, a change is as good as a holiday. The congregation climbed the steps of E wing, somewhere I had never been before.

The priest impressed me from the start. He had his flock enthralled as he switched from mirth to reverence and back to mirth again. In delivering his sermon, he spoke in a brogue as thick as the day he sailed out of Dublin Bay. His followers were entertained by a mix of blarney and charm. Dressed like a monk in a cheap cassock, he interrupted the rituals to make an earthy quip and then became serious to hammer home a righteous point to which nobody could object. Shorty had been breaking the law since he was nine years old. He went from reform school straight to jail. Yet here in church he meekly sat giving his full attention to all that the priest said. Not only Shorty. The entire congregation showed a respect for their faith that the protestant priest could not hope to replicate. On chanting through their litany the Micks confirmed their belief. Not like what was happening over in A Division. Don't get me wrong. There were protestant believers too though in the main they were not so open about it.

A greater sense of ritual existed in this service. The Hail Mary's and Latin chants were steeped in history, this being the original sect of Christianity. If Henry VIII had not wanted to divorce his wife, all Protestants could still be part of the Catholic Church.

At the end of the service, I returned with the tykes back to our yard where the proddies were shaking off the effects of an hour-long ordeal. In coming together the two sects merged into a genial mob. Everyone keen to get on together and do their time as best as they could. Chatter and horseplay spread through the yard as inmates filled the time before being locked up for lunch.

Vern Fry was looking lost. The only person now in the yard serving a long sentence. The Greek killer had been moved into number four yard. The quality of Vern's life would improve when he turned twenty-six and moved out of the boys' yard.

After lunch came the privilege for young first-time offenders. No other yard enjoyed this right. The gate swung open and two warders threw a large bundle into the yard. A hessian bag was also thrown in. Inmates ran to grab the bag and wrestle over its contents. There shouts of 'leave off,' 'give over' and 'let go or I'll job ya.' Meanwhile, the bundle was unrolled and dragged further into the yard. A post was slotted into a hole prepared for it in the ground and the other end of the net was stretched and fitted to the lean-to by hooking into cleats. Four rackets had been claimed and their holders began to whack a ball (which had bald patches and gone a bit soft) over the sagging net. Lugal and Geppy claimed their rackets from the two hijackers.

'Jeeze Lugal, we were only having a warm up.'

After two practice serves, the game began. Best of three games stayed on the court. A good game was a quick game and a bunch of umpires made sure that every game was quick. All disputed calls were awarded to the winning pair. The umpires wanted the game to end so they could get on the court themselves. Lugal and Geppy were champions. Geppy had the uncanny knack of hitting a pothole with his serve, which counted. Fifteen love. His next serve was returned but Lugal, gripping the net for leverage smashed the ball to land beside a faded white line. Umpires waved the protests away. The ball was in. Thirty love.

Rules in Yatala differed to those of the Davis cup. Though we knew all about the Davis Cup. In the 1950's, Australia won the cup eight times and were beaten finalists twice. Those two years came as a shock. The cup was held in Melbourne at the Bank of New South Wales on Collins Street. Members of the public were able to view the cup. An armed guard accompanied them down to the basement where the cup was displayed. As a message boy in Melbourne, I saw the cup plenty of times. The guard was sick of taking me down but he couldn't refuse. It was his job. I remember the Cup as a handsome silver trophy mounted on a deep black plinth. Silver shields surrounding the plinth named the winning country each year. I noted in the early years that Australia and New Zealand played as one combined team. When the ANZAC spirit was strong. There was limited space left on the plinth for the addition of more little shields. At some time in the future something would have to be done about that.

The first pair were bombed off the court. Vern and his new partner were next. Vern took his tennis seriously. He leapt, stretched and panted as he slashed at every ball. He abused the umpires, who then reversed their original call and awarded the point to him. Not far into the game, he shouldered his partner out of the way to reach a passing ball and then called him an idiot for not intercepting. His partner became a nervous wreck and fluffed most of his shots. After two games they were off the court. Ron and I, coming on next did no better.

Those not involved in the game either watched or lazed in the sun. This was the time when bets were settled. Race results on Saturday nights came via our earphones. And then we listened to the trots, live. I couldn't bet as I had no pipe tobacco, but I did well in tipping competitions. I expected to be a big winner when I could buy from the shop.

On Sunday evenings, the ABC played songs from the current hit parade. Sundays were good. A highlight of the week. In the future I decided to go more often to the Catholic Church. I would rather listen to Father Witt than the protestant priest and there was zero chance of getting pinched.

40. MISTER BIG

Holding the floor in the toilet while sitting on it, the speaker was a mild-mannered man with smooth skin and fine grey hair. Judging by his demeanour, he was a man whose life had known many disappointments. I likened him to a shopkeeper who stocked unwanted goods, or whose store suffered from a lack of passing trade. I could picture him at his counter, watching someone approach his shop and then sigh as the potential customer sidled past his door.

He was talking about a Frenchman, a showman of some repute. The Frenchman used to appear on stage in a swimming costume - an old-fashioned one-piece suit with straps over his shoulders and a hole in its backside. He stepped into a tin bath and on sitting down, sucked water up into himself through his backside. He then stood up, turned side on to the audience and bending forward squirted water out through the hole in his bathing suit. Two blokes in the karzi weren't having that. They said it was trick. A con. The Frenchman used a tube and some kind of a balloon. No, the shopkeeper said, this Frenchman was famous. He appeared in theatres all over Europe. The pair of doubters jeered. Get out of it, they said. That's a load of bull. It's a con they insisted. The retailer stood his ground. Good on him. He refused to back down despite the pressure from both men.

Skeeter, perched on the toilet seat, cut into the argument with his nasal whine.

'Hey, never mind that. Who cares? I don't care. Why should anyone care? If he was a conman good luck to him. Now listen to this. Listen. I've planned a great lurk for when I get out of here. It's brilliant. Dunno why no one hasn't thought of it before.'

Skeeter leaned forward on the bog. The chain of a cistern fixed above hung within easy reach. I had never seen that chain get yanked. Inmates were regular in their habits and used a bucket in their cells.

'I've been planning it for months. Months. Gone into every detail. Worked out all the angles. It can't fail and I'm tellin' you, it's brilliant.'

Skeeter paused now that he had our attention. He allowed himself a sly smile before continuing.

'I'm going into cars. That's what I'm gunner do. I'll set up the biggest car racket this country has ever seen. It's gunner be massive. The cops won't have a clue what's going on. They'll never work it out. Getta load of this. I'll get cars knocked off in Sydney and bring them over here. And cars from here will go to Sydney. This is the clever bit. They'll go on the back roads and keep off the highways.'

Someone in the room must've shown doubt. I didn't catch who it was.

'You haven't heard it all yet,' Skeeter screeched, his lips curled back to expose small pointed teeth. 'The cops will think the cars have gone to Melbourne. That's what they'll think, the cops in Sydney and Adelaide. But they won't be going nowhere near Melbourne. Now then,' and Skeeter calmed himself, stretched his neck and loosened it, 'who do ya think I'm gunner get to knock off all these cars? Eh, who do ya think?' Peering and switching his gaze from side to side. 'Kids. That's who – kids. Kids knock off cars for fun. They do it for nothing. I'll payem to do it. Think of it. They can have all the fun they like and get paid for it. All the kids will be desperate to get in on the action, here and in Sydney.'

Skeeter paused. The faces he scanned wore blank stares and so he hastened on.

'I know a bloke in Adelaide who'll move the cars on. An expert. He takes the numbers off the block before he lets them go. And he's got contacts, lots of contacts, yeah, you bet he has.'

At this point I interrupted. When Skeeter bullied old Ted, I felt bad about not saying something. I should've told him to back off and leave Ted alone. I didn't. Here was my chance to make amends.

'I thought you said you'd never come back to this state.'

Skeeter, infuriated, swung his eyes to me.

'I won't have to come back. I won't have to,' he shrieked. 'I'll be doing it over the phone. You think I haven't worked this out? Phones, that's what I'll be using. Now then . . . so yeah, selling cars in Adelaide won't be a problem. And I'll find a bloke in Sydney who can do the same. No worries. But I haven't come to the best bit yet.

'These kids. I'll have a boss kid in Adelaide and a boss kid in Sydney. They'll do the recruiting. No one will know who I am. I'll be outer the picture. Behind the scenes. I'll be in the background pulling all the strings. Nobody will know who I am. I'll be outer sight, living it up, keeping me nose clean.

'When it's up and running, when it's going tickety boo, I'll do a deal with some motel out on the back roads. Some run down joint. A motel that's struggling. They'll snatch me hand off. I'll get special rates. Kids can choose if they go straight through or stop at this motel. The kids can take another car back if they like. Swap cars over, ya see, and have a free night in the motel. It'll be like a holiday for them. Kids from east and west. They won't get paid much at first but after doing a few runs they can stay a night in the motel. Later there'll be bonuses. Incentives – see, that's the way to build a business.

'There'll be different bank accounts, see, for the car dealers, the boss kids and for me. You think I haven't thought it through? Stone me. As if I'd start up half cocked. Months, I've been working on this, months.'

The shopkeeper's head was down. No longer looking at Skeeter. One of the other blokes had clearly lost interest. Not me. I was fascinated. I was taking it all in.

'When it gets bigger, I'll get someone to run the show. I'll do a bit of travelling. Go to Tazzy, maybe across to Kiwiland. The cops won't have a clue. They won't know what's going on. All these cars disappearing. And if they get onto it, I'll be the last one they'll suspect. I've never done anything with cars. Nothing to connect me to cars. All I've ever done is busts (breaking and entering). They'd never dream it was me behind this big car operation. This massive scam.

'Busts is all I've ever done. But busts are small potatoes. This car thing is gunner be big. Gunner be huge. I've waited all my life for something like this. Can't wait to get started. Soon as I'm outer here, I'll be onto it. Yeah. You bet,' and Skeeter gave a firm nod to confirm his intent.

He sat in reflection for a moment before going on to say, ' but first I've got to do a few busts– for revenge.'

41. A QUIET MAN

He kept himself to himself and was different to other men in the tailorshop - shy and retiring. A very quiet man. I had seen him when passing One Yard, his hat jammed down on his head and his ears bent over like brackets to support the hat. His big brown eyes peering out from underneath its brim. He sat on the opposite side of the bench, halfway to the toilet, always glued to his chair as he sewed diligently. He never spoke to anyone and never went to the toilet. A very private person, content in his own company. He made no effort to mingle with his fellow inmates.

One day I noticed a change in him. He sat next to bad boy Dawes and there they were he and Dawes engaged in a lively discussion. Two opposites, chatting away like long lost friends. Trust Dawes to draw him out. Dawes, in his mid-twenties was held in number three yard. A proper larrikin. Never shy to air his opinion and always had plenty to say for himself. The quiet fella looked to be around fifty. I couldn't think what they talked about or what they had in common. The trend continued. The pair were always at it, yakking away like life-long pals. Their liaison went on for weeks. Then came the day of a big surprise. Ron nudged me and hooked his thumb towards where the duo sat. Dawes was up on his feet, shouting:

'Cop a load of this, will ya. Come and watch this fella. Come on, come on . . . here we go.'

As the quiet fella got to his feet sewing machines fell idle. Needles came to a halt and machinists raised their heads. Some stood to get a better view of what was happening. I saw a pair of legs go up in the air, bent at the knees at first and then the legs straightened and pointed their toes. Ron and I left our seats to round the bench and see an amazing sight. The quiet man had one hand on the back of the chair and the other on the chair's seat. His ladylike hands were supporting him from two different levels. He held the position for some time. A couple of crims were trying hard not to look impressed. But they were. Dawes spread his arms and tilting his chin upwards beamed a big promoter's smile. The quiet man lowered himself, drew the chair in behind his legs, took his seat and crouching forward then resumed his sewing. The crowd dispersed. Men drifted back to their seats. Pedals were pressed, machines revved and needles began to punch thread through the tailors' materials. We hadn't seen the half of it yet.

A week or so later Dawes rose up to his feet again.

'Listen to this, everybody. You've gotta come and listen to this. Come on, gather round,' and raising an arm he scooped it through the air in making come here gestures.

Crims left their chairs to see what was up. Those close to Dawes stopped sewing and sat in expectancy. Ron and I joined the throng. Murphy remained on his seat and carried on sewing.

'This fella here,' Dawes announced, 'says he can remember thirty things. So here's what we're gunner do. We'll make a list of thirty things and read it out to him. Then we'll see if he can remember them. Who's got a pencil, a pencil and a bit of paper? Come on, let's go, there's gotta be a pencil somewhere . . . good man Smithy. You sit here and write the list. I'll start it off. Scissors, okay. Write that down, scissors, that'll be number one. Stick number one in front of it. Next, come on you fellers give us something else.'

Somebody said pencil quickly followed by paper. Beehive came next, which Dawes said was a good one. He urged everybody to use their imaginations. The quiet man said it would be best if he didn't hear the list being made. Take a walk then, Dawes replied. The quiet man hesitated. Rather than move from where he sat he plugged his ears with his fingers and hunched over the bench, pulling his head further in.

The making of the list progressed. Dawes leant over Smithy and said, 'what's that word?'

'Knickers,' Smithy said.

Dawes said Smithy's writing was shocking awful and he couldn't spell to save his life. After a shaky start, the list grew with a range of more creative suggestions. Once completed, Dawes tapped the quiet man's shoulder and when his ears were unplugged, began to read aloud from the list.

'One – scissors, two – pencil, three – paper, four - beehive,' and he carried on until he reached the last of the thirty items.

The quiet man nodded as Dawes announced each item. Then clearing his throat, he repeated the full list in a clear and distinct tone. Nobody said a word when he finished, not even Dawes.

'If you like, I can say them in reverse order, from thirty back to one.'

And off he went, not waiting to hear if anyone had requested it. He recited the full list backwards without a single pause. On reaching number one he glanced at a ring of blank faces.

'If somebody gives me a number, I'll tell them what the item is.'

Wrighty called out fifteen, and raised his eyebrows when he heard, T-bone steak. More numbers were thrown from the ring. In repeating each number, the quiet man attached the related object to it – bottle of beer, silk stockings, Marilyn Monroe. Scanning the list Dawes confirmed that every answer was correct. It was clear the quiet man knew the list back to front and inside out. When asked the following day, he recited it again. Just as with his handstand, I never heard his memory feat being referred to. And life went on in the tailor shop as it had done before.

Sometime later, days, weeks, I'm not sure, the quiet man tapped my arm at the end of a shift. Which surprised me. We had never exchanged as much as a glance and a word never passed between us.

'You're too open,' he said, in a quiet voice. 'You shouldn't mix freely with these men. You wouldn't want them to recognise you on the outside. You should be like me. I don't draw attention to myself. When not at work, I pull my down my hat and cover my face.'

He didn't have to tell me that. And in my opinion, apart from looking ridiculous, he drew more attention to himself. Having said his piece, the quiet man moved on. Dawes was by my side in an instant.

'What did that fella say to you?'

'Dunno. Couldn't work it out.'

Dawes eyed me, not trying to hide his suspicion.

'It didn't make any sense, not to me, anyway.'

'You know what he's in for, don't cha?'

'I guess he's a homosexual.'

'No, not that. He snatches little boys and has way with them. Worth doing jail for he reckons.'

Dawes walked on and left me stranded. I watched him further ahead, put an arm around Harold's neck. In typical Dawes fashion he then loudly declared:

'How are you doin' me old china plate?'

Harold did not answer, didn't turn his head, just plodded on with Dawes's arm draped around his neck. At the gate Dawes removed his arm and they both disappeared. The quiet man had gone already. Now I knew why the quiet man was held in number One yard. The worst kind of deviant and a repeat offender. I was last to leave the tailorshop. Everyone else had gone. I quickened my steps to the gate and clattered down the stairs, wondering how Dawes could befriend a child abuser, a sick predator - a beast.

42. SUMMER

With the coming of Spring, the sun rose earlier in the morning, grew bigger, shone brighter and remained longer in the sky. By December it had evolved into a ball of fire throwing out intense heat - dry heat, scorching heat, heat that parched the air and Adelaide prepared itself for six weeks of temperatures over a hundred degrees Fahrenheit, 38 Celsius. Hot, hot in the tailor shop and hot as blazes in my cell. The air hung - it didn't stir. Not a breath of fresh air came through the bars of my window. The only relief I could gain was lying bare-backed on the stone flagged floor. At night I slept with my arms and legs stuck out from under the sheet, the pillow dampened by sweat. Boys in the yard removed their shirts to bake their bodies in the sun. A few of the quarry gang were as dark as the indigenous boys.

Grimshaw and Dutchy were gone. Prior to being released, Dutchy used to sail his chest between the gate and toilet block with Grimshaw bobbing along in his wake. I expected the pair to separate once they were outside.

Christmas dinner was everything old Ted had predicted. Two thick slices of roast beef swimming in rich gravy. Never mind the fat, I wolfed the whole lot down. Baked potatoes, oh my God, what roasting does to the common spud. Sprouts! I had never thought much of brussel sprouts but they were delicious. It may seem mad to eat hot food in this kind of weather. I loved it. The only problem being sweat that dripped from my brow into the gravy. Christmas pud, wonderful, hot and moist and I do believe the custard was made with proper milk and not that powdered stuff stirred into water.

The Sally Army adopted the role of Santa Claus. We each received a two ounce pack of cigarette tobacco. A top brand – moist and aromatic, sealed in a cellophane packet. It didn't rustle when being rolled or spill from a cigarette paper like the boob weed did. To smoke it was bliss.

There's more. More to come. That's not the end of it. The Sally Army excelled itself. All inmates received nine boiled lollies each. Each lozenge was wrapped inside its own twist of cellophane. But there was a problem. Last Christmas there were ten lollies each, not nine. Nobody blamed the Sally Army. The screws had robbed us. Helped themselves. Dug their grubby mitts into what was meant for us. Maggots, mongrels and worse, you should've heard what the screws were called.

After Christmas dinner we were lazing in the yard.

'Are you sure you got ten lollies,' Lugal said to Shorty.

'Yep.'

'You're a liar,' Geppy said, pushing closer to Shorty. 'If you got ten you're the only one in the jail that did. I don't believe you.'

Shorty laughed. 'I was talking about last year,' and to a chorus of howls, he added, 'okay, I got nine. Alright, but see if you can do this. Last Easter I still had one left. Try that. Bet none of youse can do it.'

Phillip changed the subject. 'What I would've liked for Christmas was a glass of cold beer.'

Who wouldn't? Unless it was a bottle or two. Vern said he would prefer a woman to a glass of beer. 'Any day of the week, not just for Christmas.'

'Since you ain't seen a woman in the last seven years, I spose that's understandable.'

Geppy's jibe made Vern wince, after which he lowered his head and slowly moved it from side to side.

'Not long now, Shorty,' I said.

Shorty's smile narrowed his eyes and creased his forehead into deep lines. The kind of brow you would expect to see on a middle-aged man.

'Am I still okay for your tin when you leave?'

'Did you think I would forget?'

'No. Sorry.'

And then it was New Year's Eve. I would be fast asleep before 1959 arrived. No point in trying to stay awake as I had no means of knowing when midnight arrived. The coming of the new year would be unknown to me. This time last year I was living it up on The Corso in Manly. A wild, crazy night as people jostled each other while parading through the street, cheering and laughing, full of drink. Not everyone was happy. An older guy when passing me swung his arm and king-hit me. I didn't see it coming. The punch split skin beside my nose right at the edge of a nostril. He squared up in front of me, drunker than his friend and the two women with them.

'Want some more of that. Like a bit more of it, would you?'

I drove a fist into his stomach that knocked the wind out of him. And then I landed heavy blows into his startled face. The prospect of getting hit back had not occurred to him. I bloodied his nose and made sure that at least one of his eyes would be black on the following morning. On staggering back, he stretched out his hands and grabbed my shirt. His friend wrapped his arms around him and dragged him away from me, causing my shirt to rip down the middle of my back. Though my shirt was almost torn in half not one button popped off. The two women looked distraught. They weren't looking like that when he first punched me. All four then retreated, the two women clutching each other and the injured party helped along by his protector.

Later that night Jock Garden and I met Patty Cook and the girl we called the lizard. I went off with Patty. We wandered around back streets and into a schoolyard where we did it against a wall while standing up. My first time. Better than I imagined – way, way better. No wonder people lose their heads in wanting more of it. As it was New Year's Eve and we were both a bit drunk, I didn't approach Patty later to see if we could do it again. I could be pretty dumb sometimes. Real slow on the uptake. That was a lost opportunity, made more regrettable now as I wouldn't be seeing another girl for fifteen months. It's times like these in jail when the loss of freedom hurts.

My peephole cover swung around. A warder was doing his final round, checking all cells were occupied and making sure that no one had hung himself.

New Year's Eve, the end of 1958. Goodbye to that. From the hammock I glanced at my last lolly resting on the shelf. My intention had been to keep it till Easter. As it new year's eve, why deprive myself. On the outside everyone would be celebrating. I deserved any pleasure I could get and reaching for the lolly, I unwrapped it and slipped it into my mouth.

43. WRIGHTY

Every Wednesday morning, the latest news was brought into Yatala by the escort on its arrival from Adelaide Gaol. News that the censor had blanked out in all the papers that were sent into Yatala. Apart from learning what crimes were committed, the names of men on remand and being held in Adelaide Gaol were also made known. The grapevine picked up the news and spread it around the jail. That's how I heard that Reg Magee had been busted again. He told me in Adelaide Gaol that the cops were desperate to get him. Seems like they had. But could they make the charge stick? Last time they didn't have the evidence to convict him. Had his luck run out?

A week later the charge was known. Reg became a hot topic. Crims who knew him aired their views – their opinion of him. Did they think he did it or not. I didn't believe it for a minute. Rape! No way. I couldn't see it. Reg was a good-looking guy. A snappy dresser, smooth talker - a ladies' man. Why would he need to rape anyone. It made no sense to me. Perhaps he had been falsely accused. Or might it be a case of mistaken identity. Maybe a spurned woman wanting to get revenge. Thinking more about it, I saw how the charge could be valid. Maybe she was drunk and knew if she had been sober she would have refused consent. That could be it - a likely explanation. Then I went back to my original thought of being falsely accused. A nasty case of spite. Some kind of misfit desperate for attention, wanting to see her name in the paper. She spotted Reg and thought he'll do. He needs to be taken down a peg. She wanted some drama in her life and public sympathy.

Another week passed. The latest escort now revealed details of Reg's charge. Supposedly one night in a lane, Reg watched a young woman in an upstairs room doing ballet exercises. After she switched off the light, he waited a few minutes before shinning up a drainpipe to crawl in through her window.

A shocking incident - terrible. And though a woman had been raped I couldn't see Reg being involved. I wondered how he came to be charged. What were the details of his arrest? Was he accused by name? Did the victim know him? Or did she pick him from police photographs? Could she even see her attacker in the dark of night? I was convinced of his innocence. Or was there a witness? Another person who was present in the lane that night. That could be it. Someone said they saw Magee coming down the drainpipe. The cops could produce a witness if they wanted to. Do a deal with someone and drop all charges against him, allowing him to stand up in court and tell a pack of lies. Had Reg been fitted up? That could be what happened. It made sense. The cops were desperate to get him. This way they solved a crime and nailed Reg at the same time. One solution to two problems. It's a low way to bring a man down. The lowest of the low. The cops would tell the victim they had caught the man. She would be traumatised. Open to suggestion. Plant a seed in her mind, a detail that would implicate Reg. All she wanted was justice, the case over and done with so she could get on with her life. She would be distraught, damaged and confused. She could be led along.

'We've got the man,' the cops could say. Why wouldn't she believe them?

Did the cops even need the victim's evidence. Their witness could say he saw Reg coming down the drainpipe. A witness who knew him. That would clinch it. No need for the victim to say a word. She would be relieved. Not having to give a testimony and go through the trauma again, by reliving the ordeal in front of a packed court while being grilled by a hard-nosed lawyer.

Her dignity had suffered enough. It would be a relief for her if a witness sealed the conviction.

None of this looked good for Reg. Did he have an alibi or could he disprove the evidence against him? Otherwise, he'd go down for a long time.

Then came the Wednesday morning of the escort's arrival. Ted was at the small barred window in the tailor shop.

'They're here,' he called, and men leapt from their chairs and joined him at the vantage point. Bodies jostled and shoulders bumped as men strained to get a view. I nipped in beside Ted. Men leant forward from the back standing on their toes. Necks craned in from either side. Men were crammed into the space that overlooked the square below.

Straggling through the inner gates, the escort formed a line facing our distant window. The prisoners stood a metre apart. Babcock, with his back to us, launched into his induction speech. Somebody at the window asked the usual question.

'Anyone down there that we know?'

Eyes strained to peer at the distant faces. There were squints, perusals and fixed stares as tailors scanned the faces below them lined up in the square. Looking for anyone that was known. Nobody there that I knew. Ted began to splutter.

'Yes, yes,' he said, shaking a finger at the window, 'Magee. Magee's there. Look. There he is!'

'Is he? – 'Where?' – 'Which one?'

'The tall one, third from the right.'

Ted was excited, as if glad to see Reg jailed. That's the impression he gave, pointing a finger at Magee as he opened and closed his mouth causing a hinge of saliva to work in a corner of his lips. For Pete's sake Ted, wipe your mouth.

I studied the third man from the right. It didn't look like Reg to me. The man was standing hangdog, neck drooping and shoulders hunched. His cropped hair not blond enough. That couldn't be Reg Magee.

'So that's him,' a voice behind me said.

The man below lifted his head and turning to one side, presented the distinct profile of Reg Magee. Ted had done well to spot him. I never would have picked him out. Beside me Ted was nodding. A strip of grey whiskers ran beside the ear nearest to me, where the razor had missed. Nobody else in the escort was known. Men withdrew from the window and returned to their chairs at the bench, except Skeeter who headed for the gentlemens.

I returned to tailorshop after having lunch in my cell. Murphy began to tell a story about his time in New Guinea. Japanese soldiers stumbled across a primitive tribe, and were killed were eaten. I had heard that story before but I let Murphy finish the tale. His eyes, big and wide sparkled like phosphoresce.

Then to left of Murphy, the barred gate swung open and a prisoner made a tentative step into the tailorshop. Two more steps and he stopped as the gate slammed shut behind him. Reg Magee stood marooned in his new environment. Heads turned, men rose from their chairs and a welcoming committee ventured forward to meet him.

'Hi Reg.' – 'Jeeze Reg, seven years.' – 'That's tough.' – 'What a bummer.'

He stood behind Murphy's chair. I had a good view of him. In the months since I saw him last he seemed to have aged years. Deep furrows on his brow, eyes sunken and dulled. His mouth slack. Shoulders slumped. He looked stunned, as if he'd been smacked on the back of his head with a hunk of wood. His posture had collapsed. His shoulders were narrow and sloped, like the neck of a bottle. What happened to his shoulders? They were wide and square when wearing his pastel blue suit. This was a totally different man to the one I knew in Adelaide Gaol. The change in him was shocking.

The welcoming committee gathered around Reg. Having hailed and greeted him, it paused to hear what he had to say for himself. Nothing came out of his mouth. He seemed dumbstruck.

One member looked to his neighbour, another cleared his throat. Time trickled by.

At last Magee croaked: 'It's a travesty. There wasn't a shred of evidence.'

Bodies around him murmured. Grunted in sympathy. Nobody ventured to make a comment. In an uncomfortable silence, Reg felt the need to speak again.

'It was a travesty.'

I couldn't get over his shoulders, the look on his face and the way he stood. He looked like a man who wanted to flee, but he was hemmed in by a mob. A mob wanting to hear details of his charge. No one spoke. The entire panel was curious, anxious to hear more and Reg was obliged to speak again.

'She said she recognised my voice. That's not evidence. You can't convict someone by the sound of their voice. That's all they had, nothing else. It shouldn't be allowed. That's not evidence. It was a travesty.'

Heads in the crowd nodded. Looks were exchanged. Eyes widened, lips were pursed. Reg remained stranded in the middle of the crowd. A nervous tic began to twitch on one side of his face. His eyes pleaded. They were begging for release.

'You can't convict somebody by the sound of their voice. It was a travesty.'

Wrighty elbowed his way through the crowd and confronted Magee.

'Yeah, yeah, so you said. We heard that. You said that already.'

Wrighty was nineteen. Shorty gave me the low down on him. He first went into reform school as a little fat kid. He used to sit at the end of a room reading comic books. Three older boys bullied him. They stood over him, kicked his feet while calling him names. One day he put down his comic, stood up and beat the living daylights out of his three tormenters. He's been beating up people ever since. Wrighty pressed closer to Magee.

'But didja do it?'

Magee recoiled. Men around him opened their mouths and shaped a silent gasp. They looked at each other. Questions like this were never asked. It wasn't good form. Not in front of other people. Not with such aggression. It wasn't etiquette. Wrighty didn't give a stuff about etiquette.

'Well, didja? Didja do it?' Wrighty demanded.

Magee had been struck mute. None of the men around him would have asked that question. Now that it had been asked, they wanted to hear his response. The group around him hovered, expectantly. Magee was frozen. Unable to respond. Nobody offered him any help. No one suggested that Wrighty back off. Wrighty was no longer fat. Chunky is what you would call him. His head the shape of a stone ball on top of a brick gate post. And looked almost as hard. He was right into Magee's face. Magee's tic twitched furiously. His mouth sagged open. His eyes pleaded for mercy. Everybody was eager to hear what he would say next.

'You can't convict somebody by the sound of their voice,' he croaked, looking around for support and not finding any.

Wrighty snorted through his nose, made a 'hummph' noise, then spun on his heel and walked away. Men started to drift back to their seats. The welcoming crowd deserted him. Magee was left stranded. He looked around and blinked at his new surroundings. His eyes fell on me. He showed no sign of recognition, even though just months ago I lived in the cell next to him.

His shoulders were slumped. Legs bent at the knees. Face haggard. I never saw a man look so miserable. And then he began to flounder forward, in search of a warder for guidance, or maybe for a place to hide. Somewhere where he could be alone and avoid being grilled. He needed time to nurse his battered self-esteem. He needed to grieve, to mourn for his reputation. A reputation that had just committed suicide.

44. RAY CULLEN

A couple of times each day, I left my seat at the bench and went to the toilet to have a smoke and listen to stories being told. It was nice to stretch my legs and escape the din that battered my ears. Inside the toilet I sat on the floor, rolled a smoke and tuned in to the stories being told. There were seldom any discussions. On almost every occasion, a narrator told of a caper from his illicit past and when he had finished another man then revealed what he had done. Seldom did anyone admit to having made a mistake, or reveal how they were caught and jailed. That kind of story was rarely told. All of the exploits tended to have a successful outcome. The culprit got away with it. That was the common theme. That was the type of story told. What listeners expected to hear.

When I entered the toilet, Wrighty was sitting next to a bloke I knew to be a snowdropper. Two hundred pairs of ladies' panties were found inside his house. Panties he had stolen from neighbours' clothes lines. I suspected there was more to it. I doubted he would be in Yatala just for stealing underwear. I sat across from the pair and lowered myself to the floor. Ray Cullen was squatting against the wall just inside the door. As Ray did. I never saw him sit on the floor and I never saw another man squat. Skeeter was there, naturally, seated on the ceramic bowl. He started to yap right away.

'Tell me Ray, tell me, I always meant to ask, how do you know how much jelly to use when you blow a tank?'

'I don't use gelignite.'

137

'Huh,' went Skeeter, his beady eyes darting around in his head, 'what do you use?'

'Nitro-glycerine. It's more effective.'

'Nitro, jeeze, that's dicey stuff. Where do you get it from?'

'I make it.'

'You make it,' came as a squeal, and Skeeter asked Ray to explain.

'I put two sticks of gelignite into a pan of water, and boil it.'

'Fuxsake, didja hear that,' Wrighty exclaimed, as he dug an elbow into his neighbour's ribs, 'he boils gelignite.'

The snowdropper winced, shut his eyes and held his breath.

'When the water boils, the scum that rises to the top is pure nitro-glycerine. You just have to scoop it off.'

Wrighty gave a call like, 'whoaha-whoaha-whoaha.'

'But you have to treat it with respect. Nitro is a very unstable product. When Nobel's factory in Germany blew up it killed two hundred workers.'

'Who's Nobel when he's at home?' Skeeter wanted to know.

'Alfred Nobel, the man who invented dynamite.'

'German, was he?

'No, he was Swedish.'

I seldom said anything when inside the toilet. Here was an opportunity to get in a word. 'The Nobel Peace Prize,' I said, feeling pleased with myself.

'That's right,' Ray confirmed. 'I reverse the process that Nobel used. He infused his explosives with nitro. I extract it.'

'I wouldn't be messing with that stuff,' Wrighty was adamant, and the snowdropper edged further away, expecting another dig.

'As I said, you have to treat it with respect. Strong nerves and steady hands, that's what is required. And take care where you store it and how you move it around.'

Ray raised the cigarette in his hand and put a match to it. After taking a pull on it he sent a jet of smoke spiralling from his lips. Skeeter for the moment had been rendered speechless. The snowdropper struggled to his feet and puttered out of the door, out and away from Wrighty, out to where the sewing machines were hammering away.

I was trying to think of something to say. Something to stop Skeeter from whimpering again. I hoped Ray Cullen might go on to reveal more of his past - how he and Tommy Godfrey met, or how he went about educating himself. Too late! Skeeter started to whine, complaining about Yatala's food, the rubbish we had to eat. I wished he would get a change of job. Or get released. Getting rid of Skeeter would have made my visits to the toilet much more enjoyable.

45. PINCHED AGAIN

A letter could be written every second week. On the appointed day, bottles of ink, pens and paper were left on a table in A Division's foyer. Prisoners picked up the writing materials on going to their cells at the evening lock-up. The double page of lined quarto was headed as follows.

SOUTH AUSTRALIA
YATALA LABOUR PRISON
Northfield

1. Prisoners may write and receive one letter every fortnight.
2. They must confine themselves strictly to their own domestic or private matters and are not permitted to comment on discipline or arrangements of the Establishment, or on public or political affairs.
3. They are not to write closer than the ruled lines, or across, and are not to use other than this prescribed paper for correspondence.
4. Any matter which may appear objectionable will be expunged, or the letter will be withheld, as provided by the regulations.
5. Visiting days – Once every four weeks, on Tuesdays and Fridays, between the hours of 11.45 a.m. and 1 p.m. The number visiting at any one time is to be limited to three persons.

These restrictions prevented me from writing what I wanted to say. I found it a chore when writing to my mother. I struggled to get further than halfway down the second page. It wasn't like that when I wrote to the girl. I filled all four pages in small writing.

I described my travels since leaving Sydney and enquired what she and her friends were doing. Look where I am now I wrote. The letter was also for her friends whom I also knew. It's better be remembered than completely forgotten. When I finished my mother's letter I wondered what to do next. The program on my earphones held no interest for me. I had read my library book twice and wasn't in the mood to read more of the bible.

On eyeing the bottle of ink, I decided to tattoo myself. The jail was full of self-made tattoos. I tried to think of a design as I lashed three needles to a matchstick with darning wool. The Saint was a common image - a stick figure with a halo hanging above its head. The saint was embroidered onto my socks but I wanted something different for a tattoo. A weather map caught my eye on a sheet of toilet paper. When the needles were ready, I dampened the weather map and stuck it on my left shoulder. Then propping my mirror on the hammock, I traced around the map of Australia with the inked needles. It was a good job. The spaced blue dots gave the impression of a rugged coastline. Then I made a mistake by unpicking the hammock's hem and hiding the needles in the space for future use.

At midday two days later, a warder stood waiting at my cell door. My cell had been searched. The hammock lay on the floor with unravelled blankets and sheets heaped on top of it. Come with me the warder said. I followed him out of the cellblock and crossed the square to B Division. He led me along a bottom wing to a cell near the end of it. The cell had been stripped. After taking my tobacco and matches he locked me in the cell, where I stayed for the next four days. I did press-ups and shadow boxed, walked lengths of the cell and solved jigsaw puzzles. My nerves were craving for nicotine and I decided to quit smoking right there and then. When my privileges were restored I continued to draw my tobacco ration.

On the next Wednesday afternoon I joined the line waiting to see the visiting magistrate. Our hats were at our feet. An angry sun bore down on us. Time dragged. I was second last in the line waiting to be seen. The man on my left, solidly built, looked to be in his fifties. Sweat lathered his bluish red face. He had a nice head of hair. Silver streaks ran through it as it wrapped around the back of his head. He would have been handsome as a younger man. Now overweight and out of shape, his blood pressure had blotched the skin on his face. He noticed me looking at him.

'Do you believe in Jesus Christ, our lord and saviour?'

'Not sure that I do.'

'I do. I believe. I'm a believer.' Passionate now as he ogled me. 'Jesus is my light. He'll lead me through the darkness. With him guiding me I'll come through life unscathed. I've got two sisters - both nuns. They're angels that's what they are, angels. Beautiful human beings, so pure and innocent. They'll get their reward in heaven. The Lord Jesus will see to that. God will reserve a place for them in his paradise. They will be rewarded for the sacrifices they've made. They've given up their life for Jesus, Jesus Christ our Lord.'

I turned from him to face the front.

'They're pure. Pure in spirit. Innocent, that's what they are, innocent. They know nothing of the wickedness in this world. Poverty and sickness, that's all they know. The poor, the sick and the meek, those they care for. They've got no thought for themselves. They've dedicated their lives to helping the unfortunate. It makes me weep when I think of the goodness in their hearts.'

He was talking to the side of my head. Talking like he would never stop. The warder further to my right was not looking our way. I stepped back to count the number of men in the line ahead of me. I could see another eight. Perhaps there were nine, hard to tell. The man closest to the door was tall. Also bald. My neighbour kept on babbling about his wonderful sisters. Their pure hearts, unblemished souls. Untouched by the evils in this world. So pure and innocent. On and on he went. It must have been obvious

MEETING THE KILLER OF CONSTABLE GEORGE HOWELL

to him that I had no interest in what he was saying. It made no difference. He felt compelled to speak.

The sun beat down. The temperature must've been well over a hundred degrees. Not a hint of cloud overhead. The sky a deep regal blue. The warder on duty strolled towards my end of the line. When he turned I saw his damp shirt was stuck to his back. The bald-headed prisoner was still at the head of the line. The governor and magistrate were taking their time at the table. Another gin and tonic perhaps.

My neighbour lapsed into silence. I was standing with my legs apart. I brought them together, stepped up and down, raised my arms and folded them. Then spread my legs again. No change at the head of the line. I glanced to my left which was a mistake. My neighbour pounced.

'Do you know what I would do if I met one of these screws on the outside?'

I shook my head. He drew in his chin, took a deep breath and flaring his nostrils said, 'I'd take out their eyes with red hot needles - that's what I'd do.'

His bluish red jowls were quivering. Eyes narrowed to a squint. I held his gaze.

'That doesn't sound much like a Christian thing to say.'

He swung his face away from me and looked directly ahead. His lips were clamped shut. I could hear him breathing heavily. The colour of his face deepened. A good half minute passed before he turned to face me again.

'I forgive,' he said, 'but I don't forget,' and saying this he swung his head to face the front again.

His breathing eased. Tension drained from his face. No more talk between us. He was done talking to me. I sneaked another look along the back of the line. The bald prisoner was still there. The sun could be frying his brains. When he went inside, it could be forty-five minutes before I was seen. Longer if someone argued their case.

The sun hung in the sky like a blazing cauldron. My hat on the ground at my feet. Behind me, a strip of shade beside the wall was only inches wide. There was no chance of any relief. The warder on duty strolled again towards our end of the line. Plain to see that he too was sick of waiting. All of us sweltering in the sun while the governor and the magistrate relaxed at their table.

46. NOT CRICKET

The day I turned nineteen, I could not wait to be twenty. At twenty I would only have a few more months to do. I wanted the next year to fly. I wanted it over and done with - gone. Finished. At least I was done with being eighteen.

'It's my birthday,' I said, when the porridge came around and I scored an extra dish. Brown in the opposite cell, heard what I said and wished me well. Brown informed me what I missed on other radio stations. On having a crystal set, he didn't need to listen to the ABC. I liked Brown. I liked everyone on D wing – all young guys. Happy chatter in the mornings coming through the hatches and every night at lights-out, a shout comes from above.

'Is everybody happyyyyyyy?'

Marching to work that that morning, I recognised Redda's voice from behind when he said, 'I do press ups in my cell.'

'Why do you do that', enquired another voice.

'A man never knows when he might need to defend himself.'

In the tailor shop, I took my place between Murphy and Ron. Murphy was a hold-up man, in for armed robbery. I doubted his victims thought twice before handing over their money. Murphy aiming a gun at you would be a scary sight. You would think by his frenzied eyes and upright standing hair that he had just received an electric shock. And if he started to giggle, well, money would be thrown at him. Yet by nature Murphy was shy. He didn't mix with other men. He never left his seat or talked to inmates across the bench. When walking past One Yard, I would see him close to the wire fence, standing alone and staring into space. Though he didn't talk to other men he often talked to me. Perhaps as he

considered me as just a kid. He talked about the war, nothing else
– just the Japs, New Guinea and jungle. The jungle with its snakes
and crocodiles, its mosquitoes and malaria. He hated its humidity.
His skin was always slimy with sweat. Tropical sores refused to
heal and went as deep as the bone.

He told me about a Japanese soldier found in the jungle not
long ago. The Jap was unaware that the war had ended. I read this
account in the paper but didn't interrupt. Once Murphy got going
it was not easy to butt in. And on this morning, my birthday, his
voice was calmer than usual when he began to speak.

'When you've got an enemy like the Japanese the gloves are
off. Know what I mean . . . the gloves are off. They fought a dirty
war they did. They really did. You wouldn't believe some of the
things . . . some of the things they did . . . no . . . no - honest to
Christ you wouldn't.'

His voice so low that I strained to hear.

'That's how it was. They did it to us and we did it to them. It
ain't no game of cricket - war. Dog eat dog that's what it is. There
are no rules . . . well . . . there are but no one takes any notice. Not
when you're in the thick of it. Not when you're tired and out on
your feet. Not when you're scared and can't sleep. Not when you
see your mates get butchered . . . it's hell, that's what war is. Hell.
Butchery all around you. Bodies shot to pieces. Bloody murder,
that's what it is . . . one of our blokes with his head chopped off . .
. hands tied behind his back. It gets to you . . . the killing, the fear .
. . the . . . the . . . Jesus. You did it to them before they got a chance
to do it to you. That's how it was. War ain't no game of cricket. A
bloody awful business. You can't sleep, not properly, not properly
you can't. You lie there thinking about getting killed. Always out
on your feet . . . and some of the things you see.'

Murphy lapsed into silence, sat up straighter on his chair and
turned away from me. I thought he had finished. I had wartime
memories too. Sitting by the aerodrome fence off Elm Grove,
eating tinned peaches with older boys. And once I walked down

Kerfield Street to find a magical place. Dozens and dozens of kids were running over hillocks and then disappearing underground. I joined them, racing through tunnels with squeals of delight, coming up out of a hole in the ground to plunge down into another. Such excitement. Breath taking. Suddenly I was alone. A girl came into my tunnel. 'Little boy,' she called, 'the bell has gone.' And then she left. I didn't know what she was talking about. When I came out of the tunnel all the kids had disappeared. In February '45 when I started school, all the mounds of earth had gone and the air raid shelters were filled in. The Japanese push had been stopped and Melbourne was no longer at risk of being bombed.

But Murphy had not finished.

'A dirty rotten business, that's what war is. Terrible . . . butchery. Hell. And the Japs. When you see what they've done you don't hold back. You let rip. It keeps you awake at night, thinking about killing them, or getting killed yourself,'

His voice trailed away, and he turned to slide two lengths of moleskin towards his needle's shoe. He didn't speak again that day. He didn't know it was my birthday. Only Brown and the porridge detail knew. My mother failed to mention it in her last letter. She didn't send a card.

47. QUEENSLAND

I spent the evenings in my cell using a fork and spoon as tools in embossing the lid of my tobacco tin. Pressing down hard on the lid's inside created a bulge on the other side, then turning the lid over, I worked around the bulge to further define its shape. The design I made was a snake and skull, a copy of a tattoo on my right forearm. Ron and two other friends had the same tattoo. When my father saw it he became incensed, but it was there, permanent, and nothing he could do to make it go away.

There were many imposing tobacco tins in Yatala Labour Prison.

Craftsmanship in the jail was exceptionally high, considering the work was done with such crude tools. There were tins that shone like chrome, having been coated with solder in the tinsmiths' shop. When an inmate due for release passed his tobacco tin on, the receiver accepted the gift as a real prize. Ron was also embossing his tin lid. He refused to tell me its design.

Sitting beside his vacant chair, I assumed Ron had gone for a smoke. He had been missing for ages. I fancied taking a break myself but didn't want to leave the bench before Ron returned. Two empty chairs beside each other could draw Mister Conner's attention. On his return, I asked him who was in the toilet.

'I haven't been in the toilet.'

'Where were you?'

'At the top with Abdul.'

'I haven't been up there for a while. How is his suit coming on?'

'I didn't notice.'

'You didn't notice? What were you doing?'

'Listening to Abdul. He used to live in Queensland.'

Once Ron started he couldn't stop. Abdul said this and Abdul said that. Queensland was a magical place. The winters are so mild. Girls can wear a summer dress all the year through and a man could live his whole life in a pair of shorts. Words gushed out of Ron. He jumped from one subject to another. Abdul had dived the reef. The water so clear that you can see sixty feet ahead. There are millions of fish. You swim through shoals of them. The colours of fish and coral are amazing.

'Houses are built on stilts, allowing a breeze to run underneath. They barbeque and eat outside and spend less time inside the house as in other states. The tropical rain is so heavy that you can hardly see through it. A man could take a bar of soap and shower outside his front door.'

And then Ron moved onto fruit. I had forgotten at this stage about a break in the toilet.

'Mangoes hang over fences. You can pick one as you walk down the street. Bananas grow in people's back yards, paw paws too, avocadoes, custard apples, lychee trees and macadamia nuts. There are huge pineapple farms.'

Listening to Ron, I knew we would have to get to Queensland one day. I owed him that. It's where he wanted to go from the start. If we had taken a direct route we might be there now.

Abdul said in the west of the state, black dirt makes the earth move. Telegraph poles leaning one way will lean the other way on the following week. Foundations of houses have to be deep and the props supporting a house can be jacked up or down when a house needs relevelling.

Abdul said when he gets out, he might go back to Queensland. I wondered why he was making a suit if all he needed up there was a pair of shorts. He was talking about beaches now, beaches and surf.

'Surfers Paradise, yeah, I want to get there one day.'

Ron's eyes were glowing, shining with wistfulness. He was sitting like that when I went to the toilet. From that day on, Ron often paid visits to Abdul. He always returned from his visits in a buoyant mood. No point in asking him the state of Abdul's suit.

48. CURLEY WADE

I hadn't seen Abdul's suit for a while and going beyond the section where denim shirts were made, I wondered if Mister Clements still did all the sticking, or, if by now Abdul had taken up the needle. Once past the toilet I mounted two steps to the top of the workshop. On approaching the cutting bench, Curley Wade gave me a wink. He was standing behind the bench between two stacks of moleskin. The pile on his right had been cut to shape while the other on his left had yet to be done. The scissors he held were enormous, almost as big as garden shears.

'How are you going,' he said, and laid the scissors down.

'Good. You?'

'Good.'

'That's good.'

I sensed he was in the mood for a chat and I stopped to linger beside the bench.

'Do you know what I miss most in jail,' Curley put to me.

There were a few things I could've guessed, but I raised my shoulders and let them fall. I was looking at the scissors. Anyone with small hands would find it hard to use them.

'Women,' Curley said, 'that's what. I really miss 'em. I'm very fond of women. I think they're just the best invention.'

As soon as he got out of jail he'd shack up with a woman. That's what he said. 'Can't wait,' he said.

He laid both hands flat on the bench and leaned closer to me. Then lowering the tone of his voice he spoke so only I could hear him.

'Half the blokes in here have got no idea what to do with a woman. They flop on top of her and grunt. That's no way to go about it.'

He removed his hands from the bench, stood upright and let his voice return to its normal level.

'When I'm with a woman I spin it out. Make it last. You've got to do the foreplay. Go through the preliminaries. Get her worked up. Once you get her primed she'll be ready for anything. Making her laugh does no harm. Humour and sex go good together. Women like a bit of fun. They love it. I walk my fingers over their body. What's over here, I'll say, over in this direction. Hey, this is interesting. Nice spot, I think I'll snuggle here for a while. My God, what's happening? Explain it to me. Tell me what's going on.'

Curley waggled his head and smiled. I guessed he was telling me this as he thought I was a virgin. I wasn't a virgin. I had been with two girls. The first time standing up and what I did with the other girl was flop down and grunt. I didn't care what Curley thought. Curley could think what he likes.

'Use your tongue, that's the thing. Lick them all over. But don't slaver, flicker your tongue. Lap like a cat. Once you get them tantalised you'll be surprised what they will do.'

Twinkle, twinkle went his eyes in fond remembrance.

'After we've been in bed for a while I get them up and have a dance. Nothing like a dance in the nude. Twirling a lady around the room. It's best in the middle of the day, curtains open and sun coming in. It's not the same in the dark. I like to see what I'm at. And if there's a mirror in the room, I walk them to it and introduce ourselves. I'll say, now here's a handsome couple. What are your names and we're pleased to meet you. I bow and get her to curtsey. I give the two in the mirror names. She's always Trixie from the trapeze. That's so I don't mix up their names. I'm the gypsy ringmaster. I use a deeper voice when the ringmaster speaks. I get her to talk to Trixie and we have a conversation. The two in the mirror use funny voices. Some of the things they say. Shocking, really.

'Then I point to the mirror and say, wow, look at the body on Trixie. I'm going to have her next and back we go to bed.'

Curley smiled, reliving it. He was looking back rather than looking at me. His blue eyes twinkling away. Curley the charmer. Curley the smooth operator. Loose black curls flopped on his head, dimples on either cheek.

Women seemed to go for likeable rogues like Curley.

It's hard to reconcile Curley with what he had done. Across the border in Broken Hill, he and Neil James bashed a man. Beat him up really bad. They say there was blood all over the place.

Curley relaxed his smile and released a gentle sigh. Then he blinked and the sparkle in his eyes began to fade away.

'Ah well, hey ho,' and picking up the scissors, he smoothed his hand across the cloth between the piles of moleskin. The open blades came together in executing a ten-inch slice. Then sliding forward, the uppermost blade raised itself, aimed along a blue chalked line and swooped down onto it. Snip. All of Curley's concentration now on the task in front of him. I watched him work for a while before strolling away – down the steps and past the bog to skirt beside the sewing machines. What Curley said stuck in my mind just as I knew it would.

Curly, Curly, what have you done? What were you thinking? You didn't do what you said you would do. Instead of shacking up with a woman you stuck with your mate, Neil James. Bad choice Curley, a really bad choice. Together you were a disaster. What made you think this time that you would get away with it? You should've known. When on the rampage together the outcome was inevitable. I saw your names in the paper. Cecil Wade and Neil James were today convicted of killing a doorman at the Bondi RSL.

'This is a robbery,' you said, and the doorman slammed the door in your face. A gun was lowered and shot the lock just like in the movies. In the movies the lock falls apart and the door springs open. It didn't happen like that at the Bondi RSL. The bullet deflected off the lock and travelled upwards through the door. It hit the doorman in his heart and killed him instantly.

Was it you, Curley? Did you pull the trigger? Did you take the leading role? Pop the lock with one shot and go through the door like Humphry Bogart. Is that what you thought? Or was it the hot head, Neil James, who reacted with a snarl? It makes no odds. It doesn't matter either way. It is of little consequence which of you killed the doorman. In the eyes of the law it's just the same. You were both there, in on it. Both guilty. And you'll both go down for a long, long time.

It's a waste. A shocking waste. One man dead for no good reason. Only doing his job. It wasn't his money you wanted to steal. Another man would have stepped aside, raised his hands and let you through. His family surely wish that is what he did.

You'll pay a high price, Curley, higher than you thought. You'll watch your life trickle away while growing old in jail. You will be an old man by the time you're back on the street. Past it, washed up. Wasted. It's a shame. You could have done better. You had style. You might have led a useful life. It could have been so different, but you squandered all your charm and threw your chances away.

It's a pity the better half of you was the weakest part.

You'll have plenty of time in jail to think of the women you have known. To reminisce and know what you are missing. You will never be part of a handsome couple again and when you are released, what about the ladies then. Will you be able to turn it on? The charm, I mean. Will you still have it? You'll be out of practise. Bound to be awkward. Could be embarrassing. The twinkle in your eye dulled to a wistful stare. You'll be grey haired and have wrinkled skin. It won't be like it used to be. And if you find a woman who is willing to go with you, she's bound to be a granny. Not the type to dance with naked, twirling around a room.

Or flirt with in a mirror. And will you be able to spin it out? Make it last. Bring her to the pitch of absolute surrender. Or will you flop down and grunt. Probably in the dark. That's if you can still do it.

I didn't know what lay ahead that day by the cutting bench. Neither did Curley. He thought he did but he was wrong. About as wrong as he could get. His name jumped off the page when I saw it in the paper. I will never forget that day by the cutting bench. I think he meant to give me some tips. I don't believe he was bragging. Maybe just in the mood to share a few of his memories.

On leaving Curley I returned to my sewing machine. I forgot about Abdul and my intention to look at his suit. Abdul and his suit had gone right out of my mind.

49. TARONGA PARK

A sense of unease crept over me. An intense feeling of disquiet that made me feel uncomfortable. Something was not right. I had no idea what brought this feeling on. It crept up on me gradually and then took a firm hold. I was sitting in my hammock, listening to the radio on my earphones when the uneasiness grew stronger and became more intense. There was no apparent reason for it. Then glancing at the door, I noticed a chink of light coming through its peephole. At that very instant, the peephole's cover slid back into place. A screw had been spying on me. A flush of anger swept through me. What kind of a man gets any pleasure from spying on somebody in their cell. This was my peter, my home, and while inside it I had a right to my privacy. Being locked up is one thing, being spied on is something else. I hated the intrusion, the slyness of it. I hated that a screw felt he had the right to do it. I would never know who he was which upset me even more. It's a pity I didn't insult him before he sneaked away. Called him a pervert. That's what I should have done. It didn't occur to me at the time. I would have felt better if I had done that even if it meant getting pinched.

On completion of the night check, all cell lights and the radio were switched off. The call duly came from above. 'Is everybody happpyyyyyyyy?'

I wasn't happy. I couldn't sleep. I was restless and wide awake, thinking about the peeping tom. Angry and frustrated, my resentment churned away. That's when I recalled once seeing the resentment I now felt.

Sydney zoo had just received its first gorilla. Newspapers were full of it. What a magnificent beast. It's huge size, the breadth of its chest and thickness of its powerful arms. Something not to be missed. A new attraction for Sydneysiders. I decided to go and take a look, and boarding a ferry at Circular Quay I crossed to the wharf at Taronga Park. Once inside the zoo, I had no trouble in finding its newest resident. Gawkers were crowded in front of the Gorilla's cage. They were packed together three and four deep. I stood a way off and waited for some of the watchers to leave. Nobody did. The mob remained, transfixed by what they were looking at. More people arrived and joined the throng. They stood on tip toe and peered over the heads of people in front of them. More punters arrived and wriggled their way into the crowd. No onlookers left their place. They remained in front of the cage. People were straining to get a look at this new attraction. I moved to the back of the crowd, worked my way into it and got a good view of him.

He was indeed magnificent. Standing close to the bars and on the same level as the people watching him. Just a short space between him and the rubbernecks. He stared at the crowd as it ogled him. A colossus. One could only be impressed by the size of him. The girth of his chest, the bare muscular aura of it. A tree trunk of a neck supported his noble head. His powerful arms reached far below his waist and his fur backed hands were huge. One hand could clutch a melon with ease and no doubt crush it to pulp. His nostrils were flared. Onlookers gaped at him and he in turn glowered at them. He glared at the horde of gawkers standing there before him. His eyes burned with resentment. There was no mistaking the rancour in his hostile gaze. His pride was evident too. He confronted his tormentors. Braved their stares. He refused to be cowed. The crowd was captivated. Nobody moved, as if rooted to the spot. Everyone ogled him in awe.

While glaring at the crowd, he swung an arm behind his back and held it there. Then swinging the arm around, he hurled a handful of shit, yellow shit, sloppy shit, half a bucketful of it. It splattered across the front of the crowd. There were shrieks of disgust, howls of despair. Women screamed, men groaned. The crowd quickly dispersed. An older woman with arms spread apart, looked down at the front of her dress. Though she knew what she was looking at disbelief was etched on her face. A man got out his handkerchief and rubbed the front of his trousers, spreading the slops on his legs like peanut butter over toast. People who had a ringside view tottered around, soiled and dazed - befuddled. Shell shocked. Struggling to come to terms with their catastrophe. At the scale of their disaster. Now sorry they hogged a place at the front of the crowd. Yes, that's what he did. That's what it is. Streaks and dripping globules of shit. Those that escaped the splattering quickly distanced themselves. Not wanting to mingle with the besmirched. The clean and unsoiled viewers fled. The sullied onlookers tottered around and exchanged aghast looks. In the swirling mayhem, I watched the gorilla survey the havoc he had just created. Calm satisfaction now in his eyes. He breathed in through his widened nostrils and expanded his chest. It would not have surprised me if he started to beat that chest with his fists. His dignity now restored. He let the gawkers know what he thought of them. He might be caged but not cowed. His pride was still intact. He had thrown off his frustration and no longer felt helpless. He paid the gawkers back for humiliating him.

If only I had thought to shout at that screw. That's what I should have done. I should have let him know I'd caught him as a peeping tom.

'Piss off you pervert.'

That's what I should have said and sent him scuttling away. I would've felt a lot better. Even if I got pinched, it would have been worth it. It's a pity I was slow to react when I realised what was happening. And thinking about it kept me awake. Damn, I thought, damn and blast. Unlike the gorilla, I didn't have the satisfaction of soothing my resentment. I lay awake in the hammock for what seemed like hours.

50. TANKMAN

Abdul was in the toilet, sucking on his gold tooth as he gazed at other inmates, and in particular at the crim who was speaking at the time. A happy chap, Abdul. A man with an appetite for life and determined to enjoy the part that he played in it. What others took as knocks, he endured with a shrug, accepting what befell him as one of those things that can happen in his chosen way of life. Like now, sitting on the toilet floor having a smoke and a natter with a few of his contemporaries. He might have been in a northern saloon, a tot of rum in his hand and glass of beer beside him, ready to chase it down.

He had left Mister Clements stitching his suit, and gone for a break in the prisoners' recreation room. By the way, I should confess that Mister Clements was not the warder's name. I've forgotten what he was called, but I have to call him something so Mister Clements it is. Nice fella too.

So there was Abdul, listening to this lanky crim tell of when he worked in Sydney as a window cleaner.

'We used to fly round the job. We'd be done by ten thirty and then get on the beer. The last job every week was a bookshop. It never got done right. Its window never saw a wet cloth. We dry scrimmed it every week. When the sun hit that glass it shone like a mirror. You couldn't see through it, but nobody complained so we did the same every week. But that's beside the point.

'We got a new job to do, a bank. I was putting up a ladder outside and the boss told me to leave it and go inside. I can't go in there, I said. When he asked why not, I told him that I robbed the bank earlier in the year. Somebody might recognise me, I said.

He sacked me on the spot. I mean, me and the boss were drinking buddies. I thought we were mates. He sacked me for being honest with him. I'm telling you - honesty doesn't pay.'

'I wouldn't know,' Skeeter said, 'never tried it.'

Skeeter was in his usual place on the dunny pan. And turning from the window cleaner, he then addressed Abdul.

'Abdul, how do know how much jelly to use when you blow a tank?'

'Experience,' Abdul said.

I hadn't known till then that Abdul was a tankman.

'Like, do you use a full stick?'

'Hell no,' and Abdul, showing a gap between forefinger and thumb said, 'about that much. Depends how thick the door is and size of its keyhole. You've got to plug it in properly. That's the thing. I take plasticine with me, push that into the keyhole first, then add the jelly and detonator and cover it with more plasticine.'

'Gotcha, gotcha . . . right.'

Skeeter was taking it all in. If he had a notebook he would've been jotting it down.

'Main thing though, is to move the tank away from a window or an outside wall and find some way to deaden the blast.'

Skeeter detected a snag.

'How do you move the tank if you're working by yourself?'

'Ways and means. Some people use golf balls. I use short lengths of a broomstick and roll the tank along.'

Abdul eased his mouth to one side and gave the opposite cheek a scratch, revealing once again his huge golden tooth.

'Ha,' he suddenly exclaimed. 'I did a butcher's once. I went in on a Saturday morning to get myself a sirloin. The shop was heaving. All the wives were there getting in the Sunday roast. Four butchers were on the go working like stink. A girl on the till took the money. The till's drawer was jammed full of notes. It could hardly shut properly. I thought to myself, hello, hello, I know what I'll be doing tonight.

'I got in easy enough, but would you believe, I forgot to bring my broomsticks. You can imagine a butcher's shop - concrete floor and tiled walls. Like an echo chamber. You'd hear the blast miles away. But I noticed these packets of lard on a shelf. I unwrapped the lard, spread it on the floor and slid the tank along as easy as you like. When I got the tank in the cold room, I draped a sheet of tripe over it and put a side of beef on top to stop the tripe sliding off. Then I set the charge and left the room.'

'Yeah, yeah,' Skeeter said, leaning forward on the throne, nodding.

'The blast was well muffled. Went off with hardly a pop. But when I opened the door, Oh Boy, you shoulda seen it. Tripe spattered everywhere – on the walls, ceiling - everywhere. Sausages too and some of them had exploded. Sides of beef were blown off their hooks lying all over the place. A couple of them were charred, and the smell - like a barbeque gone wrong.'

He widened his lips to swell his cheeks and put his golden tooth on display. A whopper. The window cleaner smiled too, whereas Skeeter rocked around on the throne sniggering and slapping his thighs.

Picturing the spattered tripe made me think of the ruined meat. The sides of beef blown off their hooks and sausages thrown everywhere. The waste. And the cost of it to the butcher. Maybe more in value than money in the safe. Abdul did it, he blew the safe and ruined the meat. He did the damage. But I was staring at Skeeter. It was him that disgusted me, rocking around on the toilet, sniggering and slapping his thighs. It is hard to describe just how much that man irritated me.

51. THE NEWS

Shorty had been outside for months and Lugal was soon to follow. Phillip asked what he would do first and before Lugal could answer, Geppy said I know, he'll get himself an ice-cream. Lugal confirmed by saying, 'yeah, yeah, I will.' Geppy wished he was going with him. 'Have a lick for me,' he said.

'I know what I wish,' Phillip said, 'I wish they would deport me.'

'Where to?' I asked.

'Italy.'

'So, you're an eye-tie,' Geppy said.

'I came here when I was eight. My mother still calls me Filippo.'

'Why do want to get deported?' That was my question.

'The Olympics are in Rome next year. I've got the language. I could get a job as a bell boy in a posh hotel. All those rich tourists going there for the games – easy pickings.'

In Lugal's opinion, Phillip would not get deported. Not when he came here as a kid. Not when his parents lived here.

We were in the yard by the iron fence, our shirts off and taking the sun. I wanted to ask Lugal something.

'Lugal, how did you get that name?'

Geppy threw back his head and laughed, and Lugal let out a groan.

'I'll tell you,' Geppy said. 'Kids in reform school were talking about what gun they'd like to have. Everyone named a different gun, you know, Smith and Wesson, forty-five, derringer, thirty-eight and so on. Lugal said he'd like to have a German lugal. He meant a luger, but Lugal's been Lugal ever since.'

Phillip, Ron and I laughed along with Geppy. Lugal raised his eyes and formed a half smile. I think he liked the moniker as long as nobody knew how he came by it.

Lugal's release came shortly afterwards. Within a few weeks, the escort from Adelaide Gaol reported what he had done. Inmates were delighted. Good old Lugal, that's what we said in the yard. He had gone to a newspaper, not the most popular one, its competitor – The News. The young guy who owned The News agreed to print Lugal's story. He gave Lugal a full-page spread. That page was covered with printer's ink on every copy of The News coming into Yatala. But now we knew what the censor had expunged. Lugal's article described the conditions in Yatala, especially its food – the meagre rations and poor quality. By all accounts what he described read as a damning report. The governor would be shamed into providing better food. The government might demand it. Maybe increase his budget. We might get some fruit. Proper salad instead of raw cabbage. Real potatoes more often and less watery mash. Meat with less bone and gristle, sausages with less fat. Custard made with real milk and more than a single egg each year. Bigger portions, more bread. Good old Lugal. Everyone talked about him as we waited for the improvements to take place. Weeks went by and nothing happened. There were no improvements. Food stayed the same. The governor's hand had not been forced. There was no public outcry. The public had its own concerns. It had no interest in Yatala's food. After a month of waiting, we realised there would be no change.

The article in The News did not harm the governor. Quite the reverse. The story did him a favour. He looked very pleased with himself at morning assemblies. Lugal's report helped to boost his image. Politicians approved of the job he was doing. The public was behind him. Not what Lugal hoped to achieve. Not what inmates expected. Only the owner of The News thought there was any merit in printing Lugal's story.

52. REVELATION

'Poor bugger, they're making his life a misery.'

I knew that voice. Who could mistake it. But Skeeter was not on the bog. I took another step on entering the toilet, and there was Skeeter on the floor with his back against the same wall as the doorway. Another crim had managed to claim the only seat in the room.

'It's ridiculous,' Skeeter shrilled. 'Sixteen months in separate. Sixteen. He was way outer touch. He didn't know what the hell was going on in the world. Didn't have a clue. I was going past his exercise yard and he called out – who's there? I told him it was me, and he said – what's happening out there, Skeeter.'

Six crims were in the toilet. I made the seventh. The limit was supposed to be four. Somebody should have got up and left - three people in fact.

'Not much I said, except the Russians have put a rocket into space. It's going round and round the world. Jeeze, he got upset at that. Don't give me your bullshit, he said. I get enough of that off the screws. Poor bugger, he doesn't know what the hell is happening. They're making his life a misery.'

'If you kill a cop and then shoot a screw you've got to expect a hard time.'

This came from a tall inmate, sitting across the room from where I settled down. He was inside for flying kites. A smooth looking customer. Easy to see how he got away with passing dud cheques. Though not every time, otherwise he wouldn't be in jail. It seems he passed one cheque too many.

A scrawny guy sitting next to me then chipped in. 'He didn't shoot the screw. Taylor did.'

'Makes no odds who pulled the trigger. Does it? Makes no difference.' And saying this from the toilet seat, the speaker scanned the room from his elevated post. A gruff looking character, his craggy features pocked with old acne scars. His clear-cut speech a contrast to his rugged face.

I knew who they were talking about. The warder was shot during an escape from Pentridge.

'Did he even kill the cop,' Skeeter wanted to know. 'The hat that was left behind, it didn't fit him did it? He said he didn't do it. No point denying it, is there, not amongst his mates.'

News to me about the hat. I was only twelve years old when the cop was shot. I could still remember his name – Constable George Howell. A minutes' silence was held for him at our school assembly.

The man on the crapper sent the talk in another direction.

'It's the cat that gets me. Barbaric. It shouldn't be allowed.'

'It isn't. It's against the Geneva Convention.'

This came from the crim sat beside Skeeter. Uncertainty wavered in his voice. He looked around for support, hoping someone would confirm what he said. Nobody did.

'Said he'd never known pain like it,' Skeeter screeched. 'That's what he told me. He thought he was getting cut in half. On every lash the cat's tails came right round his body. Wrapped around his ribs,' and Skeeter used both hands to swipe around his ribs. 'He said it took months to get over it.'

A pause to digest this information.

Harold sat next to the kite flyer. He'd been in jail a long time, Harold, twenty years and more. He wore number three on his back. I doubted if he knew who they were talking about. He made no comment. Harold never made a comment. He was in jail for biting off a man's penis. That's all I knew. I didn't know the events leading up to it, or what became of his victim. Truth be told, I didn't want to know.

'They're lead tipped aren't they, the cat's tails,' said the scrawny fella.

'Not now, not any more. That was in the bad old days.'

The kite flyer was a good-looking guy, though one side of his forehead differed to the other. When he spoke he cocked an eyebrow, arched it like a cat's back. Deep lines formed above it, while the other side of his brow remained perfectly smooth. On relaxing the eyebrow, it still sat higher than its twin though creases above it disappeared.

Seated on the karzi, the pock marked man spoke again in his cultured tones.

'Up to two hundred lashes, that's what those early convicts got. The cat ripped flesh off their backs. A man's spine could poke through his skin.'

'O'Meally was cut. It cut him. And he reckoned his ribs was broke. That's why it took him so long to get over it.'

As Skeeter was saying this, the man on the bowl rose to his feet and started to leave the room. Skeeter saw his chance to claim the seat and started to scramble upwards. Redda Lewis walked in from the door straight to the toilet and sat on it. The man vacating the dunny had seen Redda coming. Skeeter, part way up onto his feet, sank to the floor again. His disappointment did not curb his tongue.

'They're tryin' to break him. That's what they're tryin' to do. Don't reckon they will, though. He's a hard man. Yeah, don't worry, he's tough,' and nodding his head he went on to say, 'at least he's doing life in Pentridge. Better than this shithole. He'd be up the creek doing life here. Worst jail I've been in. Treat us like mushrooms here they do. Keep us in the dark and feed us on shit.'

The kite flyer hoisted an eyebrow and focused his gaze on Skeeter.

'If he killed a cop in this state he wouldn't be doing life. They would've hanged him.'

'Yeah, struth, you're right there. Never thought of that.'

Another lull descended. I was thinking about O'Meally and recalled the headlines on his second escape.

PUBLIC ENEMY NUMBER ONE ON THE RUN AGAIN

I straightened a leg and slid my foot across the wooden floor. The kite flyer looked down at my foot and decided it offered no threat. Seated on the dunny, Redda had his tin out and was removing its lid. Somebody had to break the silence. I expected it would be Skeeter. But no, it was Mister Conner at the door thrusting his head into the room and looking at those present. A stern look on his face.

'Alright!' he rasped and withdrew.

Roll-ups were nipped and placed in tins. Men rose from the floor and began to file out through the doorway. Not Redda, he remained seated. He had a right, he'd just come in. I had risen to my feet and was about to leave, but standing there I decided to stay. I had not been in the toilet long. Why should I leave.

Though Redda always acknowledged me, we hadn't talked one to one since coming into Yatala. He had taken a bumper out of his tin and was lighting it.

'Do you know William O'Meally?'

'I know O'Meally,' Redda said, and added, 'he's a nice fella.'

I laughed. I laughed at the contrast between nice fella and Public Enemy Number One. And I laughed because I felt comfortable in Redda's presence. I thought of him as my mentor. When he next spoke, I wasn't looking at him, nor did I notice the edge to his voice.

'I'll tell you something else - he didn't do it.'

Not aware of the shift in his mood, I was smiling when I said:

'Tell you that, did he.'

Now came a snarl, an angry rush of words spat from between his teeth.

'He didn't have to tell me . . .'

I was struck by the vehemence in his voice - a hot and angry outburst. Alarmed, I swung my eyes towards him. His lips were drawn tight against clenched teeth with danger flashing in his eyes. His features then slackened as both the colour and tension drained away from his face. A final two words burst out of him like a painful howl.

'. . . I know,' he cried, as if the words were torn from him. Let out against his will.

I took a sharp breath. Redda now looked stunned. Aghast at what he let slip, and jumping to his feet, he hurled his bumper into the bowl, yanked the chain and hurried out of the room.

What he said and the way he said it left me in a state of shock.

*'He didn't have to tell me . . . **I know!**'*

I didn't know what to do, sit down, go back to work, or remain on my feet. I feared someone would come in the room and see me looking shocked. I composed myself as best as I could and returned to my chair at the bench.

From that day on, Redda cut me dead. He didn't try to avoid me, but if his eyes met mine, he looked at me as he'd look at a door or an item of furniture – an object that required no acknowledgement. I felt uneasy around him and tried to distance myself. Whenever our paths crossed, I averted my eyes. Before going to the toilet I made sure Redda was sitting at the bench.

Life became a strain in the tailor shop. Luckily, my discomfort did not last long. I was transferred out of the tailor shop and given another job. A year passed before I saw Redda Lewis again.

53. BRICKYARD

Air was fresher once outside the high stone walls of Yatala. Crisp and clear and heady, like breathing in pure oxygen. I felt alert and energised as I breached a gap in the wall. And there beyond the barbed wire fence was the real world, grass turned brown by summer's sun, great swathes of it, stretching out into the distance where its colour faded and its definition blurred. Out there was where Vern Fry had run. Where he was shot before he stumbled and fell into a ditch. Further out the horizon, and like a line of ants, tiny silhouetted cars were creeping along its surface. Overhead a big, big sky, more expansive than I could recall seeing it ever before. Ron and I followed a warder deeper into the brickyard.

Conscious of every step I took I stabbed a toe into the ground and sent dirt flying. For eight months now I had trodden only man-made surfaces. Great to be walking over dirt. Man that loses touch with the land also loses part of himself. Indigenous people will tell you that and they have history to back them up. This is how we were meant to live, out in the open under the sky and only earth beneath our feet.

The brickyard throbbed and clanged with life. We passed two hills, one of sand the other gravel. Between the hills were bags of cement stacked for easy access. Two boys were feeding the hopper of a giant concrete mixer. They filled buckets from each hill and tipped their contents into the hopper. Two bags of cement were ripped open and added to the mix. Cement powder flew, which added to the grey coating over the boys' bodies. Cables from the hopper stretched upwards to a drum, which revolved and rumbled around at a steady rate. Its contents thumped and sloshed around on every revolution.

Behind the hills and mixer stood an open sided shed - massive. Its concrete slab about the size of four tennis courts. Metal poles rose from the slab to support an iron roof. A smaller shed lay ahead and the warder standing by it eyed our approach. Unlike other screws in uniforms of blue, he wore a khaki outfit. His shirt sleeves were rolled up high. His arms were cocked like a gunslinger ready to make a draw. The cap on his head sat at a slant. This was Gatlin, poached from industry to come and manage Yatala's brickyard. This was his realm. He ruled it. I heard he was a good bloke and he never gave me reason to think otherwise. A wiry build and leathery skin – strength of character in his face. Empathy in his gaze. Not very tall, but every inch defined him as a leader of men - organized, decisive and patently humane.

'Take them to the top of the shed where the face bricks are.'

The warder in blue led us to mount the big concrete slab. As we passed the mixer's chute, it spewed its lumpy gush into a wheelbarrow's tub. The chute was then winched higher, and another barrow raced in to collect its load. The tub just filled set off at a gallop. Action all around us. Felons on the run. Others were lifting breezeblocks and placing them onto flat-topped barrows. And there ahead a barrow raced, its handlebars held up high like those of a Harley Davidson. It swooped from the slab onto a ramp, threatening to shed its load. A firm grip on the handlebars maintained control. Once clearing the ramp, the barrow sharply turned, one of its handles at shoulder height while the other was level with the young prisoner's hip. A wide grin on his face as he swung the barrow around.

Off to the right a piece of plant shook violently, as a wheelbarrow tipped a load of concrete into its bowels. The empty tub spun around and a boy from five yard zoomed off to fetch another load. The machine's operator jacked it up and pushed it further forward, leaving behind on the slab a freshly made batch of breezeblocks.

The clanging and banging of tools and plant, the screech of hopper cables, blended with whoops and hollers made by the prisoners. The overall clamour created a vibrant atmosphere. I knew I was going to like it here. What a change from being cooped in the tailorshop. I looked around, took in all the activity and stamped my boots on the concrete slab. Glad to be rid of the kiddy-style shoes I had never liked. Glad to be outside prison walls and keen to get involved in this swirl of industry.

The prisoners were mainly young, coming either from my yard or from Number Three. Most were bare-backed - their skin darkened by the sun if not by their race. Apart from the pair feeding the hopper who were powdered grey.

We came upon rows of bricks, five at a time standing on planks. A dozen or so of these planks lay beside each other. Some were loaded with bricks while others remained empty. Our new work place lay ahead in a corner off to the right. The warder in charge, slightly built, coolly appraised our approach. Four prisoners were working at waist high stands with their backs to us. Another wielded a hunk of wood in whacking a cement mixer's drum. I recognised him from my yard but didn't know his name. Once we were delivered, the warders exchanged a few words before our escort departed. Now I could see that all five boys were from number five yard. Four were black, one white.

'Take those two there,' said the man in charge, flicking the back of his hand towards two vacant stands. Ron and I moved into place, at right angles to the other four.

'Alright Milera, show them what to do.'

'Sure thing, boss.'

The black boy smiled for our benefit and grabbed a shovel that leaned against a large upturned drum.

'Hang on a sec,' and replacing the shovel he pulled two handles towards himself on his brick making mould. 'First you gotta stick in a board, but I got one already. See,' and he took out a board, held it up and waved it around. Then he replaced it into the mould and pushed the handles back into place.

'Now you put in the red.'

He used a metal spatula to dump red powder from a tub into his mould. He levelled the red in each section with the spatula, and then with his shovel heaped cement from under his stand into the mould. And whacked the heap and flattened it with the back of his shovel. Next, he rammed the thick cement with a heavy iron tool. Gripping its shank, he thumped its head into the mould, again and again, using all the force he could muster. He pounded the tool three times into each of the five sections.

'Put your back into it, Milera.'

'Me back's goin' into it, boss. Me back's goin' right into it.'

And it was. Each time the rammer slammed down, muscles rippled across his chest. Thump, thump, thump the rammer went, up and down, up and down. Milera's body glistened with sweat. Not only Ron and I looked on. The entire gang had stopped to watch Milera's performance.

'Come on, get back to work,' the warder said, 'have you gone on strike, and you, Robinson, give these two some cement.'

'They're gunner need some red, boss,' the white boy said, and shouted as loud as he could, 'more red, more red. Hey, Mister Red, there are two new guys.'

Milera slung his rammer on top of his upturned drum, and shovelled more cement onto the top of his mould. Then grabbing a different tool, he gripped both ends of a long flat iron and raising it into the air, swooped it down with mighty thumps. Once the cement was compacted, he slung the tool onto his drum.

'Did youse get that? That's all there is to it,' and he smiled.

'Take them away then. Take them away.'

'Yeah, yeah, I'm going,' and pulling the handles forward, he popped up five red faced bricks standing on a board. On lifting the board, he held it clear of his body, turned and carried the five bricks and settled them down on a plank. The warder passed him on his way back. On reaching the end of the plank, the warder raised an arm and drove a stiffened finger into the top of each freshy made brick. The bricks split and fell apart. Then he kicked the broken remains, just for good measure.

'These bricks are soft. Clear them away and make them again.'

Now back with us Milera muttered, 'soft my arse,' as he picked up his shovel and wandered off to clear away his ruined work.

A thick mix of cement was dumped at my feet. The rest of the load was then tipped between the legs of Ron's mould. Mister Red hustled in, stirring a stick in a tub that he cradled in one arm. Mister Red was aptly named. His shirt and britches were stained red, as was his face and hands. His eye lashes were dusted red.

A forty-four gallon drum acted as my workbench. My tools were placed on top of it, plus a tub of red colourant. My shovel leaned against the drum. I started to work.

We made bricks. We were the face-brick gang, four black boys and three white. We put our backs into it. We talked and kidded around as we worked in getting to know each other. Don't ask me what we talked about, a load of rubbish probably. We thumped and shovelled, yanked and heaved and ran with bricks to stand on planks where they were left to harden. And all the while the warder in charge strutted between the mixer and my drum, puffing on a cigarette. On occasions he ventured between the planks to reject more of our bricks, and kicked them as if they were sand castles made by kids he didn't like.

At the shriek of a siren tools were downed, barrows ditched and breezeblock making machines switched off. Smoko time. I followed a mob of workers to where we sat on forms in the shade of a lean-to. Hoots of laughter mingled with a babel of raised voices. Tobacco smoke rose from all along the forms. It was great to be a part of it. A welcome change to the tailorshop. Our gang of seven faced each other from a pair of wooden forms. We clicked.

By now we knew each other's names. We got on well together right from the very start.

The white boy (Ray) said, 'the Boy's in a shitty mood today.'

Rufus added, 'he's always in a shitty mood.'

'The Boy,' I said, 'the Boy.'

'Yeah, the Boy Bastard,' Kevin said.

'Are we working for the Boy Bastard?'

My new workmates confirmed. Billy saw the look on my face and laughed. The others found humour in it too. I'd heard of The Boy Bastard, reputed to be a terror. One story told of a dozen prisoners waiting to see the magistrate. Nine had been pinched by The Boy. Just when I thought I had found a good job and landed on my feet, I learned that I was working for the worst screw in the joint. That took a bit of shine off the day.

54. SOAPY

Wally tends to the mixer while the rest of us talk about the programs we heard on our earphones last night. The Boy is having a sulk. He hates to see us idle. His annoyance can be clearly seen by a grimace on his face.

'Come on,' he shouts to Wally, 'get a move on, you're fannying around like a . . . a . . .' and he gives up in his search to find a simile that fits.

Wally is going as fast as he can. Sand is in the drum already, tumbling round and round. Cement flies from his shovel, leaving a trail of fine grey powder. Another scoop, another heave and in it goes to the tumbling mix. Next comes water from a hose - squirt, squirt and slosh. Wally uses a hunk of wood to whack the slow revolving drum, knocking clumps from where they have clung to the blade shaped flanges.

The Boy sucks on his cigarette and blows out puffs of smoke, one puff after the other, as if he is desperate to finish the smoke and get onto the next. His eyes are narrowed to slits as he paces from my drum to the mixer and then paces back, strutting like a drummer boy fuelled by nicotine. There he goes back and forth - ratta-tat-tat, tum-tee-tum - puff, puff, puff.

Wally has almost finished his first batch of cement. A wheelbarrow parked by the mixer is ready to accept its first load. Wiry Wally, dark skinned, is the darkest of my friends. He keeps his shirt on as he works. Most of us work bare-backed as it allows freer movement. Wally doesn't feel the need. Don't rush on my account, Wally. Take as much time as you like. My hands are giving me hell. Red raw and aching where skin has peeled from blisters that have burst. At night I bathe my hands in water laced with lots of salt. They say pissing on them helps. I've tried that too.

The first batch is knocked up. Wally tips part of the mix at Rufus's feet, pale skinned and freckled Rufus. Billy and Ray are served from the remainder of the load. Back goes the barrow to get refilled. Here it comes. Kevin first, then Ron and finally to me. Red powder is in my mould. Now I shovel cement. Using the shovel hurts my hands more than yesterday. I'm praying for numbness to kick in and reduce the pain. Time to pick up the rammer. I grit my teeth and raise it, then pause at the top of my swing before swooping the tool down. Pain shoots to every nerve in the palms of my hands. The Boy is standing close by and watching me.

'Come on, you're prodding like an old woman. Put your back into it.'

With the passing of time, the pain in my hands is replaced by a burning sensation that lingers for a while before it fades away to numbness.

A flatbed truck arrives, reverses beside the shed and stops by a stack of bricks. The Boy tells us to load the truck. I lay down my tools and ease on a pair of mittens, made from moleskin and faced with rubber from old tyre tubes. Two stackers come to give a hand - Soapy and Nick. Wally and Rufus climb onto the truck's tray and arrange bricks the rest of the gang have humped from the stack. It's lovely. My fingers take the weight of the bricks, no pressure on the palms of my hands. I could load this truck for the rest of the day, no problem. Lugging bricks is a piece of cake. Strolling from stack to truck and back while basking in a friendly sun. My blistered hands are grateful for the relief.

'How's tricks, Bluey?' Ray says to the driver, who is standing at the back of the truck, leaning against its tray. Bluey says tricks are good.

'Good man, Bluey. That's what we like to hear.'

Soapy, on hoisting four bricks from the top of the stack lets out a loud shout: 'Praise the Lord,' and dumps the bricks onto the truck. Back at the stack again, he gives another yell: 'Jesus is my saviour.'

Rufus laughs as he takes Soapy's bricks and Wally, shaking his head says, we get this all the time. On Soapy's return to the stack, he gives another shout -'Halleluiah,' and lifts another four bricks. Between his chants Soapy wears a good-natured grin on his face. A middle-aged man in the prime of his life. Happy in his skin. The hairiest man I have ever seen. His lanky torso is matted with whorls of long grey hair. Hair on his chest and back and tufts of it sprout from his shoulder tops. Even over his belly. Another holy chant rings out. The red-headed driver is amused. Not the Boy Bastard who mopes in a shade thrown out by the shed.

'Hey Soapy,' Kevin says, 'are you serious about this Jesus stuff?'

'Absolutely, one hundred per cent. I'm going for it all the way.'

'Really,' Kevin says, 'straight up?'

'You betcha. Straight up and dead set. I've got a young wife and a baby girl. I'll lose both of them if I don't stay out of trouble. She'll stick by me for now, but this is my last chance. I've tried all ways to go straight and now I've found the answer.' A pause, another grin and then, 'Halleluiah, Jesus is my Saviour.'

We hoist and heave and carry bricks to the back of the truck and dump them for Wally and Rufus to spread across the truck's flat bed. The bricks are stacked from its cabin towards its rear end. All too soon it is loaded. I gingerly peel off my mittens. The gang straggles towards the shed and mounts the concrete slab.

'See yer later, Bluey,' Ray calls, and gives the driver a wave.

'Yep, I reckon you will,' and Bluey yanks the truck door open, jumps onto the vehicle's step and swings a leg into its cab. Its engine fires as he turns a key and a radio bursts into life. Bluey toots as he pulls away. Soapy and Nick, still wearing mittens, return to carrying bricks from the planks to place on the outside stack.

'Come on,' the Boy urges, 'don't hang around, you've got bricks to make.'

My hands are no longer numb. Feeling has returned to them. Starting again will be the same as first thing in the morning. What I wouldn't give for a pair of padded gloves. Or better still, a week back on the sewing machine to give my hands a chance to heal. I have a board in the mould. After the red, I shovel cement from under my stand and flatten the top of the heap. I put down the shovel and pick up the rammer. The Boy has got me in his sights as he stands beside me. His lips are primed and ready to smirk. I grip the rammer's shaft and raise it to shoulder height, its iron head now poised to slam down with force. I mustn't let the Boy see how much this is going to hurt.

55. SIX MONTHS

The first six months are the worst. Phillip was first to tell me this. Then later in the tailor shop, the little guy sitting across from me said the same thing. No doubt they meant well but it failed to cheer me up. Did I have to feel as low as I did for a whole six months. Though as the months passed by, I found the weight of my gloom reduced as I adjusted to being confined in a labour prison. I thought less about the outside world and all of the things that I missed. If conditions can't be changed it's best to adapt. That's what I did. Most people do. Otherwise life is miserable. By the time six months had passed, I was managing. Getting by. Doing okay. Coping.

Having done six months in Yatala, three events then occurred that enhanced the quality of my life. The first was getting transferred from the tailorshop to the brickyard. I thrived on manual labour and working with boys of my own age lifted up my spirits. We talked and laughed the whole day through, and physical exertion helped make the time whizz by. During daylight hours, I don't believe I once thought of the outside world. There is therapy in toil and sweat.

The next event to buck me up was easter, not only as a milestone reached but also for the bonus it brought - an egg. My one and only egg in twenty months of jail. I would have preferred it hotter and not boiled so hard. It didn't ooze over my bread but had to be sliced. A bit of pepper would have been nice to complement the salt. Don't think I'm complaining. It was lovely. I savoured the white rimmed discs with their hubs of orange yolk.

The third event at six months was being able to buy from the shop. A privilege I had long waited for. I originally thought jam had to be bought. That was not the case. An opened tin of jam was issued every second week. It compensated for having no fruit. I got my fruit out of a tin and spread it over my bread.

The brand of the jam was IXL. Very clever – I excel.

Before I quit smoking, I intended to buy pipe tobacco and mix it with my boob weed. Since I quit smoking, my choice had switched to condensed milk. Other crims raved about it. The best thing yet they said. Everyone who tried it agreed. On the day of my first buy, I shuffled forward in the queue beside the admin building, feeling more excited than I cared to admit. On reaching the shop I faced a warder standing behind a counter that stretched over the door's lower half. There were no goods on display.

'Condensed milk,' I said.

He jotted my number in a journal lying on the counter and ticked a column on its page. Then laying down his pen, his hand disappeared to one side and returned clutching the can of milk. As soon as he placed it on the counter, I snatched it and hastened away to my cell.

I gobbled my meal while eyeing the can, eager to get at it, and pushing away the empty dish I began to open it. Nobody warned me how hard it was to open the can. My knife was made from a sheet of tin. To strengthen it, the top of the blade and handle were rolled and soldered into place, and serrations were hammered onto its cutting edge. The knife was fine for slicing a sausage. It was next to useless for opening a can. I sawed across the tin's lid, back and forth, back and forth, working the knife furiously. I pressed down hard on the knife's blade while sawing away. Not even a mark appeared on its lid. After labouring for an age, a faint line appeared. I continued to grind with the knife while pressing down on its blade and eventually the line developed into a scratch. I worked on the scratch and checked at times to see if it was deepening. At last the scratch became a dent and after I don't know how long a hole appeared in the dent. I worked at the hole with my spoon handle, twisting and levering until the hole was big enough to suck.

The taste of the milk was sensational - lusciously sweet and delicious. Nothing had ever tasted this good. I kept on sucking. This was ecstasy in my mouth. I kept on glugging, not able to stop and savour the milk that was getting slurped down my throat. After pausing for a breath, back went my lips to the hole in the lid. I wondered if I should I save some milk to put on my porridge next morning. That seemed not important as I made a pig of myself. I sucked until the tin was dry. Then I felt queasy. The nausea became acute and fearing I would be sick, I left the stool and stretched on the floor lying on my back. After resting for a while the nausea receded and left me with an aftertaste of the sweet and creamy milk. There would have been more inside the tin, clinging to its sides, but I couldn't get at it with the knife, not then and not in the morning. Every week it was the same. On taking the first sip, I couldn't stop until the tin had been sucked dry. Not once was condensed milk added to my porridge.

56. REFORM SCHOOL

We are the facebrick gang, three white boys and four black. The Boy Bastard is our boss. No longer the terror he used to be when he pinched prisoners on a whim. The governor failed to rein him in. He had a licence to victimise. To persecute. Everyone tried to avoid him. New prisoners were warned about him. Despite loving that part of his job he requested a transfer. Working night shifts and weekends did not agree with him. Now he worked regular hours, supervising one small gang in the brickyard. To other prisoners he became just another uniform. No longer feared. Even ignored.

Kube took on The Boy's former role. A flat faced Slav who prowled the jail squinting like a sniper, ready to pick off any target straying into his sights. Eyes to the front when passing Kube. Don't give him any reason to slap a charge on you. Kube was a nightmare. Steer clear of Kube if you can.

Losing his reputation hit The Boy hard. He found it difficult to accept. It didn't suit him to be ignored. He became ratty, and scowled the whole day through while making caustic remarks, and smashing our bricks out of spite. He drove us on, but he hadn't made a single pinch since moving to the brickyard. His job was to keep us occupied. Pinching one of us would be counter-productive. He knew us well, knew our names. We were not the random numbers he once terrorised. We ignored his attempts to rile us. We tolerated his moods. He became a frustrated tyrant.

We talked of many things as we worked, of fighters and horses, of movies we'd seen and songs we heard on our earphones. Songs by Elvis, the Everley Brothers, Chuck Berry and Little Richard.

'Buck Ram is the Platter's manager. What a name that is eh, Buck Ram, wow, Buck Ram. Wouldn't it be great to have a name like that?' And Billy scanned our faces for somebody to agree with him. Rammers pounded, shovels dug and Wally smacked the mixer's drum with his makeshift club. Billy had drawn a blank.

Kevin thought Floyd Patterson would be the world champ for years. Which led us to talk about Dave Sands. All of us sad that he was dead. The world would never know how good Dave Sands might have been. He whipped Bobo Olsen twice and Bobo went on to become middleweight champion. Sugar Ray Robinson said one day he would have to meet Sands. It would be a hard fight, he said. And when we talked about boxing, the boys all knew I was going to fight when I got out of jail.

We stuck together in the yard lazing by the iron fence bordering number Four yard. Stories told there were often based in the local reform school.

'Remember Richardson?' Ray said, and turning from Rufus to face me, he carried on to say, 'he had a box full of screws, all different sizes. He tipped them onto a bench and told you to sort them out. When you had sorted them into separate heaps, he scooped them back into the box, shook it up, tipped them out and told you to do it again. Wasn't he a prick?'

Rufus smiled in agreement, while Kevin and Wally nodded their heads and Billy only laughed.

'What about Izzy, hey, I gotta tell you about him. We used to have cows. Somebody had to get up early and milk them every morning. There was a roster. Everybody took turns. Then Izzy said he didn't mind if he milked the cows every day. So we let him. But we reckoned there was something fishy about Izzy and those cows. One morning we followed him.'

The others were grinning as Ray related the story.

'Do you know what he did, the dirty little grub? He stuck his dick into one of the of the suckers of milking machine, and Wally, didn't ya Wally, (Wally was smiling and nodding his head) Wally

183

sneaked to the milking machine and turned it on full blast. Hey, you shoulda seen it. Izzy had trouble in pulling the sucker off. It nearly sucked him inside out.'

Didn't they laugh? They surely did and Ron and I laughed along with them. Then Wally said to Kevin, 'well, he's your cousin.'

'Can't blame me for what he does. Got nothing to do with me,' and Kevin got so upset that we laughed at the indignation spread across his face.

'After that,' Ray said, 'it was back to the roster. Except for Izzy. We wouldn't let him near the cows. Whoever got up early used to punch Izzy in the head before they left the dormitory.'

They did jail easy, my friends. Reform school prepared them for it. There must be boys who were reformed by going through the system. They'll be the boys I never met. I thank my lucky stars that I avoided it. Reform school would have been bad for me. Being confined with boys like myself would have made me worse. I thought I was clever when younger and saw no reason to change. I loved the thrill of breaking rules, going against authority and taking things for nothing. Now I knew where that kind of life led. Once out of here my life will be different. I'll tread the straight and narrow. There was zero risk of me being jailed again.

57. MISTER RED

Mister Red worked in busy isolation. Stationed at his bench, he opened a barrel of colourant and transferred scoops of it into his tub. He then proceeded to break down the lumps by twirling a stick around as he stirred and stirred. A fine red mist rose from the tub and settled over him. His shirt and his pants were stained red, his hands and face too. His nostrils were red rimmed, eyelashes powdered red. Also his hat. His red stained hat never left his head. He cut a lonely figure. Adrift from our gang except when racing in to top us up with the colourant. He never uttered a word, and though vital to our job we didn't think of him as part of our gang.

'More red,' was the shout and Mister Red came galloping in, twirling a stick on the run. I guess we took him for granted. I wouldn't fancy his job. God only knows what chemicals were lurking in that colourant. One consolation of his job was he could shower every day. Three inmates left early each day to go for their shower - Mister Red and the pair that fed the big concrete mixer. One red man and two grey.

At the morning siren, we dumped our tools and set off for the smoko shed. Instead of taking the centre path we kept to the left, passing Mister Red's bench. He was in the process of opening a new barrel.

As Ron passed he enquired, 'what are in for, Mister Red?'

'I robbed a bank.'

That pulled us up.

'Yeah?' 'Didja?' 'No kidding.'

Mister Red was young, not much older than us. He didn't look a bank robber type. You wouldn't think he had the spunk to rob a bank. We wanted to know the ins and outs - what prompted him to do it? How did he go about it? Did he do it by himself? Rufus and Billy had walked on, but realising five of us had stopped, they returned to join us. Mister Red began explaining why he did it.

'Ever since being a little kid I wanted to be a legionnaire. I thought it would be fabulous. Men from all over the world coming to join the legion, having to bond together and learning to speak French. They could give themselves any name they liked,' he said with a wistful look on his face.

'I wanted to be a part of it. The legion takes care of its own. It won't give you up. If the law comes after you, the legion will whisk you away. Once you're in it you belong. Don't you think that's great? The legion takes care of you once you've been accepted. They respect you for what you are and not for what you might have done. Legionnaires make friends for life. Everyone a foreigner with their own language. All these nationalities lumped in together and having to rely on their foreign comrades. After you've done your time, you can keep the name you've given yourself and become a French citizen. You're given a French passport and can live in France if you want to. Everything about it is fabulous, yeah, I reckon it is . . . keep that going, will you?'

Kevin passed him the match and Mister Red raised a fag and placed it between his lips. The cigarette was stained red.

'Thanks. Anyway, this is the thing, just when I'm old enough to join (puff, puff) the French are in Indo China getting their arses kicked. Getting slaughtered. The Indo Chinese are ripping into them. I thought to myself, if I join the legion now I won't get to Corsica. Not Djibouti either. They'll ship me from Australia directly to Saigon. I didn't fancy going to war not as soon as I joined. So, I decided to rob a bank.'

The boys had out their tobacco tins, those not smoking already. I hoisted myself onto his bench and sat swinging a leg.

'I put a lot of thought into it. I reckoned I wouldn't need a disguise if I wore outlandish clothes. I had on a pair of yellow daks, a purple shirt and red shoes. An orange beach hat too. My Driza-Bone was open, not buttoned up. My theory must have been right. In court not one of the clerks could identify me. Can I use your matches again? (A pause as he relit.) Ta. The robbery went as smooth as silk. I told them not to be nervous. Nobody needs to get hurt, I said and I gave them a stick of chewing gum before I locked them in the vault.'

'What kind of a gun did you use,' Ray asked.

'A shotgun.'

'Sawn off?'

'Nah. Double barrel, full length. It was under my Driza-Bone. Anyway, when I got outside the getaway car had gone. The driver had panicked and driven off. If it wasn't for him, well, I wouldn't be here would I? Crazy. He didn't have to do that.'

'Then what happened?' This was Ray again.

'What? Dressed like I was, running down the street with a shotgun in one hand and bagful of money in the other. They got me, didn't they?'

We didn't get to the smoko shed. Not that day. We were still with Mister Red when the siren sounded again. Coffee was his name. He hadn't said a word for months but once he started he sure could talk. An odd fella. Next day he was back to his usual self. Head down, busy, busy, dashing in with his tub while stirring it on the run.

I wondered if he joined the legion when released from Yatala. If he did, he may have reached either Africa or Europe. Not Saigon. The war was over. The French pulled out, both the regular army and legionnaires. They were chased out. The French beat a hasty retreat out of Vietnam.

58. WINTER

Winter came in June, mild at first and then a cold snap drove the temperature down. Icy air poured in through my window. I wished my window was fitted with glass instead of iron bars. My cell felt like a refrigerator. Everything in it was chilled. On taking off my boots, the coldness of the stone floor came up through my socks. Two blankets on top of me at night failed to keep me warm. The cold got to me from underneath. I placed a folded blanket between the hammock's canvas and bottom sheet. Then I was cold on top. I wore pyjamas every night and left my socks on. My trousers were laid over my legs and jacket over my shoulders. Older guys wore their pyjamas as underwear – three collars at their neckline with the bottoms of their pyjamas pants hanging over their heels.

I always felt hungry since moving to the brickyard. Cold weather made it worse. I asked every morning for two bowls of porridge and scored maybe twice a week. If the porridge arrived hot that was an extra blessing. A hot breakfast helped the day get off to a good start.

There were no bare backs in the brickyard and jackets were worn throughout the day. A new prisoner, a barrow boy, worked with his jacket off and shirt sleeves rolled up high. He was jailed for bashing his infant son. He beat him up really bad. A tough looking guy. Both of his arms had been slashed with a razor blade, roughly a dozen cuts between each wrist and elbow. None of the slashes required a stitch.

Keeping a grip on the iron tools was difficult early mornings. It's a wonder I didn't get more blisters. On thumping the rammer down, I feared the skin on my hands might tear.

Often it poured, and tennis could not be played on Sunday afternoons. One such afternoon, a deluge came down in sheets and formed pools across the yard. The surface of the pools danced as if being raked by a machinegun fire. A swirling wind whipped round the yard and changed the rain's direction. Inmates inside the lean-to were getting wet at both ends of it, also through the wire mesh at its front. Boys squirmed to work their way deeper into the throng. The rain did not let up. It belted down. A new boy's back was pressed against the wire mesh. He looked too young to be in jail. A timid youth, fresh faced, almost girlish. I heard that he cried in his cell every night and looked to be on the brink of crying now. His back and shoulders must have been drenched. He was not wearing a hat. I couldn't think why not. His hair was plastered to his scalp. Water ran down his face and neck. His lips were blue. His shirt so wet that it wouldn't be dry when he wore it the next day. He didn't struggle or try to move away from the wire mesh, but cowered where he was. Nothing could be done for him. He wouldn't want a day like this in his life again.

Cold water shaving was not pleasant in this kind of weather, especially as my razor blade got blunter through the week. Then there was the yellow soap that didn't care to lather. At the start of winter, I switched from a morning shave to do it during the midday break. An idea popped into my head at the start of July. Why not shave in coffee. Tea was served with breakfast, also the evening meal. Coffee came round at lunchtime. You could tell the difference between the two as tea was much sweeter and coffee had grits in it. After pouring coffee into my bowl, I splashed it over my face. Then dipping my hands into the bowl I rubbed the soap between my hands. I couldn't say I raised any foam but rubbing my hands over my face was warm and slippery. The razor glided over my skin. No jerks, no nicks nor scraping. The closest I could get to having a perfect shave.

When I first used whiting to clean my teeth I knew there must be a better way. And I found one, immediately. Yet it took me a year to realise I didn't need to shave in cold water. Which worried me. Had my brain been dulled. There was nothing in jail to make me think, nothing to tax me mentally. I had no decisions to take. Nothing I had to work out. My days were organised for me. I realised I needed to find a way of exercising my brain. Do more jigsaw puzzles. Learn something. Memorise lines from a book. Not the bible. That didn't appeal. Poetry would have been ideal. I could remember from school, a few lines of The Charge of the Light Brigade.

'Guns to the right of them, guns to the left of them, guns ahead of them volleyed and thundered. Into the valley of death rode the six hundred.'

It would've have nice to learn the whole poem, but I doubted there were poetry books housed in the prison library. I could have asked Robins to search for any poetry books. Confined in my yard, he was the sole library assistant and distributed the books around the jail. I'm sure he would have searched for me. If I thought to ask him. Thinking: I had to do more of it and exercise my brain.

59. PINCHED AGAIN

As soon as the hatches were opened, the bottom of D wing burst into life. Greetings were called to fellow inmates and raucous chatter filled the air. Bucket lids clanged when dropped to the floor and boots clomped around in overhead cells. On stooping to peer through my hatch, Brown greeted me from his cell lying opposite me. Oh, he had had a wonderful night, listening to programs on his crystal set. He had heard a new song by the Everley Brothers. It would take the ABC weeks before it played that song. Brown had no time for the ABC, the station permanently tuned to our earphones. He described his crystal set as a tiny gadget with wires attached. I couldn't picture it and didn't have the faintest idea of how it worked.

'Where do you hide it in your cell?'

'I don't hide it. I keep it on me.'

'What about the body search?'

'It's in my hand when I take off my hat.'

One program he enjoyed was about an American satellite sent into space. Explorer 1 was its name.

'It circles the earth twelve times a day, can you imagine that?'

'No, not really. . . how's your mouse?'

'Great. She'll be taking bread from my hand any day now. She's coming closer to me, the little darling.'

'How do you know it's a she?'

'She's a sheila alright, no risk. I can tell by the way she looks at me. A right little flirt she is.'

Someone like Brown lives on every street in every town in the country. Instead of having the fastest car and biggest TV screen, Brown had a crystal set and a pet mouse. I didn't mind his bragging. To tell the truth he amused me.

My porridge arrived on the hatch. I asked for two dishes but had to settle for one. The detail bringing the porridge around was fair in its distribution. By changing its route each morning, everybody had a turn of getting their porridge hot. Mine was only lukewarm that day. I had a decision to make. Eat the porridge before it went cold or wait for the sugar ration that was due to be delivered that morning. A difficult choice. Unsweetened porridge was bland. Cold porridge was grim. What should I do. Which option to take.

Meanwhile, Malley Kite's morning chant echoed throughout the wing.

'Are you up yet, Milera, you lazy prick. Get your black arse out of bed. Come on, get up, you lazy fucken bastard.'

On and on he went, calling to Kevin Milera on the landing above. It happened every morning. Malley's start to the day - his ritual. Apart from being crude, his insults were quite creative. The same swear word could appear several times in the same sentence. First as an adjective, then a verb and again as a noun. At times he referred to Kevin in the female gender, either as a whole or parts thereof. One phrase he repeated (much like a chorus) came in the plural tense.

'Hands off cocks, on socks.'

While listening to Malley's chants, I couldn't decide what to do about my porridge. My eyes fell on my shaving mirror. I held it out of the hatch to see if the sugar detail was in sight. A warder spotted the mirror and stomped towards my cell. I whipped in the mirror and sat on my stool. In a flash he was at my hatch.

'You're pinched,' he snapped, on looking in at me.

'Me – what for?'

'You know what for,' and he was gone.

I started to eat. Might as well, no sign of any sugar. A bag of it dropped on the hatch flap as I swallowed the last spoonful. The denim bag was the same as used for the tobacco ration. Tobacco strands were often found threaded through the sugar, and grains of sugar could be mixed amongst the boob weed. You would see the tip of a roll–up flare when sugar grains caught fire.

After breakfast I tidied my cell, rolled the hammock and folded my bedding. I expected to be sloughed up. A warder opened my door and swiftly moved on. Good - even though pinched, I hadn't been locked in my cell.

The next day I got pinched again. You wouldn't read about it.

Some people never get pinched. They go through their entire sentence without seeing the magistrate once. Like Ron, for instance. It happened during the lunch break. On taking my dish from the kitchen hatch, not only bread sat on its lid but also a cake. A fruit slice, my favourite – a slab of sugared currents between two slices of pastry. On walking across the square, an older bloke in front of me asked if I would like his cake. You bet I would. I nodded at him, vigorously. Once inside the cellblock, he held his dish to one side and I grabbed his cake and slid it into my jacket pocket. A voice boomed from behind.

'Nine-three-six.'

I stopped. Babcock, the senior warder, had planted himself against the wall just inside the portal. His lips were twitching in delight.

'Put your hand into that pocket,' he said, pointing a finger, 'now bring it out again.'

I considered withdrawing an empty hand but decided against it. Not a good idea to rile him. He plucked the fruit slice from my hand between a fingertip and thumb.

'You're on a charge, nine-three-six.'

Once again, I was not sloughed up. Which pleased me no end. On the next Wednesday afternoon, I stood in line waiting to see the visiting magistrate. My hat at my feet in front of me. Pratt, the screw that made the first pinch marched me into the office. He stood on my right. We faced the magistrate and governor, seated behind a desk. Babcock in his usual spot stood to my left at the end of the desk. The governor, looking downwards, read my name from a list spread on the desk before him.

'The charge against the prisoner is insubordination. All right Officer Pratt.'

Pratt said he had been abused every morning of the week. Foul language and insults were shouted at him. He said he caught me in the act, shouting filth while holding a mirror out of my hatch. The magistrate poked his hearing aid. Gave it a wriggle. Patted it twice.

'Well, what have you got to say for yourself?'

I explained about the sugar and porridge and how I used the mirror to see if the sugar was in sight. My explanation was clear, detailed and lucid. I finished by saying that Officer Pratt jumped to the wrong conclusion. When he saw my mirror, he assumed I had been shouting. He made a mistake. I didn't shout anything. I never uttered a word.

That's when Babcock butted in.

'I, myself,' he said (as if at times he was somebody else) 'when coming from A Division at night have often heard filthy language coming from that cell.'

Keeping my eyes on the magistrate, I said, 'my cell is on the bottom of D Wing, directly behind this building. It can't be seen from the square, or coming from A Division. You can't see the wing at all, not its bottom level. It's not visible. If there was any swearing, no one could tell where it came from. It's not possible. That can't happen.'

I nailed his lie. I caught him out. In a proper court of law that would be perjury. People can be jailed for committing perjury. Silence hung in the air. My eyes never moved from the magistrate. He blinked, dithered and gave his ear another tap. Glancing at the governor, I saw he was staring at me with his lips pursed. Not so much as to blow a kiss, more like he had just sucked a lemon. On my last pinch, when caught with tattoo needles, the governor said a lot of tattooing had been done in the jail. At last we've caught the culprit, he said. A statement just as viscous as it was ridiculous. As if I could wander around the jail with needles and a bottle of ink, going from yard to yard, or from one cell to another. It's what the governor often did – made the charge more serious with some outrageous remark. Babcock had beaten him to it, but the Governor now cut in to rescue the situation. He addressed his question to Pratt.

'Are you sure this is the prisoner that shouted the abuse?'

'Absolutely, sir. No doubt about it.'

The magistrate dipped his head and applied his pen to the journal. As he wrote he pronounced, 'I find you guilty. You will lose two days remission and forfeit all privileges for two weeks.' And looking up, he added, 'alright, you can go.'

The governor interjected. 'The same prisoner is on the next charge.'

Then Babcock, with his upper eyelids lowered to half-mast, slipped out his tongue and ran it the length of his top lip. Taking a taste of himself. If he was made of chocolate, he would've gobbled himself up. He then declared:

'The charge is trafficking.'

The magistrate enquired: 'What have you got to say this time?'

'Nothing.'

'Nothing?'

'**Nothing,**' I repeated, harsher and louder than before.

I glared at him. I let him know what I thought of him. A disgrace. A weak tool used by the governor to rubber stamp every charge that was brought before him. He got the message. He didn't need his hearing aid to understand my meaning. He blanched before replying.

'I'm surprised you've got nothing to say. You defended yourself very well on the last charge.'

'Didn't make any difference though, **did it?**'

The words came out with a rush, loud and filled with anger. Down went his head to the journal and he mumbled as he wrote.

'If you have nothing to say, I have no alternative than to find you guilty. You will forfeit two day's remission and all privileges for two weeks.'

My breathing became heavier. I might deserve to be in jail but I didn't deserve extra time because of a lying screw. Or because somebody gave me a cake. Pratt was still beside me. He should have left the room after laying his charge, but he stayed behind to watch the show. All I wanted to do was get out of the room. Get out of their rotten kangaroo court. I had not intended to say another word. It surprised me when the next words I heard were coming out of my mouth.

'Is that accumulative or concurrent?'

The magistrate's pen stopped moving and raised an inch off the page. With his eyes fixed on it he said: 'Concurrent.'

It was a famous victory. A concurrent sentence was the same to me as being found not guilty. Not one prisoner had been acquitted in the last ten years. When dismissed I swanked from the room, delighted with the outcome. Pratt escorted me back to my cell. He told me to empty my cell and put my accessories on the wing. He avoided my eyes as he took my matches and tobacco. He knew he had made a mistake and he knew I knew that he knew it too.

60. BLUEY

'Must be a while since you had a smoke.'

The Boy knew I had been pinched. Maybe there is a list, or perhaps my name was mentioned in the warders' mess. Taking a drag from his cork tip, he gave me a knowing look, dropped the cigarette to the ground and turned his back to me. The cigarette was almost new. Hardly been smoked at all. Suddenly he spun around and narrowing his eyes, stamped on the cigarette with his boot. I gave him a big smile, a genuine smile that took him aback. Not what he expected. The leer that was forming on his lips shrivelled up and died. He didn't know that I'd quit smoking. Spinning around, he headed for Wally's mixer, stamping his feet down hard with every step he took.

As much as he tried to annoy, he was no longer the terror that he used to be. These days he was just another screw. Losing his reputation came as a blow to him. It made him bad tempered – irritable. Why didn't he come to work with a smile on his face. It would be in his own interest. Have a bit of banter with us. Enjoy his job. Be happy. Be more like Jock the Scottish screw who kidded around with prisoners that he supervised. It would be better for him to be a happier person. He could enjoy his life.

But no, something in his nature made him want to be a shit.

As The Boy stomped back and forth puffing a new cigarette, Bluey's truck reversed in to stop by the stack of bricks.

'All right, get it loaded.'

We downed tools, pulled on mittens, and together with Nick and Soapy stepped out from under the shed's roof. Bluey jumped down from his cab and wandered to the back of his truck and leaned against its flat-topped tray.

We carted bricks, seven of us, in batches of four or five at a time. Rufus and Wally arranged the bricks across the truck's flat tray. After taking a few loads, Ron upended fifteen bricks and stood them in a line. Then pushing his chest close to the stack, he stretched his arms wide apart and wrapped his fingertips around both ends of the line of bricks. Then tipping the line from the stack, he held the bricks together as they lay across his chest and arms. Turning slowly, he trundled the bricks and dumped them onto the back of the truck. The record was fifteen bricks. Ron, Ray, myself and Kevin had all managed to do it. Rufus and Wally had no chance. Their arms were too short. Billy could not quite make it.

'Let's see you do it,' Rufus called to Billy.

'I've done it already. I've done fifteen bricks.'

'But you couldn't get them to the truck so that doesn't count. Let's see you try again.'

Billy rose to the challenge. He lined up fifteen bricks on the stack and clutched each end with his fingertips. His knees sagged as he took their weight, and taking a deep breath, he turned towards the truck whereupon the bricks spilled. His chest was grazed, and one brick bruised his shin that made him hop around and swear. The Boy showed him no sympathy.

'Stop arsing around, Williams. Just take what you can carry.'

Billy's glare dared anyone to say another word. Nobody did. In the ensuing silence, Ray nudged Soapy and said: 'How did you get that name, Soapy? What's the story there?'

Soapy paused with a bashful smile before deciding to answer.

'Well, I agreed to do a job for these Greeks. I had to knock off a semi load of cigarettes. One of the Greeks showed me which semi to take. The cops were onto me right away. I don't know if youse know the back lanes in Parramatta. Like a maze they are. I was swinging the semi through those lanes with sirens blaring around me.'

Soapy carrying bricks. He dumped them onto the truck. An older bloke amongst boys. White teeth and cheeky grin. Bronzed face. Acne scars made his face look like beaten copper. He had a noble head, Soapy. Short hair brushed forward in the style of Julius Ceaser. Soapy's profile could've graced an old roman coin. Probably more suited there than in a police record.

'Well,' Soapy continued, 'I made it to the Greek's place. As soon as I drove inside, they yanked the roller shutter down. One of the Greeks cut the ropes and the others hauled off the tarp. And there on the trailer was a full load of . . . Persil.'

Bluey the driver was loving this. The Boy remained po-faced.

'The boss said to get down a carton. He took a packet from the carton, stuck his knife into it and poured Persil onto the ground. This is not cigarettes, he says, this is soap. And looks at me like I'm to blame. Just then the cops arrived.'

Soapy rolled his eyes.

'Well, when I got up to Long Bay, all the fellas in the yard were calling out - here comes Soapy. How yer going, Soapy. What do ya know, Soapy? So that was it. I've been Soapy ever since.'

We carried on loading. The Boy beside the brick stack was standing close to Bluey. They didn't speak. They never did. Never exchanged a word. Wally and Rufus piled bricks right to the end of the truck. Bluey said that would do. That's enough, he said. And the Boy, walking forward yelled: 'Alright, you can knock off. Get back to making bricks.'

We peeled off our mittens and dawdled in under the galvanised iron roof. Nicky led the way still wearing his mittens. Soapy hung back. I turned to see what he was doing and saw him pass something to Bluey. I mounted the slab and waited for him and together we walked towards the planks.

'What did you give to Bluey,' I said, when we were past the Boy.

'A letter to my wife. Bluey will post it for me. I don't want any screw to read what I say to my wife. That's private. None of their damn business.'

His grin put a crease into both pitted cheeks. 'Halleluiah,' he shouted, and wandered off between two planks loaded with red-faced bricks.

As I returned to my stand, Bluey was easing away, one hand on the steering wheel, an elbow out of the window. Elvis Presley doing a number on his radio. Bluey was off with his load of bricks up the road to Elizabeth.

61. THE BOY BASTARD

It was time for another race to see who made the fastest batch of bricks. Six of us poised and ready to go. Empty moulds and tools arranged, spatulas stuck in the red, shovels propped against our drums and boards in place for an easy grab. Wally was the starter.

'Go,' he called and we were off. The Boy with a sour expression watched us having fun. On throwing my shovel aside, I was slightly ahead and raising the rammer upwards I drove it down fifteen times, in three lines of five across each section of my mould. Wang went the rammer onto my drum and I reached for the shovel again. Kevin just behind me and the others not far away. I had the farthest to run to my plank and needed a bigger lead. I slammed the flat iron down with force, then slung it on top of the drum, yanked both handles upwards and carried the board with its five bricks and ran as fast as I could. Kevin almost beside me. He lost ground when he swung a boot in attempting to trip me. Down went my bricks onto the plank and I raised my arms in victory.

'Dead heat,' Kevin said.

'You're joking.'

Everybody now at the planks. Kevin still claiming he had drawn and no one admitted to being last.

The Boy Bastard eyed our return.

'You're not here to play games. Those bricks will all be soft,' and off he went to wreck our bricks without doing a single test.

'Clear this mess away and make those bricks again.'

On trooping down between the planks, shovels in our hands, I remarked to Kevin that his bricks probably were soft.

'That's how you managed to keep up with me.'

201

'Piss off. I've never made a soft brick yet.'

The Boy was still not happy. Smashing bricks usually calmed him down for a while. Not this time. Lately, the Boy had been in a permanent state of angst. Something was eating him. Not a happy chap, not happy at all. I thought he would get an ulcer if he didn't pinch somebody soon. Ray suggested his wife was playing away from home. There were other opinions, none were complementary and some scandalous.

The Boy was not a boy anymore - The Boy only in name. Age had begun to weather him. He had gone puffy around the eyes. His belly gone pot-shaped. His shoulders were slumped and his neck stuck out like that of a turtle. His posture had collapsed. Maybe it was going to seed that soured him.

Next morning the Boy greeted us in a buoyant mood. Whistling as he strolled between the mixer and my drum. Swinging a leg like a schoolboy with his shoulders held back. Arms at a gentle swing. Not puffing a cigarette. We had never seen him like this before. Something was up.

The six brickmakers were chatting as Wally knocked up his first mix.

'Leave that for a minute, Robinson, I've got something to say. I've had a word with the governor and he agrees with me. There should be a quota for this job. So, starting from now there is. You have to make six hundred bricks a day.'

'What.' 'Huh.' 'Noooooo.' 'Hey, that's not fair.'

Kevin recovered first to ask, 'what happens if we don't.'

'You'll be on a charge for malingering.'

'What about when we load the truck,' Billy thought to ask.

'I've made an allowance for that.'

No more easy days. They were gone forever. We would be hard at it all the time and no idea how to pace ourselves. Queries and comments swirled around in our bewilderment.

'I suggest you make a start. You're wasting precious time.'

A gap was left from yesterday's bricks to allow the Boy to take a count. We made bricks, muttering amongst ourselves as we worked and decided to go steadily, hoping to reach the target just at the day's end. Otherwise, our quota might increase. The quota effected Wally too. He had to churn out more cement. And Mister Red, already stretched, came under extra pressure. The Boy watched us scurry around. He was loving it, and strutted along on his usual beat, then pausing by Wally's mixer, he plucked a cigarette from its pack and offered it to his lips. When lit he took a leisurely draw and blew out a stream of fumes.

At smoko we did more figuring to judge if our pace was right. And checked again at lunchtime after taking another count. We estimated we were on track and six hundred bricks were within reach. Though when loading Bluey's truck, the target would be more difficult.

By afternoon the lines of bricks had steadily grown longer. We were on schedule and working at a steady rate. That's when The Boy took a stroll down between the planks. His intent was obvious.

'Look at the Boy,' I said.

Only Ron and I could see. The others turned around to look. All seven of us watched as his stiffened digit speared into the head of my last brick, causing a chunk of it to split and fall to the ground. Hard and well-made bricks split. Soft bricks merely crumbled. The Boy put in his boot, demolished the set of five and moved along to the next plank. We knew then that six hundred bricks were the least we would make each day. Soapy wandered past him, lugging five bricks on a board. Soapy had seen it all before. Nothing new to him, seeing the Boy on a rampage. But Soapy didn't know yet about our new quota. He wouldn't feel its impact for another two days. Nicky would feel it too and Mister Red already stretched would come under extra pressure. In one foul swoop The Boy had skittled all of us. Back now treading his path with a smirk, the Boy tootled along. He paused to check his watch. No doubt to decide when he should smash more of our bricks. He drew on his cigarette, exhaled and gave a little sigh.

62. BOOKS

Ron and I walked through the gate, counted and accounted for as we entered the yard. A miserable day weather-wise, though at least the drizzle had stopped. Ron said he had to see Robins. Where's Robins, he said, swinging his head around to search as he plunged deeper into the yard. I quickened my pace to keep up with him. I've got to see Robins, he said. I scanned the yard for Robins too.

'He's down by the karzi.'

'Where?'

'There, on the left,' although by then Ron had spotted him. He raced off towards the toilet block. I struggled to keep up with him. Robins was talking to John McCreary, one of the boys who fed the concrete mixer's hopper.

'Hey Robins,' and before Ron reached the pair, he called again, 'Robins, don't change my book this week.'

Robins gave him a blank look and McCreary frowned at Ron's intrusion.

'I want to keep that book,' Ron said, 'I'll tell you when to change it. I want to keep it for another week, another week at least.'

Ron told Robins where he lived - the number of his cell. Have you got that, he said?

'I'll tell you when to change it. I'll remind you again next week.'

Robins, a college boy type, smiled at Ron's persistence.

'Chill, Ron. I've got it. I'll leave your book. No need to remind me. Just let me know when you've finished with it.'

'Right. Good . . . thanks,' and Ron was happy to leave the pair to continue what they were talking about.

I asked what was special about the book. It was special alright. Special to Ron. Queensland, that's what it was about. 1959 was Queensland's centenary year. A hundred years since the colony split from New South Wales. The book had just come out, practically brand new. It had everything in it, Ron said, history, facts and figures - the lot. Everything you wanted to know about the sunshine state. Ron was pretty excited. He couldn't wait to get locked up and get back to that book.

From that day on we heard plenty from that book, both at work and in the yard. Ron would quote snippets from it at any random time. A population rising from 28,000 to a million and a half. A coastline of more than four thousand miles. Of Captain Cook's ten landings, nine were made in Queensland. Ron said Cook named every feature on Queensland's coast, be it mountain, point, island or bay.

Wally at his mixer said, 'like Maroochydore, I spose.'

In the yard, Ron reminded Robins to leave the book in his cell. Don't change it, he said. By the second week Ron had conveyed lots of facts from that book.

Kevin said to Robins, 'get that book off Ron. I want to read it next.'

'Me too, I want to read it,' Rufus said.

Other boys in the yard badgered Robins for the book. Robins told Ron he needed to exchange it. Others were wanting to read the book.

'Leave the book where it is.' Ron was serious.

He studied its contents in his cell – read and remembered facts and figures and passed the details on.

'The Dutch and Spanish touched Cape York a hundred years before Cook. They didn't claim it though. That was their mistake.'

The Boy cut in to say, 'give it a rest. Concentrate on your bricks. That's what you should be thinking about. They'll be rejects, I can tell. Your mind's not on the job.' And the Boy rushed down beside Ron's plank and destroyed his last set of bricks. Just to prove a point.

Ron couldn't help himself. Out of the blue he'd say something like, twenty two million sheep, or six million head of cattle. I can't remember the half of it. He said the book's title was 'Triumph in the Tropics.' And did we know that France could fit three times into Queensland.

One Saturday morning, sitting by the iron fence, Ron said Britain once sent its convicts to America - fifty thousand of them.

'Fifty thousand?' Ray said. 'That's a bit steep.'

'Must be right coz it's in the book.'

'That'll be how those red necks got there,' Wally offered with a grin.

'What's that got to do with Queensland?' Ray wanted to know.

'Everything,' Ron replied, 'after the War of Independence they couldn't send more convicts. They were stuck. Lucky for them Captain Cook then discovered Australia. Problem solved. They started shipping convicts here. So you see, if not for the War of Independence Australia wouldn't be populated.'

As soon as the words were out of his mouth, Ron realised what he had said.

'I mean, I mean . . .'

Billy was onto him. 'I know what ya bloody mean. Just like whitey ain't it? The same wherever he goes. Moves in on the black man's country then takes it over. First America, then here.'

Billy was fired up. Nothing like this had happened before. Ron's mouth fell open but nothing came out of it. Awkwardness amongst us, downcast eyes, glum faces. Silence. Billy's hazel eyes were blazing. Muscles worked at both sides of his jaw. Ron in shock and appalled at what he had let slip.

'Billy,' I said, 'America wasn't the black man's country. He came later. The Indians owned America.'

Billy swung his attention to me. His nostrils were flared, lips curled. He was pumped. Not in the mood to be contradicted. I braced myself for what might happen next. Wally leaned closer to him, stretched out a hand and placed it on Billy's knee.

'He's right, Billy.'

Billy looked to Wally, distracted. Puzzle lines creased his brow. It dawned on him that what he believed was not correct. His version of history was wrong. He became quiet and looked upset, tugging at an ear lobe. It wasn't Billy's fault.

It's easy to get the wrong idea with a lousy education.

Ron looked relieved in the ensuing lull. Though a general unease continued to linger. Ray cut into the silence.

'Wonder what movie we'll get after lunch,' and flicking Billy's shoulder he said, 'you never know, might be cowboys and Indians.'

Billy answered him right back. 'I'd like to see the Indians stick it up those cowboys. Just for once.'

Ron eased off Queensland after that, though he kept the book and reminded Robins to leave it in his cell. When Robins saw Ron approaching he said, I know, you don't have to tell me. Leave the book where it is. And Ron would wink and say, 'You've got it. You've got the message.'

Ron offered me a loan of the book. He'd get Robins to switch it and then return it later. Okay I said. The book was interesting. A history of the state, its growth and development up to the present day. It covered the trials and successes of its early explorers, the hardship of its convicts and gains made by settlers. It once was thought a white man could not live in the tropics. A claim made in the book. Its editor was Raphael Cilento, a knight of the realm no less. Not a common name, Cilento, not in Australia at that time. I wondered if he was related to Diane, the actor. She came from the sunshine state and went on to marry a Scot by name of Sean Connery.

Ron was smart in asking Robins to leave the book with him. Robins swapped all the books on a weekly basis. He serviced every cell in the jail. He and one warder managed the library. Prisoners had no choice of the book left for them. It could be a western, pot boiler, factual, pulp fiction, comedic, a classic or war story. Any subject except crime. Books on crime were not allowed. Binned on their arrival.

A few good books were left in my cell - Elmer Gantry, Not as a Stranger and Bhowani Junction. Those titles come to mind. The best book I read was Voss, written by Patrick White. His next book was even better though I didn't know that then.

Patrick White used words like Picasso used paint. He let you see what you knew in a different light. Picture this, his writing said.

By now I had finished the bible. Read as a challenge and something to do. I read every page, scanned every line - read it from cover to cover. In my opinion the Old Testament was the better book. Its authors were more creative. Always something happening. Men begat men and went on to live for hundreds of years. Seas were parted, a bush could burst into flames and people were turned into salt. Nothing like that ever happened in the New Testament. It was dull by comparison.

It didn't occur to me to do what Ron had done. I could have asked Robins to leave me only good novels. He gladly would have done it. I only had to ask. But I read every book that was left in my cell, sometimes twice, boring or not. It irks me now on looking back that I didn't make use of Robins.

63. RECREATION

Huckle brought her into the yard - a naked woman carved on a match. Have you seen this, he said, knowing full well that nobody had. The reaction from the initial group caused more boys to join the group that was gathered around him. He was mobbed. Overwhelmed. Shy retiring Huckle, the lonely moocher in the yard was now a minor celebrity.

'Where's it from?' 'Who done it?' 'How did you get it?'

Question after question came as eyes ogled the figurine.

Huckle had done it himself. His standing rose amongst those who once discounted him. Voices were saying, 'let's see, let's see,' when what they really wanted to do was hold her in their fingers and study her.

Look at Huckle now. Beaming. Lapping up the attention being given to him. He handed the match to Vern Fry. Vern gripped the base of the match on which the naked lady stood. His gaze was intent. Mine too. So was everybody's. The red head of the match had become a ball, held above the lady's head by her extended arms. Standing beside Vern, I studied her as she was slowly twisted around. Shapely legs, rounded hips, narrow waist and an opulent bust swelling out above it.

A guy in the cobbler's shop had taught Huckle how to do it. He explained the methodology.

'You look through the box for the thickest match. And if you twist your old razor blade, it'll snap to make a pointed blade. Before you start carving, you choose one edge as the front. Get it?' And holding up a match from his box, he said, 'so these two edges will be her hips, this edge her backside and the front edge will be her face and tits.'

Everyone was at. Whittling matchsticks in their cell. Not only boys from Five yard, but inmates all over the jail. The original whittler had instructed other shoemakers too. Word spread. The craze caught on. Why wouldn't it.

I found her most fragile part was just above the ankles. I snapped my first attempt. A shame, as I ruined the thickest match in the box. My third attempt was the best result. We showed our ladies in the yard and in comparing them, awkward efforts were criticized, even ridiculed. Huckle suggested carving techniques to those wanting advice. He said the expert's lady was in a class of her own. Instead of a lumpy bust, she had a distinct pair of breasts.

I doubted this could be done on the sharp edge of a match. Then Huckle said the expert also carved a mace. The red head of the match became a wrecking ball, and between it and the handle were three links of a chain. If he carved three links of a chain on a match, I guess he could carve a pair of breasts on its sharp edge.

Matchboxes rattled throughout the jail with versions of naked ladies, and men in their cells snapped razor blades and applied themselves to their craft. Like the yo-yo and the hoola-hoop craze, everybody was at it.

Meanwhile Kevin and I were engaged in another diversion. We shared a newspaper clipping that listed all the Melbourne Cup winners. On alternative nights, we took the list into our cells and memorised a further ten names. At work and in the yard, we chanted the winner's names together - 1861 Archer, 62 Archer, 63 Banker, 64 Lantern, 65 Toryboy. Chanting the winner's names helped lodge them in our memories. We had reached 1900, won by Clean Sweep. Our aim was to know the complete list before the next Melbourne Cup, run in November.

We gambled too. Kevin won consistently. His understanding of horses helped to explain his luck. He loved horses. Not only to bet on. He said he would like to be a trainer. One thing he would never do was race a two-year-old. Phar Lap never ran as a two-year-old. That's what Kevin said. I suggested he get a job as a stable boy. Once inside the system he could work his way up from there.

'Nah. They wouldn't give me a chance. If I started as a stable boy I'd be shovelling horseshit for the rest of my life.'

I could pick winners for fun when nothing was at risk. But when it came to gambling, I was hopeless. I missed my condensed milk when I bought pipe tobacco to use as gambling stakes. But there you go. That's what I did. Gambling was an interest I shared with other inmates in the yard - a form of recreation. And life would be a dreary affair without any recreation.

64. MAX STUART

Kevin often told me of things that affected him during his early years. Nothing in great detail - a snippet, the bare bones of an event that left its mark on him. He remembered his father and uncles sitting around a tin bath, scooping their cups into the bath and drinking goom. They drank and laughed until they fell backwards off their chairs. What's goom I asked?

'Meths and water.'

When a little kid, one of his aunties was hard on him. She took a delight in finding fault and slapped him on occasions. He said she was an old bag. Not long ago, he and Wally were big winners at the races. They swaggered home broadcasting the extent of their success. Word of their luck passed around the mission. It wasn't long before the aunty rushed up to Kevin. I hear you've had a good day, she said. We sure did Auntie, Kevin replied. He pulled a roll of notes from his pocket and peeled off a tenner. Then he lit the bank note with a match and raised it to light a cigarette, and dropped the embers at her feet.

'You shoulda seen her face. Best tenner I ever spent.'

Another time he told me that the missionaries confused his people's folklore. Another auntie (I think she was an auntie) told him that Jesus came to Australia. He walked beside a lake where the women were fishing. Jesus said he was hungry and asked the women to give him a fish. The women refused. Jesus replied by saying that nobody will eat that fish in the future. The fish became full of bones making it inedible.

He said in his language a white man was called goonya. Goonya means fat, he explained. When a dead body is put in a tree and its skin falls off, the white stuff covering its bones is goonya. When his people saw their first white man they thought he was a dead man walking. They pointed at him and said, 'goonya.'

I often walked with Kevin when returning to B Division. He used to name the black guys approaching us from the opposite direction. That's Malley Kite's uncle, he said, when an older man went by. Long white hair and a white pointed beard made him look artistic. I imagined Albert Namatjira would look like Malley's uncle. He didn't. When I saw Namatjira's photo, he looked like what he was – an indigenous man raised in the bush.

Then there was Heron. A good-looking man, proud and erect, who padded past like a cat. Cords of muscle were prominent on both sides of his neck.

'That's Heron,' Kevin said, 'he killed two men.'

Wally from behind said, 'more than two.'

I asked how he killed them.

And Wally again, 'with his hands.'

Campbell was a big guy, thick limbed, more solid than Heron. Once he had passed I asked Kevin if Campbell had killed someone.

'Campbell? Nah, he wouldn't hurt a fly. Grog's his problem. When he's drunk and wants more drink he'll grab a fella on the street and pin him to the wall. Calls him a thief. You're a thief, he'll say. When the fella says he isn't, Campbell says, yes you are, you stole my country. You can't take my country for nothing. Give me something for it. Give me some money. Give me your watch. All he wants is a bit of money so he can buy more grog. Campbell would never hurt anyone.'

One day a thin and dark-skinned man came ambling towards us. Kevin named him in awed tones. This is Max Stuart, he said.

'Who is Max Stuart,' I asked after he had passed.

'Max Stuart, you must know Max Stuart. He's famous. Seven times he was gunner hang.'

I had never heard of the man. His case would have been the reason that pages were blacked out in newspapers I read. I often passed Heron and Campbell. Malley Kite's uncle too. He'd raise a finger and smile as he passed. I only saw Max Stuart once and didn't give him a second thought. Not till years later.

A movie called Black and White was released. It centred on the Max Stuart case. Nine-year-old Mary Hallam was found dead on a beach, murdered. Black trackers said the killer's footprints belonged to Max Stuart. He signed a statement with a cross as he couldn't read or write. He spoke only Pidgin English. He was found guilty and sentenced to hang. A priest conversant in Stuart's language said he didn't make that statement. He would not phrase words that way even if he knew what they meant.

A young newspaper owner became involved in the case. The same man who printed Lugal's story about conditions in Yatala. His paper's banner headline read:

PRIEST SAYS STUART IS INNOCENT

Rupert Murdoch only had one newspaper to his name. But Rupert was ambitious and he had the nose for a story. Murdoch's paper, The News, did not sell well in Adelaide. That was about to change. Continual pressure from The News led to the hanging being deferred. A retrial was held. Stuart was found guilty again and sentenced to hang for the second time. More pressure from Murdoch. More bold and outraged headlines. The News funded a search to locate missing witnesses. An appeal was granted and failed. The national press picked up the story but Murdoch was its driving force. What would have been a quiet hanging was now the cause of heated debates all over the country.

Lawyers defending Stuart faced financial ruin. Back and forth they went to court in further retrials. The News asked readers to make donations towards the mounting costs. Stuart's hanging was reinstated, then put off and reconfirmed. Murdoch became a thorn in the government's side, both at state and federal level. The last chance of appeal reached the Privy Council in London. The News helped raise more funds. Again, the appeal was turned down. The News asked why an English court should interfere in Australian affairs. The Prime Minister told the State Premier to make Murdoch shut up. Murdoch was threatened with seditious libel, a charge as serious as treason. After a meeting between The News and government, Stuart's hanging was commuted to life imprisonment. Murdoch then ceased his protests.

Capital punishment was later abolished in South Australia. Legal Aid was introduced and lawyers no longer bore the cost of defending cases they had drawn in a lottery. Referrals to the Privy Council were no longer made. Australia established a Federal Court, based in Canberra.

Murdoch and Stuart were good for each other. Murdoch saved Stuart's life and Stuart's case established Murdoch in the public eye. And Rupert learned a valuable lesson. If you go against the government it is likely to fight dirty. Even threaten you with the law. It's best to stay on the right side of a government. Something that Rupert perfected. By promoting a certain candidate and helping to win the election, he made sure the government stayed friendly towards him. Rupert used this ploy as he moved from country to country.

In the Black and White movie, David Ngoombujarra took the part of Max Stuart. Charles Dance played the prosecutor and Robert Carlyle and Kerry Fox acted as Stuart's lawyers. Ben Mendelson took the role of Rupert Murdoch.

When released from Yatala, Max Stuart became a tribal elder. He was presented to the Queen as such on one of her visits. During her long reign, Elizabeth met people from all over the world. I wondered if she remembered meeting Max Stuart.

65. GUYS LIKE US

Mister Red had gone for his shower together with the pair that fed the big concrete mixer. Wally was sloshing water around in his mixer's drum and other gang members were winding down after a hard day's work. Breezeblock making machines stood idle after being hosed clean. The concrete mixer was motionless, its drum tilted at rest and its hopper cables though still taut were relieved of their strain. Wheelbarrows having been washed clean were laid on their sides, and flat-topped barrows were scattered across the shed's concrete slab.

At the siren's wail, an exodus made for the gate. Ray and I walked together. I don't recall what amused us as we wandered through the shed. It concerned an incident that we made more laughable by adding twists to it. What about if, one of us said in suggesting another slant, and we both laughed at the thought of it. Or said the other, on proposing a turn of events that made us both crack up. We laughed at each suggestion, and added further outcomes that were completely absurd. On reaching the wall where our inmates stood, we were still laughing at the source of our amusement. Once through the gate and inside the walls we waited for the rest of the gang to be counted through. One boy wandered from the group and rounded a nearby corner. He beckoned others to follow him. Ray and I were amongst the few that slipped away to join him. Around the corner a prisoner sat in a small yard, his legs stretched out on either side of a big rock. Rocks were piled around him. He held a mason's hammer in his right hand. He picked up a rock, placed it on the big rock, hit it with the hammer and broke it into little rocks. Then he picked up another rock. We stared at him through the bars surrounding the yard. We watched him cracking rocks.

An inmate called, 'hang in there, Johnno.'

Another voice added, 'good man, Johnno. Don't let the buggers grind you down.'

Johnno did not look up, but continued to pick up and crack rocks. His downcast eyes were focused on the task he had to hand. He did not react to the calls of encouragement. He seemed unaware of our presence.

'Get back here, the lot of you.'

It dawned on one of the screws that some of us had strayed. By now the entire brickyard gang were inside the walls. The warders herded us into line and off we marched to A Division. Ray and I continued to add twists to our distraction, sniggering as we dug each other with our elbows. From the body search, we tramped through A Division and were counted into our yard. We were laughing like fools through the lean-to, and in still high spirits when flopping down by the iron fence.

Ray released a long sigh that came out like, 'hhheeeeeee,' and plucking out his tobacco tin, he flipped it into the air. As the tin fell, he spun it off the back of his hand and on catching it, removed its lid and clamped it underneath the tin in one smooth operation. It must have taken hours in his cell to perfect that trick. Then taking a pinch of grouse, he tweaked it and laid it along the crease of a cigarette paper. While absorbed in this task, he said:

'Just as well we do jail easy, coz let's face it, guys like you and me, we're gunner see plenty of it.'

Focused on his roll-up, he didn't see the surprise on my face. I didn't know anyone thought like that. Even knowing he would get caught, he meant to continue doing what he had always done and to hell with the consequences. I didn't know how to respond. I sat mute, watching him make his cigarette. I was convinced the time would come when he would be sick of jail. He would regret wasting so many years of his life. I intended to point this out to him.

On getting his roll-up lit, he flicked away the match, inhaled, and extruded a fat smoke ring. And smiling, he turned to face me. He might not like what I said but I thought he needed to hear it. Would he feel the same about jail when he was forty or fifty years old? That was a good way of putting it. Why not change his ways before reaching that stage of his life. Just as I was about to speak, Wally and Kevin arrived.

Ray asked if they had seen Johnno, and started to tell them how we saw him cracking rocks. Then Ron, Billy and Rufus came along to join us.

'Did youse see Johnno in separate?'

When they said they hadn't, Ray repeated what he had been saying to Kevin and Wally. The chance to tell Ray what I intended had gone. I doubt it would've changed him. Not at first. But later and hopefully not too late he might recall what I said and then act on it.

We lounged by the iron fence until called for the evening meal. By the next day I had forgotten whatever it was that had amused us, and I never gave another thought to what I meant to say to Ray. It was just another day. Another day of sweat and toil. Another day of knocking out six hundred bricks.

66. JOCK

I passed Jock the Scottish screw several times a day. He worked in the section where breezeblocks were made midway between the concrete mixer and the facebrick-gang. I knew him and he knew me though we had never exchanged a word. Jock held a black belt in judo, not that anyone would know judging by his scrawny build. The scrawniest part of him was his neck. His Adam's apple bulged as if a walnut was stuck in his throat. A walnut still in its shell.

Jock was a likeable screw. He treated prisoners as equals while overseeing their work. He kidded around with them. Inmates wished more screws could be like Jock the Scottish screw. He saw me when I first arrived, pale skinned, tentative and wearing a nice clean uniform. A new boy in the brickyard. Later he saw me swagger past, bronze skinned, toughened up and wearing dirty moleskins. The toughest part of me were my hands. Real navvy's hands, gnarled and hard as teak.

It's fair to say I loved my hands.

At night I lay in my hammock studying my palms. I admired every lump and bump, every horny ridge, and also the troughs weaving between the hardened and yellowed mounds. The surface of each opened hand looked like a craggy landscape. It's hard to believe human skin can toughen to that extent.

The state of my hands filled me with pride.

There is nothing more honest in this world than a pair of calloused hands. They can't be bought at any price. They can't be hired, can't be borrowed. They can't be stolen. There is no way to copy them. Calloused hands can't be faked. There's no easy

219

way to get them. It takes manual labour and time. Hard yakka and plenty of it. There is no alternative.

A tight grip on iron tools absorbed the shock of every blow I struck. A grip that acted as buffer between sinew and joint, muscle and bone. My fingers were also calloused. All of my digits were square edged, and yet my fingers tips were smooth – smooth and sensitive. I liked to run the tip of a finger over the hardened contours of my other hand, and wished my hand was able to caress bare female flesh. Glide the rough over the smooth, thrilling the stroker and the stroked. If only. The thought of it brought on a pang.

At that very moment, a tapping on the wall wrenched me from my thoughts. The tapping came from an empty cell, or it had been for the last two days. I leapt from the sheets, grabbed my stool and ducking under the hammock, placed it by the window and stood on it. I recognised the voice calling out to me.

'Who is it? Who's there?

It's me, Lugal,' I called.

'Can you give us something to smoke?'

I said I would tap on the wall when I had it ready. And spreading a piece of clean denim, I plonked a clump of tobacco on it, peeled off eight or nine papers and included a bunch of matches. I sawed off a chunk of soap and added it to the bundle to give a bit of weight. After securing the bundle with a length of darning wool, I tapped the wall with my mug and returned to the window. Leaning into the cut away, I stuck my arm through the bars and lowered the bundle towards the ground. It wasn't easy to swing due to the thickness of the wall. Only my forearm reached through the bars. And I should have added more soap as the bundle was too light.

'The string's not long enough.'

'It's coming. Just wait.'

Each swing hurt my arm as the bundle gained more height.

'You've got to let out more string.'

'Just wait will ya. Jesus, Lugal, it's coming.'

My arm jammed through the bars was beginning to hurt. And standing on my toes, with legs and body stretched, I swung the bundle back and forth. It gained height on every swing and at last I felt the wool go slack.

'Got it. Thanks.'

'No worries.'

When leaving my cell in the morning, slop bucket in my hand, Lugal's cell remained locked. At lunchtime it was empty again. He had been moved twice which was unusual. As he was held in three yard, I never learned why he was pinched. I never spoke to Lugal again.

Life in the brickyard carried on. The Boy enjoyed smashing our bricks. He timed it so we had to rush to reach our quota by the end of the day. A week passed. At the Monday morning break, I walked with Kevin towards the smoko shed. Jock the Scottish screw lingered ahead of us. As we neared, he said he would like a word with me. I remained with Jock while Kevin continued to the shed. I had no idea why he wanted to see me.

'I was on night duty last week,' he said, looking me in the eye. 'I was leaning against D wing's wall having a smoke, when something almost knocked off my hat.'

I dropped my eyes to his Adams Apple. I knew that a few years ago, a crim sneaked up behind Jock and whanged him over the head with a shovel. One of those occasions when a black belt in judo is no damn use at all.

'I went and looked at the board to see who was in those cells. And I thought, aarrrcck, I was enjoying a smoke, might as well let them have one too.'

I raised my eyes to his again. He watched me looking at him, a neutral expression on his face. I didn't say a word. We stood facing each other. Voices from the smoko shed drifted to where we stood. Nothing stirred around us on the deserted slab. Jock broke the silence between us.

'Alright, you can go.'

I suppose I should have thanked him. That would have been the right thing to do. Kevin didn't ask why Jock wanted to see me, and I didn't tell anybody what Jock said. From that day on when passing Jock, nothing like a knowing glance ever passed between us. As if I didn't know how he once nearly lost his hat.

67. BULLA

A loud shout called out my name. It rang out above the thump of the concrete mixer's drum, rumbling overhead. I turned to look from where it came and there was Bulla Rigney, a wide grin splitting his face. He raised an arm and waved at me from twenty yards away. Then stooping he lifted the handles of a flat-topped barrow and set off on a run, swinging the barrow around while holding its handles up to shoulder height. This was not new to him. He ran the barrow like an old hand. Bulla had been in the brickyard before. I was convinced of that.

When back at my stand with the facebrick gang, I said I had just seen Bulla.

'Know him, do you?'

'Yeah, we were in the lock-up together. And you, you know him too?'

Kevin replied, 'Ohhhh yes, we all know Bulla.'

Apart from Ray the others confirmed with grunts and raised eyebrows. Billy said everyone knew Bulla.

'One of these days he's gunner get it,' was the comment from Wally.

As we worked we talked about what we heard on our earphones the previous night. Floyd Patterson getting beaten came as a huge shock. The Swede didn't look like a fighter but what a punch he had. And horses, we talked about racehorses. How they ran and might perform on their next outing. We discussed the form of sprinters and stayers. I thought Mardine could step up and win at a mile. The Melbourne Cup was coming up and likely winners were discussed. Jockeys and trainers were mentioned, also the weights, the weather and other factors that could influence the result. At a nod from me, Kevin and I began to chant.

'61 Archer, 62 Archer, 63 Banker, 64 Lantern, 65 Toryboy, 66 the Barb . . .'

We knew all ninety-eight winners, and chanted their names as we shovelled and thumped. As we often did. By now all winners were firmly lodged in our memories. When our bricks were made and laid on the planks, the Boy walked down and rejected them. He said our minds were not on the job. I wondered if he had lasted a day without wrecking any bricks. During smoko, we discussed if that had ever happened. Probably not we decided.

At the end of the shift and by the stone wall, somebody slapped me on the back.

'Been long time,' Bulla said.

He said it was good to see me and gave me another slap. I thought it was you, he said, slap. He seemed pleased to see me. Slap. Once through the gate we joined the line marching beside F Wing's wall.

'Do you know what that is?' Bulla said, pointing at a low structure standing by the cellblock wall.

It was something I saw every day but never much considered. Raised a few feet above the ground, it was covered by a hatch flap. It could have been a coal bunker, or low storage shed. I had no idea what it it was used for.

'That's the Black Peter. They can't use it no more. One fella he went crazy in there.'

'What is it?'

'Black Peter. You can't see nothing inside. Can't stand up. You gotta sit or stand like this,' and Bulla bent his knees to crouch. 'When he was in it, this fella used to throw a button up into the air. Then crawled round to find it and throwed it up again. All day he done that. One time the button went up and didn't come down again. He went crazy. Later the screws found his button stuck in a spider's web.'

We were side by side at the body search. Once inside A Division, Bulla peeled off to the right and headed for number Three Yard.

The Black Peter was news to me. Nobody else had mentioned it. I asked inmates in the yard. Nobody knew anything about the Black Peter. Not even Vern Fry. Bulla had been here before, definitely. No doubt about it.

68. ELIZABETH

The bricks we made were used to build a new town north of Adelaide named in honour of the queen – Elizabeth. It's where the ten-pound poms will live when they arrive here on a ship. That's what Bluey the driver said.

'It only costs them ten quid to get here. We pay the rest. It ain't right. I don't want my taxes used to pay the fares for immigrants. This is our country. It's not for them.'

At which point Wally added, 'now you know how we feel.'

Bluey had nothing more to add after Wally's comment. But Ray agreed with Bluey, though Ray had never paid tax in his life.

I said one day in the future I would like to see Elizabeth. There were nods and general agreement. Everybody felt the same, to go and see the town built from our labours. Ray said the streets should be named after us and his would be the main drag. How many bricks had we made and how many were needed to build a house? Other questions and issues were raised regarding Elizabeth and our bricks. Bluey at the end of his truck smiled at our rambling. Nick Janawouski thought we were nuts.

'You've got to get away from these bricks not go chasing after them.'

I scratched 936 onto the face of some of my bricks with a pointed stick. I wondered what the odds were of finding one of those bricks. If they were ever used. A bricklayer might discard them when working on the job.

At the smoko break I made a prediction.

'I reckon the Boy will take a trip up to Elizabeth. Just to see what our bricks have built. He'll take the credit for it of course.'

'Don't say that,' said Ron. 'He might increase our quota.'

'Then we'll be up shit creek,' came from Billy.

'In a barbed wire canoe,' Kevin hastened to add.

'With tennis rackets for paddles,' came from Ray.

Cliches: they can't be restricted, can't be quelled.

Wally closed the subject by saying:

'He doesn't need to take a trip Elizabeth if he wants to increase our quota.'

69. DAYS LIKE THESE

Sometimes jail is just as good as any other place

Where life can thrive and hopes are high and when you're young and fit and Getting ten hours sleep at night and living clean by keeping clear of cigarettes and alcohol and cannot Ever over-eat or burn the candle at both ends and

Every day you exercise by doing press ups in your cell and Feel the benefit of it that Stays with you and Stays with you and never Sick or Tired or Stressed you Take the seasons one by one and when you've done twelve months or more and you can see your way ahead to do the time you've yet to do

Then it's great to be alive and when you wake you just can't wait to

Leap out from between the sheets and

Fling yourself into the day and get out there and

Slam and Pound and Bash and Thump and make six hundred bricks a day and

Feel the power Surging through your veins and all your sinews too and

Dripping sweat you laugh and joke and horse around with all your friends and

Bug the screw who gets annoyed that you are feeling so Damned good and he will Never understand just why you like the work you do

That is preparation for the day you walk out through those gates to

Live the dream and Claim your rights and when at night in your own cell you think of all the girls you'll know and men you'll knock out in the ring and

When you sleep you sleep the sleep the soundest sleep that's known to man because you Know what lies ahead and you're prepared to

Bide your time until the day they let you go to

Join the world and Live your life and Chase the dream and Work and Strive and don't slide back and Train and Fight and Climb the ranks and Make your mark and Let them see

AND SHOW THEM ALL.

Days like these are a joy.

70. FIFTH PINCH

Ron and I were on the court playing Vern and his partner. His latest partner, a reluctant partner. Tennis brought out the worst in Vern. It meant so much to him. His only form of exercise. His one passion. When a point was lost or the game began to slip from him, Vern's partner bore the brunt. Partners were sacked, partners resigned. A nicer fellow you couldn't meet without a racket in his hand. At twenty-five Vern had mellowed since being jailed at seventeen. He said he longed to be free. He would do any work, live anywhere if he had a wife and family. I had no doubt when he was free he would be no threat to the public. Not like the Greek, who tried to stab a man with a fork. Not like Kitchen either, who went for a man with a knife in the tinsmith's shop. I'd worry about those two when loose. Also Heron, the proud indigenous man who killed at least two men with his hands. His calmness was chilling. Other killers I couldn't judge. I wouldn't like to say. I saw no sign of malice in them, no matter what they had done. The pharmacist was a safe bet, the same as Vern. He gave out medication in the foyer of A Division. Considerate with fellow inmates when giving them pills and medicine. On passing, I would hear him give instructions in a friendly tone - three times a day after meals, or take one every four hours. He had been a small-town cop in the Northern Territory. Normally a cop in jail would have a hard time, but Mac (everybody called him Mac) had never dealt with criminals on the outside. Domestic violence and drunkenness kept him occupied. One day he came home early and found his wife in bed with another man. He shot them both dead on the spot and handed himself in. If a gun had not been strapped to his hip the pair would probably still be alive. There are all kinds of killers. Up in Balcaldine, somebody poisoned the tree of knowledge.

So there we were on the tennis court, me and Ron against Vern and his latest partner. The new kid's racket edged the ball and sent it sailing over the fence. Vern needed to calm down. That could happen to anyone. Being nearest to the fence, I waited by it for a warder to come round between the fence and perimeter wall. Minutes passed. At last a screw came dawdling around the corner of number Four yard. When closer I saw the mood on his face. He was not having a good day. He looked fed up, disgruntled. It was plain to see he begrudged working on a Sunday. He wanted to be somewhere else. As he neared I made my request.

'Can we have our ball, please?'

I added the please due to the expression on his face. The please had no effect. Glaring at me his face reddened before he snarled:

'Do think I'm only here to throw your balls back to you?'

I knew I should not have done it. I should've kept my mouth shut. But I couldn't resist it. The contrast in our moods triggered my response. Him being a free man and having a rotten day, while I as a prisoner was in a carefree mood. That's what prompted me to say it.

'Yes,' I said, a loud resounding YES, as soon as he asked the question.

He went rabid.

'Go to the gate,' he screamed. 'Go to the gate,' his face contorted with rage. His whole body began to shake. When raising an arm to point the gate, his arm, hand and finger trembled violently. He was almost frothing at the mouth.

'Go to the gate, go to the gate,' his whole body shaking as he yelled.

I went to the gate. The warder there on duty, must have wondered what I did as did inmates in the yard. After waiting for several minutes, the irate warder arrived, breathing heavily. He told me to follow him and stomped into the cellblock. He turned right onto B Wing and halfway along the wing veered into an empty cell. I followed. Two other warders were already there. I was ordered to strip. Once naked, I splayed my legs and bending forward placed my hands against the wall. The position where a warder could check that nothing was hidden up my backside. As if.

While leaning against the wall, I could hear murmurs and whispers behind me. And then a slap of leather, as someone came running along the wing. I lowered my head and looked to the door from underneath my arm. A warder rushed into the cell. One hand gripped a baton strapped to his belt. Another warder, just inside the door, shook his head from side to side. I realised I'd been brought here for a beating. For some reason it had been called off. I could hear movement behind me, shuffles, steps and more whispering. Then a voice told me to dress. When I turned around to fetch my clothes there were three screws in the cell. One had gone already. Another two followed, leaving just one officer and not the screw who made the pinch. When I was dressed and booted, he asked me the number of my cell. On the walk to B Division he didn't utter a word. At my cell I carried the stool outside with bedding and pillow on top. Out went the hammock and cutlery, earphones and library book, the enamel bowl, towel and soap. I surrendered my tobacco tin and box of matches. Pinched again, for the fifth time.

I knew I had had a lucky escape. Not just from the kicking. That was the least of it. I would have recovered from that. There would have been further repercussions. To justify beating me, the screws would say I lashed out first and had to be restrained. That would fetch me solitary, seven days on bread and water. And if I was charged with assault, an extra six months in jail. Those six months would be spent in separate confinement.

Considering what might have happened, my imagination began to run wild. What if when fending them off, I hooked one of their eyes and yanked it out of its socket. What then. Grievous bodily harm of a screw. What would I get for that? Five years? Seven or more? It gave me the shivers to think how lucky I had been to avoid further charges. On the following Wednesday, I fronted the magistrate. The charge was insubordination, made by the warder who locked me in my cell. Not the hothead who pinched me. I said nothing in my defence. The usual punishment applied, loss of privileges and loss of remission. The warder walked me back to my cell. He didn't speak. He did not engage with me at all. He was just an ordinary screw. There were no stripes on his arm. But he took control of the situation. The other screws were up for it. They were ready to give me a kicking. He overruled the hothead and calmed the others down. That took some doing. He had principles. He was a decent man. I owed him.

I followed him along D Wing to where my accessories were stacked outside on the wing. At the door of my cell I turned to face him and looked him square in the eye. He gave no response, showed no emotion. He remained calm and composed. Before turning to enter my cell I gave him a nod of appreciation. Again, nothing in return as he shut the door.

I never saw him again. I looked for him during assembly, at the body search, when filing to the kitchen and on being locked up. I would've given another nod to express my gratitude. But he was nowhere to be seen. I wondered if he had quit the job.

71. ANNOYED

A pair of short powerful arms handed me my lunch at the kitchen hatch, their pale skin downed with light ginger hair. Redda Lewis's arms, I felt sure of that. He must have been transferred to the kitchen from the tailorshop. On accepting a lidded dish with a chunk of bread on top, I turned to traipse across the square towards B Division, and once inside the cellblock, I walked the length of D wing and froze on reaching my cell. It had been trashed. My hammock had been flung on the floor with disheveled blankets and sheets heaped on top of it. Dirty footprints covered the sheets, going in all directions. My pillow lay on the floor in front of the tangled heap. A pair of dirty footprints showed where a screw had jumped. I lifted the pillow, turned it over and saw that he had jumped on both sides of it. Then placing my lunch on the corner shelf I surveyed the chaos. My bucket's lid had been slung to the far end of the cell, lying under the window. The toilet paper was scattered. Towel and soap were on the floor and enamel bowl kicked aside. My water jug (minus its lid) stood in a pool of water. My earphones were dangling on their cord. Salt and whiting were lying in heaps on the corner shelf, their wooden tubs empty. Knife, fork and razor were swept against the wall. My spoon was on the floor. This was not a random search. This was wilful destruction. A screw did it because he could. Because he assumed the right. I sat on my stool and faced the door while eating my lunch, preferring to ignore the mess. At the end of the break I went back to work without tidying my cell.

At assembly I told my friends about my cell being trashed. I said I couldn't understand how his boots were so dirty. None of my friends could offer a reason. A Kiwi standing in front of us overheard what I said. He turned around to enlighten us.

'The wings get mopped every morning. His boots would've been wet.'

Ahh, so that was it.

We were back in the brickyard at the hottest time of the day. Shirts were off. Sweat flew. I pounded and thumped and ran my bricks to place them on my plank. The Boy Bastard chose to pick on me that day. He rejected more of my bricks than others in the gang. My bricks were well made and firmly compacted. When he leered at me I think he knew the smile I gave him had to be forced. And off he went down the planks to ruin my latest batch. I noticed the gold ring on his left hand. Somebody loves him. Or did at the time they were married.

After the siren's wail and making our way to the gate, two prisoners started to fight. They grappled and swung each other around and slapped and clawed each other. One pulled the other's hair. The scuffle involved a nightclub owner and Bluey. Not Bluey the driver, another Bluey, who had been a jackaroo. I expected he would have been handier with his fists but they fought like two little kids and embarrassed themselves. I grabbed Bluey and dragged him aside. Another inmate clamped his arms around the nightclub owner. We were too late to prevent the fight from being noticed. Jock the Scottish screw rushed in with another warder. Gatlin arrived just after them.

Wagging a finger at the combatants, Gatlin said, 'don't let that happen again. Hear me? Think yourselves lucky you're not on a charge.'

The other screw, not Jock, looked upset at not being able to make the pinch. Gatlin closed the matter by saying, 'it's lucky that no one could get hurt.'

Bulla now beside me, gave a friendly nudge.

'Ha, the peacemaker. I ain't seen a fight like that since granny slapped her sister,' and he threw back his head and roared with laughter.

Once through the gate and on the march, Bulla tried to persuade me to go into his yard. I didn't want to risk getting pinched and I said would stay in my own yard. He kept at me, insisting that I would find it interesting. No, I said and repeated it twice. On nearing the body search, he stuck out his elbows and flapping them, started to cluck and squawk.

'I didn't think you was chicken,' he said.

That did it. Once through the body search, I followed him into the cellblock and took the exit on the right. Two and Three yards were laid out the same as numbers Four and Five. I followed Bulla into the yard on the left. The screw that counted me through the gate didn't know me. Which was a relief. Bulla led me to the lean-to. At the water bag, he unhooked its canvas spout and filled the tin cup and after drinking from it, he handed the cup to me. As I sipped, he told me what he did when sloughed up in his cell.

'I keep a needle in my jacket and I stick the needle in my boot. Then I pull a button off my jacket and throw it over the needle. Close at first, then further away. When I get my eye in, you'd be surprised how far I can throw the button and get it over the needle.'

I drank another cup while listening to him. When I hung the cup back on its hook, Bulla said, 'let's go for a walk.' He set off at a brisk pace and cut through the middle of the yard. When I caught up with him, he spurted off again. There were more prisoners in this yard than in Number Five. Plenty of guys I knew, friends who were once in Five Yard, Shorty and Lugal amongst them, having both come back inside. Workers from the brickyard too. I was too busy chasing Bulla to take a good look round. At the end of the yard, Bulla turned and started back by the iron fence. Once again, he strode ahead of me. When the Kiwi noticed me looking at him, he averted his eyes. Other inmates too, turned their heads and avoided looking at me. I became conscious of being shunned. The reason had to be because I was with Bulla. I couldn't understand it. Those from the brickyard knew I worked with four black boys. That we were friends. What was so different with Bulla.

I realised too that Bulla wanted to lead me rather than walk alongside. He wanted to show me off. And then Brown, my neighbour, ducked his head when I looked at him.

'Let's go this way now,' and back by the lean-to Bulla shot off towards the wire fence.

I said I wanted another drink and went into the lean-to. Bulla didn't hear me and kept walking. He returned after a while, sheepish. He knew he had upset me. He tried to get me talking as I stared through the wire mesh. I didn't see Shorty or Lugal, nor Jammy Just, who must have been there too. I did not expect to see Malley Kite. Malley had been released, leaving Bulla as the only black face in the yard. A coolness now between us. It would have been fine if he walked with me. That's what I expected. I resented being led as if I was a trophy. The call to the gate couldn't come quick enough for me.

Those arms were there again at the kitchen hatch - Redda Lewis, definitely. On crossing the square I felt annoyed. Annoyed with myself for going into Three yard. Annoyed with Bulla for tempting me and then showing me off. Annoyed with inmates who snubbed me. I was so annoyed with the whole affair that I didn't know what annoyed me most. On reaching my cell I stopped at its door and stared at the devastation. I had forgotten that my cell had been trashed. The state of my cell perfectly matched the kind of day I had had.

72. SAND HEAP

During the morning smoko break, I often lay on the hill of sand rather than sit in lean-to's shade amongst the brickyard gang, and stirred by the warm rays of the sun, I lapsed into pleasant thoughts while watching the clouds move overhead; the wispy streaks breaking up or being devoured by larger clumps that moved at a faster pace, and letting a handful of sand trickle between my fingers, I imagined myself resting on a lonely beach.

At the shriek of the siren, I rose and plunged down through the sand. A new prisoner stood at the foot of the dune, watching my descent. He intercepted me and addressed me by my name.

I had no idea who he was and gave him a hard look.

'You got two and a half years,' he said.

Who was this guy? Coming onto me like he did. I narrowed my eyes at him and taken aback, he began to explain himself.

'I saw your name scratched on a wall in a cell at the court.'

I brushed past him and left him standing. I didn't remember scratching my name on any wall at the court. But it puzzled me. He must have seen my name on a wall and nobody else would have done it. It must have been me. I thought back to the day I was sentenced. How I went numb when the judge said he had considered the birch. The birch! I didn't know in South Australia that people could get flogged. It sounded so medieval. Or something that happened in other parts of the world. But here in Australia too. I was shocked. And then on hearing my sentence, my mind went completely blank. I found myself in a tiny naked cell - stunned. That's when I must've scratched my name on the wall. I had no memory of it. And wondering how I did it, I decided with my belt buckle, the only possibility.

On another occasion while lazing on the dune, somebody came and plonked themselves down right next to me. Close to me, too close.

'We know each other, don't we?'

His face was blurred by the sun, and raising a hand to shield its glare I recognised someone who I never expected to see again.

'Piss off Dognuts.'

Now he knew how he knew me. Leaping to his feet, he raced down the dune and on reaching the bottom he accosted a warder. I watched him gabble to the screw before he turned to point a finger at me. The screw walked him to Gatlin and after a brief discussion, Dognuts was taken to the gate. That was the end of Dognuts working in the brickyard. I never saw him again.

The first time I heard Dognut's name was a sorry day indeed. Huckle mentioned it. Ron and I met Huckle and Baker in a public bar. They were playing pool and we challenged them to a game of doubles. We got on well together and often met from that day on. One evening by the Torrens, as we sat sharing a bottle of Doctor Penfolds sherry, Huckle said he knew a lad called King. Listen to this, he said. King had been in a pub with a mug called Dognuts. The mug bought all the beer. When paying for each round, he pulled a roll of notes from his pocket that was big enough to choke a horse. Dognuts bragged about knocking the money off.

'We're gunner take it off him. He can't go to the cops because he stole the money himself.'

We could be in on it if we liked. Ron and I could pretend to rob King, while he and Baker took the money off Dognuts. King would stay with Dognuts to make sure he didn't go to the cops. King would say he'd been robbed too. Ron wanted no part of it. He didn't want to get involved. I talked him into it. What can go wrong, I said.

'Like Huckle says, Dognuts can't go to the cops because he stole the money himself.'

On the prearranged night, four of us hid in a clump of bushes on the banks of the Torrens. We watched the pair approach. I asked Huckle to point out King. When the pair reached the bushes, I leapt out, grabbed King and dragged him to one side. Dognuts turned to run but Huckle fell on him. They wrestled and staggered around like two drunks having a dance. Then they fell over and rolled in the dirt, Huckle on top, then Dognuts and then Huckle again. Ron, King and I crouched, watching from a distance. Baker stood over the scuffle without getting involved. Minutes passed. Baker danced around the pair like a referee at a wrestling match.

'What's Baker doing,' I said, 'wait here,' and I went to give a hand.

Dognuts was lying on his back. One hand clutched the top pocket of his lumber jacket. I pushed in beside Huckle, put a knee on Dognut's chest and levered his fingers off the pocket. Then dipping into it, I grabbed the money.

'I've got it,' I said, and the four of us skedaddled.

When in the lockup, Huckle told us what happened next. After we had gone, Dognuts said to King, 'aren't you going with your mates?'

King told Dognuts to get stuffed and before walking off, punched him in the mouth. The only time Dognuts was hit during the robbery. Dognuts went straight to the cops. It turned out he didn't steal the money. He bragged to King that he had to make a big man of himself. The money was a payoff from being sacked from a job. It was made up of a week's pay, another week in lieu of notice and also accrued holiday pay. If Dognuts said he had earned the money nobody would've robbed him.

The cops picked up King that night, and the rest of us the following day. The easiest pinch they will ever make. The worst of the whole affair and what preyed on my mind was that I talked Ron into it. He didn't want to get involved. I persuaded him. How do you make that up to a friend. Getting him twenty months in jail. I didn't have the remotest idea.

73. THE VISIT

It was hot. As hot as it can get. Dry heat that scorched and burnt, heat that parched the throat. A touch of humidity would've been nice. Back in my cell for lunch, I took off my boots and socks and padded around with bare feet on the stone slabs. Then sat on my stool at the corner shelf, ate the beans and potato mash with torn pieces of bread. Drank the coffee I sweetened with spoon-fulls of sugar. Then peeling off my shirt, I bundled and placed it on the floor to use as a pillow and stretched out on the cool slabs to take my midday nap. Each day I woke just seconds before the siren's piercing wail, my body clock now synchronised with the prison timetable. Within a few minutes I was fast asleep.

Rudely interrupted, I was wrenched awake. Dazed and confused I raised myself and resting on an elbow, turned to look at the door. It was open. Inside it stood a pair of legs.

'You've got a visitor.'

It took a moment to translate what the warder had said and sitting up I pushed my woollen socks away and slid each foot in turn into its own leather sheath. Then tied the laces. Once on my feet I shook the shirt loose and threaded my arms through it. The warder had left the cell already. I slapped on my hat and followed him, tucking in shirt tails as I advanced along the silent wing. At the end of the wing, the warder paused to close the gate and led me to the portal of B Division.

The sun outside was ferocious.

I felt its bite the instant I stepped out into its glare. And tugged my hat brim lower. The warder began to cross the square, leaving footprints behind him in the melting tar. I followed his tracks. Apart from the warder's footprints, the asphalt was littered with small black bubbles, some of which had burst.

A damp patch stained the warder's shirt between his shoulder blades. Hair on the back of his neck had bunched into damp clumps. The visiting block lay ahead to the left of the inner gates, its iron roof ablaze with the sun's reflection. On drawing closer I could see that all the booths were empty. I was led to the fourth slot along.

'Take off your hat.'

I dropped my hat on the concrete base and stepped into the open backed booth. Shade inside the cubicle was easy on the eye, though air trapped under the hot tin roof was warm and heavy to breathe. Air only fit for shallow breaths. At least the heat was less intense than outside in the square. An opening at the front of the booth was covered with chicken wire and it faced its twin on the other side of a narrow passageway.

A minute at least elapsed before anyone arrived and then she appeared across from me. It shocked me to see how old she looked. Her listless eyes peered out from a deeply lined face. Sighing before she said my name, she paused before she launched into a stinging rebuke.

'I've travelled nearly a thousand miles and sat up all night on a train.' The pitch of her voice climbed higher. 'I haven't slept a wink. I came here early in case I met somebody that I knew. What could I say about being here? What reason could I give?'

She could have lied. It's not like she didn't know how.

'The Governor was good enough to let me wait in his office. He said you've seen a magistrate five times!'

Fire now in her eyes. 'Five times,' she shrieked.

I shuffled my feet and tried to explain.

'Plenty of men in here have been before the magistrate.'

'I don't **want you** to be like other men in here.'

'You don't understand,' I started to say, but she cut me off.

'You're right! I don't understand.' Now crying, blubbering as she spoke. 'After a dreadful night on a train, then having to hear what the Governor said. It was like getting a slap in the face.'

She was complaining to the wrong person. What I would have given to spend all night on a train. Just then a warder appeared in the passage and walked between us. I didn't want a screw to see me while my mother was crying. He walked on through, eyes to the front. I tried to calm her.

'The rules in here are petty. I haven't done anything serious. Outside they wouldn't amount to . . . to anything.'

She had been well primed.

'The governor said there's a code and if you can't live by the code in here how do expect to obey the law once you've been released?'

All I could do was shrug. When she got a bee in her bonnet nothing could stop it from buzzing. I wished she hadn't come. I resented her for coming.

Suddenly I became aware of another presence. In the booth to my mother's left was a young woman. She stood close to the chicken wire, looking across the passage as she softly spoke. I could hear the tone of her voice but not make out the words. My mother and she were the only women I had seen in eighteen months. She was not beautiful. Not beautiful in the classical sense and not in a pin-up way.

But she was deliciously feminine.

The texture of her skin so different to that of a man. So smooth and delicate, and the structure of her face was nothing like a man's. Her features were unmistakeably feminine - her mouth, her nose, her cheek bones and especially her neck, which was long and slender. That neck would look out of place if seen on a man. On her it was perfect. I strained to hear what she was saying when a screech startled me. I swung back to my mother. Her eyes were glinting with fury.

'I've come all this way, all this way, and you're not even listening to me.'

'I am, I am,' I lied . . . 'I'm listening,' I said.

She was crying again, softly weeping.

'To think over the years, all the tears I've shed over you.'

That made me feel bad. I had put her through it over the years - neighbours, teachers, other kids' parents - the police. She looked sad, sadder than I remembered her ever looking before. She could never hide her feelings. They always showed. Her face not able to mask what she felt inside. Not the highs nor the lows. There had been highs, earlier, mainly when I was a child.

'Thanks for coming,' I said, though I wished she hadn't. 'How is everything at home?'

She began relaying family news and talked of people that I knew. At each pause I prompted her with another question. She had my full attention. Once we spoke at the same time, then stopped, then started again, our words tumbling out on top of each other.

'No, you, you go on.' – 'You first.' – 'No, you, what were you going to say?'

There was no natural flow to our conversation. In trying to pull together we were tugging opposite ends of the same length of rope. Our conversation rushed and stalled. Gradually it evened out and became more natural. She stopped crying and pulled herself together. I sneaked a glance at the other booth.

The young woman, so close to me, was prettier each time I looked. It was wonderful to look at her. To watch her lips as she spoke. To note the purity of her skin. To see how her eyes shone. I could have looked at her all day. And she was indeed beautiful. Three faint lines often appeared in the centre of her brow. They were there and then they weren't. Smoothed over, then returned – slight imperfections in the texture of her skin. Yet they were charming. I liked them. They made her look more fragile, more human – more humane.

I wanted her to look at me. I willed her to look at me. I zapped a message across the passage. Look at me, look at me, I commanded her. But she was oblivious of me being there. Unaware that I existed. She only had eyes for the man directly across from her. She had a lovely smile and she often smiled. Sometimes a smile not fully formed - a half smile, a suggestion of a smile, a twitch of her lips. When she held a long lingering smile, I realised I was smiling too. Disaster! I swung back to my mother. She looked hurt. I fully engaged with her and got her talking again. I had to make sure I only glanced at the other booth. Take a peep and then return to what my mother was saying.

The heat had had a different effect on the two women. My mother looked bedraggled. Strands of damp hair stuck to her forehead. Beads of sweat above her lips formed a liquid moustache. She told me many summers ago that women did not sweat. Horses sweat she used to say, men perspire and women merely glow. The young woman was glowing. She was all aglow. The flush on her cheeks made her radiant. Her eyes the clearest I'd ever seen. They shone. I stood in awe of her. Transfixed.

My mother broke the spell by giving another shriek.

'Why won't you look at me?'

I tried my best to repair our ruptured conversation. It took some time to get her engaged again. I didn't dare turn away and gave her all my attention. A chance to look at the young woman came as the warder passed through the passage. I let my eyes go with him and once he had gone, there she was. She was nothing like the fantasy women who came into my hammock at night. Nothing like them at all. They had curvy hips, tiny waists and voluptuous breasts. This young woman was slender. There was no visible cleavage in the neckline of her dress. Her breasts made modest bumps in the fabric covering them. Though her lower body was out of sight below the wire mesh, I felt sure her hips didn't curve outwards from her waist. Yet she had her own allure. I could hardly drag my eyes away. She glowed, she throbbed, she mesmerized. A real live pulsating woman. She exposed my fantasy girls for what they really were – make believe tarts - false images, nothing like the real thing. I had to get back to my mother.

Either my absence had not been noticed or she made allowance for it. I picked up the gist of what she was saying and made a suitable comment.

I wondered who the prisoner was in the next booth. The man she had come to see. My visit was due to end first and I would see his number on passing him. Perhaps he was someone I knew.

The visit progressed. As I listened to my mother's news I sneaked a glance now and then at the other visitor. At times I checked the booth on my left but it remained empty. Or maybe a person in it was standing back from the wire mesh. My mother must have realised that I wasn't always with her. That my gaze wandered at times. But I was doing the best I could.

She laughed. The young woman laughed. Her peals of joy tripped along the passageway and tinkled up to the iron roof. My eyes swung of their own accord. Her head was tilted back, exposing the length and curve of her throat. My God, that throat. I couldn't asses her character from the faintness of her voice. But the laugh. She laughed with childlike innocence and told me all I needed to know. The pure joy that she expressed could only come from a nice person. I hoped the man she came to visit was good to her. Her lover. I knew that by now. It was made obvious by how she gazed at him. She would be true to him, I could tell. I hoped he wouldn't twist her when he got out of here.

I had been away too long again. Her face might have been chiselled from stone. She knew I had lost her, ignored her, gone missing. I hadn't meant to. It just happened. All I could do was sigh and smile a weak apology.

The tin roof hummed to the beat of the sun. A trickle of sweat ran down my chest, gathering speed as it fell. Suddenly it stopped. Disappeared. Maybe it met a fold in my shirt and became absorbed. While wondering what had happened to it, I missed what my mother said.

'. . . gone to New Zealand.'

'Who's gone to New Zealand?'

'Your brother. He's gone with a team of shearers.'

'Where did he learn to shear sheep?'

'He's gone as a wool boy. He gathers the fleeces once they're shorn. He heard about the job at Dalgetys. We're not happy about him going. I said no to him at first but he got angry. He was desperate to go. He was only sixteen when he went. I don't know if we've done the right thing. But we tried to keep a hold of you and that didn't work.'

I had to agree with her there. 'No, that didn't work.'

'Those shearers are rough. They're hardened drinkers and they gamble. I don't want him to grow up too soon.'

'He'll be fine,' I said, voicing a conclusion that my mind had yet to reach. 'He'll be fine,' I said again just to emphasise.

'Do you think so?' Peering at me. 'Do you really think so?'

'Absolutely. I'm sure he'll be fine.'

'I hope you're right,' was her meek reply.

I liked what I was doing now. It's nicer giving support than being criticised. I was happy to reassure. 'He's sensible. He'll be fine.'

'I hope so.'

Our conversation now took on a more natural flow. We talked easily, with warmth and understanding. I gave her all my attention. We were totally engaged. It might have been like this from the start but for that pig, the governor.

On occasions I sneaked another glance at the other booth. Just a peep. I didn't want to slip up again. I hoped the man she came to visit wouldn't let her down. I wanted to know who he was, more than ever before.

A woman walked behind my mother heading for the gates.

'Someone went behind you. She's leaving.'

'Don't worry. The normal visit is twenty minutes but I get half an hour because I've come interstate.' And then with a serious look she said, 'when you get out of here, will you come home?'

So that was it. That's why she came.

My plans were vague. I had not intended to go home. Once outside those gates I felt all my problems would be gone. I would find a place to stay, get a job and join a gym. From there everything would fall into place. But I relented. Common sense kicked in. Home would be the best place for me. A roof over my head. No rent to pay. No pressure to find a job right away. I'd have time to find my feet and get established. I wouldn't be broke. No need to do anything stupid because I had no money. It made sense to go home.

'Yes,' I said, 'I'll come home.'

'The only thing is . . . I'm not sure where home will be. Your father might be getting a move, a move back to Melbourne. It's been talked about. We'll know quite soon if it will happen.'

'It doesn't matter, Sydney, Melbourne, wherever. I'll come home.'

The lines on her face had faded, become less pronounced. She lit up. Her mission accomplished. Happy now for the first time, she wanted to talk of earlier days. When she was a young woman and I was innocent.

'Do you remember when?' she said.

I did, and expanded on it. When life was simple. Happy days that rolled on one after another. There were no complications. My father often was not there during the war. He worked in communications with the Americans. It pleased me to see her happy. She would leave in a better frame of mind than when she arrived. I threw a quick glimpse to the right, and saw with a pang that she had gone. The other booth was empty. I would have liked to see her go. To take a last look at her. The man she came to visit, he'd be gone too. I would never know who he was.

And then a warder intervened from within the passage. 'It's time,' he said.

She acknowledged him and said, 'I suppose I have to go.'

She smiled and said goodbye. Once outside the booth she hesitated, turned and waved and then she was gone.

I now faced three empty boxes. The one to my left had not been used.

'Okay nine-three-six.'

Not the same warder that brought me here. I picked up my hat, put it on and followed him across the square. Over the blistered tar once more, under an unrelenting sun.

It was my only visit. It came a few months before my release, completely out of the blue. I was pleased she came and pleased she left in a better mood than when she arrived. Having put her through it over the years, I determined to make it up to her. Stay out of trouble. Paint a ceiling, mow the lawn. I was glad I saw the young woman. I would never forget her. A woman like that would be good for a man. Good for me. But not for a long time yet. First, I had some living to do. Catch up on all that I had missed. Later it would be nice to meet a woman like her.

Though not the same warder who fetched me from my cell, he wore an identical shirt – wet between his shoulder blades. I remembered I had to put on my socks before going back to work. Or else my feet would sweat and then squelch in my boots.

74. NORTH WIND

Those north winds in Adelaide, they're something. They don't come often but when they do, oh boy, an experience you will never forget. They must begin up near the equator and gathering all their strength together they make a dash for the south. Once over the Arafura Sea and reach Australia's coast, they roar across its red centre, picking up dust and grit on the way and hurling it into the air to form a huge billowing cloud. And driving south, due south, they reach Adelaide at last and sandblast everything in sight.

A slight stir in the air precedes their sudden attack, and after wreaking havoc, they fade away and allow calmness to return. Citizens rub their eyes, blow their noses, grab a broom and start sweeping.

The brickyard gang stood by the gate, waiting for the quarrymen to leave from its other side. A flutter stirred the parched air and without further warning the north wind came roaring in. It struck me full force in the face. I dipped my head and let my hat take the brunt of it. I stared at my feet as the squall howled overhead. Those at the front of our gang must have really copped it. Beside me a German inmate was muttering under his hat:

'Dis country . . . dis country.'

With a hand on top of my hat, I turned to take the blast on my back. Ahead of me a sea of hats was dipped to protect their owners. Amongst the khaki brims and crowns one bare face defied the storm. Its owner peered through narrowed eyes as his people had done for many thousands of years. Then Bulla began to elbow his way through the men ahead of him. On reaching me he said:

'We could have a bloody good night when we get outer here. Me and you together. Buy a flagon o'wine as dark as my face, sit under a tree and drink it. Then we fight.' He threw back his head and laughed. 'Not Marquis of Queensbury rules. We fight anything goes. You can kick – wrestle,' and raising a hand like a claw, 'gouge, bite, anything you like. No holds barred,' and pausing to smile he went on to say, 'you gotta advantage over me coz you got all your teeth.'

He was laughing at the prospect of it. I laughed too, at something that would never happen. He sensed I was not laughing with him. He stopped laughing and leaned closer to me.

'But I beat you English. I beat you.'

'English? What are you talking about? I'm not English. I'm from here. I'm an Aussie.'

Bulla stood up straighter, stretched himself to his full height and tilting back his head, looked down over his broad flat nose with scorn in his eyes. Pride tempered his voice when he spoke.

'A cabbage can grow in a lettuce patch but that don't make it a lettuce.'

His defiant eyes held mine in an unblinking stare. I was groping for something to say, to give some kind of response. Humans are born not planted I thought, but before I could put the words together Bulla had gone. He barged past me and left me standing. Other inmates were pushing past too. The gate had been opened.

Once inside the prison walls we were protected from the storm. When all of the gang was through the gate we marched to A Division and the body search. I could see Bulla ahead of me, eight or nine bodies between us. All of his limbs were swinging from their elastic joints. A man completely relaxed. Untroubled. Not affected by the rift now existing between us.

I had never heard that expression before - a cabbage in a lettuce patch. I've never heard it since. I have no idea where Bulla got it from.

I saw him a few times after that though we didn't speak again. I can't remember which of us was released first. Wally could have been right in what he said about Bulla. One day he might get it, if he continued to get drunk and fight with the police. He ran the risk of one day taking a fearful beating. I hoped for his sake that would never happen.

75. YOU'LL BE BACK

During my last few weeks in jail the thought of being free was constantly on my mind. Sleep became difficult as my release date neared. I lay awake as flights of fancy swirled around in my head. A lifetime of pleasure awaited me out in the big wide world. During the day I found it hard to keep a smile off my face. What's up with you someone would say and I realised I was standing there with a dopey smile on my face.

I had a plan of what to do as soon as I was free. I would take a bus to the city and walk its busy streets. Mingle with a crowd, rub shoulders with strangers. Nobody will know who I am. They won't know where I have been. To them I will be just another pedestrian. Meanwhile I'll be taking it in – people around me, shops and stores, window displays, office blocks – the whole panorama of the free world. I will be readapting, re-acquainting myself with with being free. I'll wander through a department store and check the merchandise. Ask a person in sales for a price. They'll be obliged to answer me. To them I'm another browser. Maybe I'll comment on an item or perhaps the weather. Act natural. Then sip a cup in a café while looking through a window at people passing by. Flick through the morning paper, a paper that's never been tampered with by a prison censor. Later I'll buy a train ticket. Once on board the train, I'll wander through its corridors, looking into carriages before choosing a seat. Watch the countryside go by. Maybe strike up a conversation with another passenger. By the time I reach Melbourne, I will be integrated into the outside world.

During my last few days in jail I received the treatment that leavers are prone to get. Leavers who have been inside for a while.

'How long now?'

That's what they ask, my friends, boys in the yard and other inmates when they hear the question asked.

'Six days,' I say, 'four, three,' - whatever.

'You'll be back,' they yell, 'you'll be back.'

It's part of the leaving ritual.

Curley Wade went outside not so long ago. As he passed the line heading for the kitchen, someone asked the question.

'How long now, Curley?'

'Five days,' he said, raising a hand with all of its fingers spread.

'You'll be back,' came the call from all along the line. 'You'll be back, you'll be back.'

Even the screw whose nose was shaped like a tomahawk blade, he felt obliged to join in too. 'Oh, you'll be back. You'll definitely be back.'

Curley waggled his head, shrugged, raised his arms and spread his hands.

'You never know. Who can tell? I might just get out there and create a bit of mischief.'

After Ron had been released I still had more than a week to go. Now I was getting it at work, in the yard and passing through the foyer of A Division.

How long now, they ask, and I tell them how many days are left.

'You'll be back,' they say. 'You'll be back.'

I play the game. I shrug. I grin. I make a face as if to say who can tell. But in my head, I'm saying, 'pig's arse I'll be back. I'm never coming back. Once out of here I'm gone forever. You won't see me in jail again. I've better things to do with my life.'

And finally the day arrives. After rolling the hammock, I strap it to the wall. Fold the blankets and place them on top. Bundle the sheets and pillow slip and dump them on the floor. I'm checking out. No slop out for me today. I am left in my cell when other doors are unlocked. I hear everybody leaving the wing on their way to slop out. Then silence. Time passes, time drags. It seems like hours have passed. At last I hear a key in the door. A warder leads me along the wing and out into the square. We enter a door in the admin building further along from the shop. Another warder hands me a bag that has my clothes inside it. I strip. Pulling up my y-fronts feels snug and comfortable. Gliding my arms through nylon sleeves is pure luxury. The shirt is tight across my back and underneath my arms. Tight across my chest when I fasten the buttons. My trousers are light and airy. The cotton socks are a delight. My feet have been clad in wool too long. My slip-on shoes are weightless. I could have jumped for joy. Finally my jacket - also tight. I leave it unbuttoned. The warder tells me to sign for my clothes.

'What about the rest of my stuff?'

'Your mother took it when she came to visit.'

'Oh.'

Then out of the door. On the far side of the square, a man in whites is leaning against the kitchen wall, smoking. He raises an arm: Redda Lewis. I hail him in return. He said he'd be pleased to see me go and now he is seeing me do it. Redda is halfway through his sentence and looking good. He is forty years old. I learn more of him later.

It was true what the boy from Melbourne said. Redda had been married to Pretty Dulcie Markham, the Black Widow, or as journalists chose to call her, the Angel of Death. At least six of her lovers were murdered. All were criminals. In the last killing (a triple shooting) Dulcie was shot in the hip as she lay in bed. Less than three months later she was married to Redda Lewis while still lying in that same bed. Dulcie was glamourous. She dressed and moved like a model despite being a prostitute since the age of sixteen. Four months after their marriage, a St Kilda report stated that Redda Lewis, hitman, died on his doorstep from a shotgun blast. The report was false. It wasn't a shotgun. Six shots were fired. He was hit in one hand and his stomach. Though critically wounded, Redda was not dead. The man charged with the shooting later walked free from court. The witness Redda Lewis failed to appear. Twelve months later he was shot again on Spencer Street in Melbourne. This time Redda was shot in the back. When the police asked who did it, Redda replied:

'Don't you fellers worry about it, I'll see to it myself when I get fixed up.'

Dulcie left Redda and moved to Sydney where her latest boyfriend was charged with possession of an unlicenced gun. Dulcie testified in court that the revolver belonged to her. She needed it for protection as Redda had threatened to come to Sydney and cause her serious trouble. Shortly afterwards, neighbours heard piercing screams before Dulcie fell twenty feet from a Bondi apartment. Apart from broken ribs, she received a pierced lung and was placed in an oxygen tent. One report stated that Dulcie was thrown through a window. Another claimed she had been pushed from a balcony. Dulcie told the police, doctors and reporters that she rolled down a flight of concrete steps. Nobody believed her. There was nothing to link Redda to Dulcie's fall. At the time there was no mention, or even a hint of him being involved. Once she recovered, Dulcie cut all her criminal ties, settled down and married a sailor. Her husband said she was nothing like her former self. She became an ideal wife.

These events took place in the early fifties, before I knew Redda.

At forty-five Redda was dead.

He died of a heart attack. Not the end that many saw coming for Redda Lewis. No doubt it surprised him too. At the time he was working as a labourer under the name of Alan Moore. It would seem that Redda had done enough jail and was trying to lead a normal life. But Fate had other plans for Leonard David Lewis.

William O'Meally, convicted for the the murder of Constable George Howell, spent twenty-seven years in jail. The police did not like O'Meally. He once did jail for assaulting one of their officers. Before he died, George Howell said the man who shot him had a red face. Moreover, he and O'Meally both lived in Bonbeach and they knew each other. If O'Meally fired the gun, Howell would have named him to his colleagues before he passed away. At his trial, O'Meally was sentenced to life without any chance of being released. Later, the prosecutor at that trial became influential in gaining O'Meally's freedom. He moved from Melbourne to Queensland where he died at the age of ninety-two. O'Meally also wrote a book, published by Unicorn in 1980. Entitled THE MAN THEY COULDN'T BREAK; the book is no longer in print.

Once across the square, I was led through the inner gates. The governor's office lay on the right. The warder knocked on its door, opened it and ushered me through. On following me inside, he closed the door behind him. The governor stood to face me. His hand came towards me with its thumb upright like a shark's dorsal fin. Instinctively I grasped his hand.

'Good luck,' he said, while shaking my hand.

I wrenched my hand free, shook his off as if I had picked up a snake. He looked at me with his lips pinched, surprised at the rejection. I wondered over the years how many men had he conned into shaking his hand. That's after doing all he could to make their lives difficult.

'This letter confirms your release,' and handing it to me he added, 'you can go now.'

The warder escorted me from the office into the sallyport. Another screw opened a partition hinged in one of the gates. One step through that opening and I would be free. The deep breath I took happened unconsciously. I had not intended to do that.

76. FREEDOM

Two steps out of Yatala's gates I heard my name being called, and turning I saw my mother standing beside a car that had one door swung open, and there through the windscreen my father sat with both hands gripping the steering wheel. Disaster. They shouldn't be here. What made her think that coming to meet me was a good idea. As soon as I asked myself I knew. She didn't trust me to come home even though I said I would. She had badgered my father to take time off work and come here to collect me. All my plans were ruined. I would be trapped in that car for the rest of the day. She rushed to hug me. My arms, straight and wooden hung by my sides. All the joy drained out of me. She clung to me like a limpet as I stood motionless. My father leaned across the front seat and called through the open door.

'Come on, we've got to get going.'

I trudged to the car, got in, and flopped on the back seat. We were off, driving along the road where I should have been in a bus. Turning to face me and eager to please my mother said it was wonderful that I was coming home. I couldn't pretend. I blankly stared at her as she continued to prattle. I glimpsed my father's stony face in the rear vision mirror. I knew he hated making this trip just as much as me. My mother stopped talking when I turned to face the side window. Out there was the real world, so close yet out of reach.

I was in it just for a minute and then whisked away.

I should have been on a city street jostling in a crowd. Easing myself back into a normal life. Not here. Not cooped in this car. It was a family reunion too soon, going straight from jail into another form of captivity. I wanted time to myself. To adjust. To get used to being free.

We skirted around the city, driving through barren suburbs. I wanted to be in the city where things were happening. And then a line of shops, housewives on a path, and a child being dragged along by an impatient mother. The scene had gone before I had time to take it all in. I would have liked to stroll the path and look in shop windows. Buy an ice cream and lick it. Too late now to ask to stop.

'Wasn't it good of your father, to take time off work and drive you home?'

'Mmmm.'

We bypassed the city and circled round to reach the Adelaide hills. Then climbing beyond a straggle of houses we began to weave through the bush. It's strange, I never once thought of the bush when I was in jail. I never reflected on camping and shooting I did with Ron and our friends. I longed to be out there now, amongst the gums, under their foliage and taking in their eucalyptus scent. I felt imprisoned, trapped inside the car. I wanted to stretch my legs. I wanted to feel free.

A sign for Hahndorf appeared, the German village I'd heard of. I asked if we could stop for coffee.

'We've got to crack on,' my father said.

We cracked on. Hours passed. I asked again for a coffee break. He said we would soon have lunch as we drove straight through a town. The café where we stopped for lunch was miles from anywhere. We parked at its front door. Seated at a table, I scanned the cardboard menu smudged with dried food. My father chose a sandwich - cheese and onion, toasted. My mother said she would have the same. Choice was limited.

'Haven't you got any salad?'

The woman said she supposed she could rustle up something. On slouching away, her skirt was hitched up on one side and drooping on the other. Carpet slippers on her feet. The salad when it came was limp. Tomato not freshly sliced. Wilted lettuce. One edge of the ham had a yellowish tinge. I should have gone for the toasted cheese. Its aroma wafted across the table as I rolled a wad of lettuce around in my mouth. I had planned to eat lunch in a cafeteria. Place my selections on a tray and savour my first free meal.

After a pot of tea we left. Back on the road the day dragged on. I didn't notice the border. We reached Horsham, a town that looked productive and moneyed. Utes and trucks were parked with sedans on both sides of the road, noses to the curb. We drove straight through. Country folk ambled the paths doing what they had to do in their own sweet time. People greeted each other and stopped for a chat. Why didn't we stop for lunch at a place like this?

Then another long haul. I had the fidgets. I wanted to stretch, walk, do something - do anything. On a train I could have stretched my legs and strolled its corridors.

By the time we reached Stawell I felt thoroughly dejected. The same wide streets as Horsham. It pained me to look at life out there. It's no fun looking at freedom when you are confined. From Stawell we reached and passed through the town of Ararat. No sign of Noah or his ark – ha, ha.

Light began to fade as we reached the fringe of Ballarat. We drove into the city on the widest streets you ever saw. Fine old heritage buildings, with verandas to shelter winter's rain and summer's sun. Lots of activity. Plenty of cars on the road. We stopped in traffic beside a pub and through its window I could see the six o'clock swill taking place. Men jammed against each other, tossing down glasses of beer. Shouting to make themselves heard. Bodies were crammed at the bar where barmaids poured beer from large glass jugs. I had forgotten about this evening ritual. The pub was brightly lit as dusk began to fall. Darkness, a strange phenomenon to me. I had never been outside in the dark for more than twenty months. Darkness for me meant the day was done. Nothing happened until the next morning. Yet here in the fading light, men in the pub were able to enjoy hours and hours of leisure before going to bed. Night life never occurred to me. When I thought of the outside world the sun was always shining. Once through the city we began our homeward run.

We reached the Melbourne suburbs and threaded our way to my grandfather's house. He rented it when he moved to Sydney to live with us. Where he died. My parents were living here while looking to buy another house. My mother and I went into the house while my father garaged the car. My brother greeted us. He was just a kid when I left home. At seventeen he was a man. More developed than me at his age. More mature in his outlook too. Confident in his manner. Assertive when he spoke. 'Yes, he had eaten,' he said when asked.

'I'll do a fry up,' my mother said, 'there are left overs in the fridge.'

The food when served looked and tasted no better than jail food. My brother joined us at the table. I don't recall what we talked about. I had become weary, more tired than I had been for ages. The day had exhausted me. I was looking forward to sleeping in a proper bed. When the time came to retire, my father said to follow him. We went out the back door, down the steps, and from there he led me to the garage. He squeezed past the car and drew aside a tarpaulin that hung from a rafter.

'Tomorrow we'll get you settled in. This should do you for tonight.'

Between the tarpaulin and workbench, a camp stretcher had been prepared.

'There are two switches for the lights. This one here will turn them off.'

On leaving, my father paused to slide the tarp closer to the wall. I undressed and laid my clothes on the workbench. And switching off the light, I slid between the covers. I did not expect to be sleeping on canvas. Those days were supposed to be gone.

77. WET EDGE

I slept in late, slept like a dead man. On waking I realised where I was - on a camp bed in the garage. Daylight crept around the edge of the hanging tarpaulin. To my left were tins of paint, stacked on a shelf beneath the bench. I wormed my way from the bedding, got up and put on my clothes. When dressed I went into the house and found my mother alone. My father and brother had gone to work.

'Good morning, did you sleep well? . . . Good, I'm pleased to hear it. Today we'll get you settled into a room of your own. Now, what would you like for breakfast? Cereal, toast, or if you like I can do some eggs.'

'Eggs. I'd like eggs,' and to the options she gave, I chose to have them fried.

She fussed around me as I ate and sat at the table sipping tea from a half pint mug. Did I want more toast. She had marmalade and vegemite, honey and blackberry jam. Was I sure? It's no trouble. More coffee? She couldn't do enough for me. Strange to see this woman, usually so sure of herself now in a nervous tizz. She said she was pleased to have me home. It's wonderful, she said. Her mood did not match her words. I sensed concern in her attitude to me. I wanted her to trust me. To know I had changed. Believe in me. And do as she once urged me to do – justify my existence.

How did I plan to spend the day? And mopping up yolk with a piece of toast, I said I had not decided yet. Smiling and attentive, she doted on me. I remembered what I promised myself when she made her visit. Make amends for the trouble I had caused her over previous years.

'When I've finished breakfast, I'll give this ceiling a lick of paint. It looks tired.'

'You don't have to do that.'

'I want to. I saw some emulsion in the garage underneath the bench.'

She confirmed they had a pair of steps and said I could use old curtains to lay down as drop sheets. On going to the garage for paint I found a four-inch brush. Step ladders were there too. I cleared the dining room except for the table and sideboard. I could move the table when painting and work around the sideboard. Before starting, I changed into a pair of shorts and left my feet and top bare. And I dampened a cloth to wipe away any spillages. My mother left me to it.

Above the windowed wall, I criss-crossed the paint then laid it off in long horizontal strokes. I moved the ladder twice on painting the first strip. Then re-arranged the drop sheets and climbing the ladder again, I feathered the paint into the existing wet edge. On completing the second strip, I was moving the drop sheets when my mother re-appeared at the door.

'Will you come outside for a minute?'

Before going to the porch, I wiped my fingers with the cloth and removed a blob of paint from my chest. She was talking to an old woman, who stood on the elevated path at the front of the house. I joined my mother on the lawn.

'Here he is, my eldest son. He's been working interstate,' and to me, 'this is Mrs Henderson, my mother's best friend.'

The little old lady dressed in black smiled to reveal her false teeth. Do you remember me, she said, nodding her head up and down.

'No, I'm sorry.'

'Your mother often brought you here when you were a child. You used to play with my granddaughter, here, on this lawn where you are now, looking for four leaf clovers.'

'No, I don't remember.'

263

'You were such pals. Don't you remember her?'

'No.'

'She had golden hair and big blue eyes. Every time she visited me she'd ask if you were here.'

I spread my hands and shrugged.

'Oh, Lizzie you must be proud, he's grown into such a nice boy.'

Never before in my whole life had anyone called me a nice boy. Not that I could remember. Her words trickled through me like warm milk and honey. It made me feel cosy inside. I knew my cheeks were burning. A quick glance at my mother saw her beaming with delight. The little old lady, pleased with the effect she had caused smiled from above the privet hedge. This harmless old lady embarrassed me. The more she smiled down on me the more my face reddened. I tried to ignore what she said. It didn't mean anything, just a compliment to my mother whom she had known as a little girl. She was bound to say something like that. It's what old ladies do. It had nothing to do with me. Yet the feeling persisted - a kind of self-satisfaction, like I had won a prize. But what was I thinking? A nice boy is something that I never wanted to be. Nice boys were soft. I always wanted to be tough in all senses of the word.

The little old lady was telling my mother of her granddaughter's whereabouts. She lived in Bendigo and was engaged to a nice fellow who worked in a bank. Everybody was nice in this old biddy's opinion. What she said about me did not mean anything. So why did it unsettle me. How could she do that? In trying to discount what she said, I belittled her in my mind.

I knew these old crones dressed all in black. Black netting that hung down from her hat almost covered her eyes. Her face heavily powdered. Rouge on her cheeks to brighten the pallor. Garish lipstick. A smudge of it on her teeth. Back stooped. White cotton gloves on her hands to protect them from the sun. These old crones waited too long before they took to wearing gloves.

The sun has done its damage already. The backs of her hands would be leathered, her fingers gnarled and sinewy. Inside those gloves her hands would be like the talons of a hawk.

Watching her talk to my mother, I knew I should ignore what she said. Banish it from my mind. The women were talking about my grandmother when she lived here.

'I'll have to go,' I said. 'I'm painting a ceiling and I don't want to lose the wet edge.'

'It's lovely seeing you again after all these years,' and she flapped a white glove at me.

When pulling the screen door open, I heard her say it again - 'nice boy.'

Something stirred in me again. She seemed determined to unsettle me. Up the ladder again, brushing, I wondered which bedroom would be mine. I tried to remember the layout of my grandfather's house but what the old lady said interfered with my thinking.

78. BUCK'S NIGHT

Ron arrived in the afternoon. He came in his mother's car which surprised me. I didn't know he could drive. He bounced into the hallway on the balls of his feet, Hawaiian shirt flapping and his hair slicked back with grease. He greeted me as if we hadn't seen each other for years. His hands could not stay still. His body jerked around in throwing off excess energy. His eyes shone. His face was animated. Back in the real world Ron had become energised.

'You'll never guess, Johnny is getting married. Yep, I know, surprised me too. On Saturday . . . yeah, this Saturday, two days' time. He put off his buck's night till you came home. It's tonight.'

Johnny was youngest in our gang, a year younger than the rest of us. Getting married at nineteen. It seemed insane. I had not seen him for almost two years. Johnny - the youth as we called him, getting married. Bizarre.

'He put his girlfriend in the club. First time for both of them, on the beach one night. How's that for luck? Him being a good Catholic boy, he's doing the right thing. Anyway, I've gotta go, my Mum needs the car. We'll pick you up at seven o'clock.'

He was turning and ready to leave.

'Ron! What was the train trip like?'

He hovered in the doorway, 'coming home you mean?'

'Yeah.'

'Great. I'll tell you about it later,' and with that he was gone.

When I told my mother, she supposed the drink would be flowing. I could see what she was thinking. It was written all over her face. She was worried I would get drunk and do something stupid. I said I wasn't going to drink. I had no interest in it. When she asked where we were going, I said I didn't ask.

They called at seven. We blasted off in Ian's car, five of us together, just like it used to be – Ron, me, Ian, John and Johnny. I felt sorry for Johnny, getting married at nineteen with an ankle biter on the way. I had just done a stretch in jail but he was committing himself for life. It was all over for him. Probably stuck in Melbourne forever with a family to support. It beat me why he looked so happy.

I could see we were heading for Tullamarine. I asked where we were going. Ian said up the road for a bit till we got out of town. He pulled off the road when we reached open country. John popped the boot lid and he and Ron extracted a keg. Ian climbed over a wire fence and asked me to give a hand. On joining him we relieved John and Ron of the keg. Johnny passed a collapsible stool and while the keg was getting tapped, he returned to the car for glasses.

'Is there anything else to drink, lemonade or something?'

That brought a laugh. I said I meant to stay off the beer. Johnny looked hurt.

'You'll have a glass with me, won't you? Have a glass to wish me the best.'

It didn't seem right to refuse. Besides, there was nothing else to drink. We talked about the early days, before I moved to Sydney. We used to ride out here with sleeping bags on our backs and twenty-two rifles tied along the top bars of our bikes. We shot rabbits, cooked them over an open fire and ate them. Slept under the stars. I sipped my glass while the others were chucking beer down their throats.

Talk moved on to the period when Ron and I were in jail. Oh, what a time they had had. Parties, girls and wild times. The mad things that they did. It's a wonder they didn't land in trouble. They also fished in the bay, camped out and used their twenty-two's. Took trips over the border, from Echuca through to Deniliquin. I listened to what I had missed. To what I could have been doing. Ron laughed along with their stories. He didn't seem to mind.

Remember when – yes, yes, oh yes – yes, they certainly did. And what about the time – Oh God, as if they could ever forget. Johnny's face was lit up. He didn't seem to realise those days were gone forever. The tap on the keg was getting lots of attention. I helped myself to a second glass and listened from the edge. They had been with different girls. At one time Ian and John went with the same girl. She was a goer, they said.

All three of them owned cars. They had their own rifles and fishing gear. They wore smart clothes. Pricey too, by the look of them. Between the telling of tales, visits were made to the keg. Later as the moon glowed and stars were glittering, Ron asked John for the time. Only Ron and I were not wearing a watch.

They reminisced, the four of them of when I lived in Sydney. They hooted and howled in recalling various incidents. Getting merrier and merrier. Their raised voices carried out into a black expanse that would have been heard for miles around. And they laughed. Laughing in chorus while nudging each other and throwing back their heads. Doubling over with it. Shrieking long and loud enough to make themselves gasp for breath. Except Johnny. Johnny had gone quiet. Like me, he had become an observer. I could see his eyes in the moonlight were brim-full of wonderment, of joy, like a little kid at his birthday party watching his pals enjoy themselves. A smile playing on his lips. The others laughed and laughed. They laughed at things not laughable. Laughing because of the mood they were in.

By the time the beer affected me I no longer cared. All five of us now in a party mood. I recall wrapping my arm around the imminent groom's neck. I may have kissed him on the cheek. Johnny was always the sensible one. Four of us had the same tattoo. Not Johnny. And Johnny refused to get involved in our more dubious exploits. What lay ahead for him didn't seem fair. But he was taking it on the chin. He didn't seem to mind.

In the din and revelry, I lost all sense of time and what was happening. I have no idea what time we finished. I don't remember coming home or how I got into the house. Or found the bed that up till then I had never slept in.

That's where I woke next morning, suffering from the after effects of the previous night. My head thumped. I felt ill. Seized by an urgent need, I got out of bed and rushed to the toilet, getting there just in time. I leaned over the bowl and heaved and heaved again. Great volumes of liquid gushed from my mouth. My body convulsed with every lurch as I emptied my stomach. Hands pressed against the wall - head stooped. I thought it would never end. Tears trickled down my cheeks.

And then a mighty thumping began to beat the door.

'Listen to you, listen to you. You said you weren't going to drink.' Bang, bang. 'That's what you said.' Bang, bang, bang. 'You said you weren't going to drink. Next thing is - you'll be in trouble with the police.'

By now I was dry retching. Though there was nothing more to come up my stomach kept churning. My throat ached, my head pounded. Tears were flowing. I remained leaning against the wall, feeling worse than I had ever felt before. As if I might never recover. At least my mother had gone. The banging on the door had stopped.

The retching eased and ended. My stomach calmed. I remained propped against the wall till I judged it safe to stand upright. And wiping my eyes with the back of a hand, I tore a strip of tissue and wiped the rim of the bowl. Then lowered the seat, yanked the chain and went back to bed.

Lying there with a parched throat, I thought of getting up to go for a glass of water. That's when I must have fallen asleep. It was nearly eleven o'clock when I next awoke.

79. THE CITY

I rose from bed the instant I woke, not wanting to miss the morning rush. I had always planned to visit the city and walk its busy streets. Today was the day to do it. My brother left the house as I was frying eggs. He walked every morning up Lincoln Road to catch a tram at the junction of Mount Alexander. My father was busy shaving. I aimed to beat him out of the house.

On finishing my breakfast, I walked to the trough of Buckley Street. When approaching the bus stop, I imagined for some reason that people were looking at me. Looking at me and judging me. I felt my cheeks redden. The spring went out of my step and I didn't know where to put my eyes. This was stupid. There was no reason for it. But I floundered on with eyes down, aware that my cheeks were burning. I stood apart from the other people, not caring to mingle with them. Feeling marooned. Making myself a target for prying eyes. One man reading a newspaper held it up so that it concealed his face. I wished I had a newspaper that I could hide behind.

I was the last to board when the bus arrived and stood beside the driver with my back to other passengers. At the next stop, people clambering onto the bus forced me further down the aisle on pushing their way in. Crammed between bodies of either sex, I could feel my face getting hotter. Hot enough to sweat. At each stop, people piling onto the bus wedged me tighter into the crowd. My face must have been crimson. My anguish lasted for the entire trip. At last we reached the terminus and I walked to the railway station and bought a return ticket. After boarding the train, I stood and faced a window. Then chugging through the suburbs, I stared at the backs of houses, at rickety fences and jumbled back yards. There were factories too with odd windows smashed. At every stop the platforms were packed. Commuters jostled each other as they pushed their way onto the train. I remained anonymous standing by the window. An unknown observer. Taking it in. Remembering. Yes, all of this was familiar to me. Once I had been a part of this.

On reaching the city, I emerged from under the clocks and crossed Flinders Street. I felt relaxed within the crowd on passing Young and Jacksons, being swept along by a horde of workers. People coming the opposite way were forced to weave through any gaps they could find. I was carried along past Flinders Lane and turned left at Collins. Fewer pedestrians here. I could walk without being jostled. Those heading east were closest to the curb. Typists and clerks were scattered amongst various other workers – lawyers and accountants, businessmen, chemists, telephonists, sales assistants, insurance people and tellers from different banks. I tried to guess the occupation of people approaching me. Not an easy thing to do. A man who looked like a CEO could be a lowly clerk with a high regard of himself. Who could tell. And people looking at me would not know I had been in jail. Though I wished I had worn a collar and tie.

Comfortable now, I swung my arms in the thick of the crowd and marched to the city's thrum - cars burbling in traffic, the tramp of feet and clanging of trams combined into an overall clamour. I revelled in the buzz of it. At the corner I waited for lights to change and headed north on Elizabeth. Turning east at Bourke, I continued to reach Swanson Street, then crossed the road and made my return. I knew this city and its streets, having been a message boy here for two years. I knew its lanes, its arcades and indistinct short cuts. I could go from Flinders through to La Trobe and not use a single street running from south to north. Once I got stuck, till I found a roomful of typists on a building's second floor. I ploughed between their desks before skipping down a back flight of stairs. It became my favourite route. I used to give a wave as I sliced through their midst, acknowledging the smiles and disregarding the frowns.

On busy, busy, Bourke Street, I felt like my old self, striding out and confident. Like someone who belonged. Back on Collins the crowd had thinned. Time was getting on. I spotted a girl further ahead coming in my direction - a girl or a young woman. She carried herself in a self-assured manner, sashaying like a model on her approach to me. As she neared the sway of her hips became more pronounced. I judged she was two years older than me, two years at least. She didn't just look at me, but grabbed my eye, and moved her body as if to the pulse of sensual music. So confident, so sure of herself. When closer and staring at me, she formed a gorgeous smile and as we were about to meet she slowed her pace as if to stop and I, with startled eyes and burning face blundered on straight past her.

I was not ready for something like this. Too late I realised what I had done and regretted it. What a fool. I had thrown away a golden opportunity. If I had stopped who knows what could have developed from there. Even if we only talked and nothing more came of it, I would have done what I should have done and not felt bad about myself. On the other hand, if I had stopped, I might have become tongue-tied, gawped at her and made a bigger fool of myself. She was too experienced for me. That was the truth of the matter. Her boldness unsettled me. Threw me off balance. And walking on I felt deflated, let down - flat.

The rush hour was drawing to a close. Fewer people were on the street. I wondered what to do next in this city I knew so well. Where could I go, what could I do. Nothing came to mind. I wandered on aimlessly. When walking down Market Street I didn't realise at the time that I was going home.

80. GET A JOB

I stayed up late at night. Got up late in the morning. At breakfast I circled possible jobs in the morning paper, then laying the paper aside, I hoped there would be better jobs advertised tomorrow. My options were limited. I had no trade. No history of work. I couldn't say where I had been. There was a two-year gap to fill. I would have to lie - say I'd been working in the bush, or moved from another state, which was not a lie and probably the best ruse. I wondered who would give me a chance and put me on the payroll. Time passed. I skulked around in this strange new world feeling I didn't fit in. I wasted the days, frittered them away. But I liked the nights, being out in the dark with streets all to myself. I walked from one street light to the next, looking at houses as I passed wondering who lived behind the curtains. I varied the routes I took each night in getting to know the neighbourhood. I walked for hour after hour. The heavens sparkled above me with a million pricks of light. Each night I found the Southern Cross in its latest position. A line between its pointers and tail always pointed due south – a hundred and eighty degrees. The Cross could also tell the time if one knew the formula. A compass, a clock and national emblem all combined in one. A mighty constellation.

Back home I munched biscuits and sipped hot chocolate, watching television till its transmission shut down. I took a grim delight in keeping unsociable hours. Glad to escape the strict routine that had ruled my life. Now I chose when I went to bed. I got up when it suited me. But I had to get a job.

The telephone at my grandfather's house had been disconnected. With a pocketful of pennies and the paper circled with jobs, I made my way to Puckle Street. A telephone box was sited outside the local post office branch. I placed my pennies in the chute and dialled the first number. When the call was answered, I pressed the button and watched my pennies drop. Click, I got cut off. Pressing the reject button did return my coins. I loaded the chute and tried again. Click, the same thing happened again. On my third attempt I tried a different number that had the same result. I thought I should report the fault and get the telephone repaired. Inside the post office, six people were waiting in line for their turn at the counter. I decided to wait and took my place at the end of the queue.

One old dear at the counter held up the line for ages as she mumbled to the clerk. When her transaction ended, she fumbled in her bag for a purse and on finding it, sifted through a handful of coins and selected those that made up the precise amount. Then laid them on the counter one by one. On reaching the front of the queue, I said the telephone on the street was out of order.

'No one else has complained.'

'Well, I tried to make three calls. When each call was answered, my three pennies dropped but I got cut off.'

'Three pennies,' he shouted, 'where have you been? It's been four pennies for more than a year.'

I felt the skin of my face burn, and turning around I scooted past the queue and fled into the street. On rushing along the footpath, I paused to dump my list of jobs into a rubbish bin. And so another day passed without me getting a job.

There were more than twenty pages of jobs in the Saturday Morning Age. Plenty of jobs, all kinds of jobs, jobs for everyone. But would there be a job for me? Who would employ me? I felt tainted, unworthy. Lacking in experience and nervous about asking. I marked six possibilities in the situations vacant and proceeded to a telephone box. Not on Puckle Street. A gruff voice answered the first call and asked if I could keep up with two bricklayers. I answered yes. To his other questions I said, no problem. I gave him my address. He would pick me up at six thirty on Monday, on the corner of Waverley and Buckley Streets. Getting a job was as easy as that.

On Monday morning, a battered utility vehicle pulled into the curb. I got in and sat beside its two occupants. Not a word of greeting, not even a grunt. Off we went. The man beside me, half turned to give me a brief glance before facing the windscreen again. The driver's gnarled hands gripped the steering wheel. That would be the boss, the gruff voice on the telephone.

As we drove towards Broadmeadows, something loose under the ute rattled constantly. Then I lost my bearings. Still no talking. We reached the suburban limits, where houses were being built on vacant blocks of land. Footpaths were not yet laid. We pulled up at the site, a half-built house some five feet high. The boss gave me a shovel and a bag of tools from the back of the ute. Scaffolding ran along the length of the back wall. A cement mixer stood between a heap of sand and stack of bricks. Behind the mixer, a sheet of galvanised iron covered bags of cement.

'Hop to it,' the boss said, as I stood in front of the mixer. 'Well, what are you waiting for?'

'Where are the electrics?'

'God, strike a light, how do I find 'em,' and pushing me aside he said, 'petrol, ever heard of petrol,' and he fired up the mixer and got it running.

That set the tone for the day. The mix I made was too thick, and bricks I stacked on the scaffold were too close to the wall, or too far from where they worked, or spaced too far apart, and the remix was still too thick. The other bricklayer, an immigrant, kept his head down as he spread mortar and laid bricks. The boss grumbled and cursed all morning. I wouldn't stand for these insults before going to jail. I would've told him to stick his job. But I bit my tongue. Kept working. I thought if I answered him back, it might lead to an argument that could become physical.

275

Then I would be in trouble. The boss was a big slob. He could see I was fitter and stronger than him and could give him a slap. But he could read me. He saw I would take the abuse and kept it up all morning. By smoko I was fit to explode.

The bricklayers sat by the sand, pouring tea from their flasks. I walked around the corner to relieve myself, and standing there I knew I had reached my limit. One more insult and I would belt him and then there would be hell to pay. I walked off the site, leaving behind my sandwiches and thermos flask. I tramped down the road, around a corner and zig zagged through the streets. A bus stop had to be somewhere, or somebody I could ask. I reached more established houses and then a shop, once out on a limb, but now in the midst of a growing community. Busy too. Cars parked outside. Housewives doing their shopping inside. General produce was on display, also fruit and veg, newspapers, magazines and a post office agency too. I waited my turn to be served and bought a cherry ripe. I asked for the nearest bus stop. The shopkeeper, Greek or maybe Maltese was happy to oblige. All smiles and happy chat. His punt on buying a remote store had paid off. Once on the fringe of the bush, now a part of suburbia.

A safe on the floor behind the counter had its door open. Banknotes inside it were piled high. Turning my back to the counter, I noted the glass louvres fitted above the door. Entry would be easy. Gelignite would be stored at the Maribyrnong quarry. Laying a charge was a simple task. No need to move the safe. It was fine where it was. Plenty of papers and magazines to stack on top and stifle the blast. I had no intention of acting on these observations. I was finished with that kind of life. Yet I saw how somebody fresh out of jail, feeling confused and down on his luck would be tempted. I never understood that before. There were plenty of ex-prisoners less fortunate than me. They had no home to go to. No one to help or lend them money. Nowhere to sleep. Though I felt isolated, they were truly alone.

I ate my cherry ripe on the way to the bus stop. The bus went into the city from where I took a tram. A sign beside my seat read:

YOU MIGHT RATE WHERE YOU COME FROM
BUT DON'T EXPECTORATE HERE

The tram clanged past Flemington, Ascot Vale and Moonee Ponds, bypassed Windy Hill and reached the junction at Lincoln Road. One thing the day had taught me - finding another job would not be a problem.

81. MOONLIGHT

At the end of the dance, a girl dashed from the floor, leaving her partner open-mouthed. A look of shock on his face. It was the speed in which she fled that drew my attention to her. The floor was being cleared, though not entirely, as several couples remained where they were, waiting for the piano player to start the next number. Most of the couples stood apart, gauging each other with small talk and discrete looks. Others were holding hands, while one boy mimicked a python coiled around its prey. Back to the girl I had been watching, the girl who missed the last two dances. She was trying to look unconcerned and failing in the attempt, as girls on either side of her accepted requests that were made to them. The girl was tall, well made, and unsure of herself. Couples were populating the floor. On the stage the singer and pianist were discussing what to play next. Sheet music was being turned, page after page. The girl was still there. The piano player hit the keys and the singer raised his microphone and leaning closer to it, began to croon. A foxtrot again, every dance a foxtrot. Couples circled the ballroom floor, the plodders, the competent pairs and the flash twirlers.

As girls were swerved and spun around I wondered how they managed to cope with male led navigation. How did they manage to keep their feet from being trodden on. It remained a mystery to me but I was prepared to give it a go on the next dance.

Yes, she said when I asked her. We took up position. A few bars from the piano and the singer with the dreamy eyes flicked the microphone's flex from underneath his feet and added his velvet tones to the piano's melody. We were the slowest movers, the slowest on the floor. Linked couples glided past, swaying in harmony. I didn't dare increase my speed and I thought by taking shorter steps I wouldn't tread on her again.

'Do you come here often,' I said, and cringed on hearing the words coming out of my mouth.

Every now and then, she said. My first time, I told her. My hand in the small of her back not pulling her too close, and her hand enclosed in mine felt soft and pliable. When she noticed me looking at her, she formed a lovely smile that made her really attractive. At the end of the dance I asked if she could bear to do it again. Yes, she said, she could. During the next number, I asked if I could take her home and yes - yes, she said again.

I held her hand as we left the hall. She suddenly resisted and stopped in front of the crowd pushing from behind.

'I have to get my coat.'

'Of course, sorry, I didn't think.'

She steered me to the cloakroom flap where we waited for other girls to retrieve their coats. In exchange for a ticket, she accepted her coat from an elderly lady dressed in black. As I watched her fingers work each button into a slit, I realised I should have helped to put her coat on. Once outside, I told her I didn't have a car.

'That doesn't matter, we can take the red bus.'

The bus travelled down Buckley Street and up past Essendon High School. There were other couples on board, couples that came from the dance, and singles too. I took her hand when we left the bus and walked along a concrete path. I began to feel awkward and uncomfortable. Apart from Ron, all of my friends owned a car. I thought not having a car would be a shortcoming in her eyes. And I had no small talk. At a loss as what to say, I suddenly blurted out, 'I just got out of jail,' as if that explained my awkwardness.

Her step faltered. 'It wasn't for rape?'

'No, it wasn't for rape.'

We carried on in silence. I saw a vacant block of land ahead, lying between two houses. On reaching the block, I led her off the path. She came along, willingly, deeper into the paddock. I stopped and drawing her close to me, kissed her on the lips. Then eased her lower by pressing down on her hips. She sank to the grass, where on reclining I loosened her coat-buttons and slid my hand up under her dress. I pulled her panties to one side and then I was there. It was quick, too quick, all over and done, finished as soon as it started. The rush of pleasure came too soon. I wasn't ready for it. It took me by surprise. And having come and gone, it warded off any thought of more desire. While lying there I knew for her that there had been no pleasure at all. It wasn't supposed to be like that. I struggled up onto my feet once erect, I gazed down at her pale white thighs all aglow in the moonlight. When she saw me staring at her, she grabbed the flaps of her overcoat and pulled them together to cover herself. Too late perhaps for modesty. Or did she stop me looking at her for some other reason. I waited until she was on her feet, until she fastened her coat, and I led her across the grass and back to the concrete path. We walked on in silence, not holding hands as we did before. Just minutes ago we had been as close as two people can get. A gulf now lay between us. She knew I'm sure that after this night we wouldn't see each other again. Not a word passed between us. At her gate I leaned closer to her and brushed my lips across her face. Then I turned to make the long walk home.

I knew her name at the time and now can't even picture her face. All I can remember are her pale white thighs in the moonlight. That and the brief disappointing act. I would have been kinder to her if I had not been embarrassed.

82. THE GYM

It was all happening in the gym. The heavy bag getting thumped, speed ball going rat-a-tat-tat and skipping ropes slapping the deck on every single spin. Two fighters were sparring in the ring. One guy lying flat on his back flexed his stomach muscles for the whomp of a medicine ball. Another in front of a mirror, took on his image with short and snappy rips and hooks. Fast hands, very fast. A fighter threw combinations at a trainer's glove - whack, whack, whack, and again – whack, whack, whack. Exercises were being done - press ups and sit ups. A smaller fighter, lightweight or feather, threw his fists at the floor between his parted legs. A trainer and others at ringside were watching the action inside it. One watcher, gloved up and ready to go waited for his turn in the ring.

Propped on my fingertips, I kept my back and neck straight while dipping my chin to the floor, then rose until my arms were stretched to their fullest extent. Up and down, up and down not keeping count but going on until my strength gave out. From there I danced on my toes, shaking my arms and body loose. Then walking across the gym and back I watched beginners beyond the ring working in pairs. They shuffled forward and shuffled back, throwing and blocking each other's jabs. Repetition, repetition, executing the drill until it became instinctive.

I skipped, though didn't attempt to cross my arms while twirling the leather around. I aimed to get that right at home before attempting it in the gym.

The skinny young kid waiting to spar was now inside the ring. Back pedalling as he jabbed, he danced clear of trouble. Then planting his feet, he blocked the punches, or ducked and weaved in avoiding them. Then going into attack, his fists switched from body to head after ducking his opponent's punch. Tricky, this kid. The muscular fighter was no slouch. Both fighters looked classy. Speed was what the kid had apart from bags of skill. Very impressive. When the kid was trapped in a corner, he spun around his opponent and smacked him with a left hook as he danced away. I wanted to learn how he did that.

I liked everything I was seeing. This gym was better than one I used when living in Sydney. This was what I had hoped to find. The ideal place for me to develop into a top fighter.

The bell rang to end the round and the fighters took a minute's rest. I asked the trainer if I could do a few rounds in the ring.

'Sure, put these on,' and taking gloves from the ring's apron, he tucked their laces inside before handing them to me. I slipped them on, also the headgear. I had heard him earlier named Charlie. Charlie the champ maker, that's what he was called.

'Haven't you got a mouth guard?'

'No.'

'I'd prefer you had one.'

'I'll be okay.'

He shrugged, checked his watch and rang the bell. Sparring continued in the ring. This round continued much like the first, the muscular fighter pressing as the kid counterpunched and danced away. His counters came in a mix of stinging combinations. As Charlie later said, counterpunching is counterattack.

At the bell, Charlie waved his arm to usher me into the ring and as I slipped through the ropes, he said: 'Leonard, we've got a new guy for you.'

The solid fighter ducked through the ropes and jumped down from the canvas. I said I thought I'd be sparring with him.

'Have a round with Leonard first.'

He made me look a mug. Like I was chasing a phantom as I punched holes in fresh air. Or not so fresh, as an odour of stale sweat permeated the gym. I decided to stop chasing and held my position. He peppered me as he danced around. He was far too quick and slick for me. He blocked or avoided every punch I threw. At the end of the round, I climbed through the ropes.

'Done some boxing before, have you?'

'Yes,' I said.

'Okay, forget everything you think you know and we'll start again.'

Charlie led me to where beginners were going through their routine. He teamed me with a tall fourteen-year-old. I swallowed my pride as I knew this was necessary. We shuffled forwards and shuffled back, block and jab, block and jab. We continued the workout until I could have done it with my eyes shut.

At the end of the session and under a shower, I felt invigorated. Everything about the gym filled me with optimism. I was getting somewhere at last. The gym would become my second home. Things were starting to come together after a long frustrating spell.

That's when I heard the laughing. There were three of them, all good fighters. One had qualified for the Olympics. It was him, the Olympiad, pointing at me as they laughed. Laughing at my expense.

'What's so funny?'

'Don't you own a pair of shorts?'

I looked down at myself. My torso was bronzed by the sun but from my waist down to my toes my skin was lily white. The only white skin on others was a strip around their buttocks.

'You look like a chocolate ice-cream on top of a stick.' 'Yeah, a stick of chalk.'

They chuckled at the sight of me. I made no response. Summer had just gone. I couldn't see any way to explain why my legs and feet were so white. Might they guess where I had been? I felt a rush of blood rise and colour my face. Once again the odd man out, different to everyone else. An outsider. Someone who didn't belong. It happened all the time. Wherever I went, whatever I did, always ended with me feeling like an alien. It was grinding me down. I didn't know what I had to do to make this nightmare end.

83. ALIENATED

During my last few weeks in jail the thought of being free kept me awake at night and distracted me during the day. My mind was in a permanent state of exhilaration. The thought of my freedom tantalized me. It was going to be fantastic.

It didn't happen like that. My release turned out to be a huge disappointment. The outside world was foreign to me. I couldn't deal with it. I felt like an alien. It went wrong from the start. Met at the gate and trapped in a car for the rest of the day. My first few meals were dull. I slept my first free night on a canvas stretcher inside a garage.

I couldn't relax in peoples' company. I withdrew into myself. I became estranged. Isolated.

Aggression in people surprised me. The boss on my first job was a nasty piece of work. I didn't know how to cope with him. And then there was a driver. He stopped with a screech of brakes, got out of his car and abused me. He said I was slow in crossing the road and asked if I'd like a punch in the face. I turned and walked away from him to avoid any trouble. And I saw a woman on the street beating a small child. Really laying into him with ugly anger on her face. The poor little kid was howling. To think that the woman beating him was his own mother. Shaking him like a rag doll in the midst of a crowd. Then there was the post office clerk who enjoyed making a fool of me in front of other people.

I knew the world hadn't changed. It was me. I couldn't relax, couldn't adapt. I couldn't act naturally. I wanted to be myself again, not uncomfortable and beset by awkwardness. I wanted to recover my self-worth. There had to be some way to do it. Nobody else could help me. It was something I had to work out for myself. If I knew what I needed to do I would have done it immediately. But I was floundering, feeling lost.

I did my jail easier than Ron did his. No doubt about that. Now our roles had been reversed. He seemed so well-adjusted. Comfortable. Happy with how things were. I remember how he bounced in to greet me when I arrived home. Totally at ease with himself. I wanted to ask him how long it took to settle into a normal life. But I didn't want him to know how screwed up I was.

I hated being different to everybody else. Feeling as if I was being watched, being judged. Stranded, cut off from other people. It never used to be like that. I never used to care what people thought of me. That was their problem, not mine. I did whatever I wanted to do. Tough, if they didn't like it.

Now I wanted a normal life. To fit in. Take my place in the world. But I didn't know where to start or how to go about it. There had to be something I could do to improve the quality of my life. If only I knew what I had to do to make that possible.

84. GREAT TO BE ALIVE

As soon as I woke I knew that life was wonderful. It happened the instant I opened my eyes. Just like that. Wow. And lying there in bed, ready to throw off the covers, I realized this was nothing new. My life had been really good for some considerable time. I had been too busy enjoying myself to appreciate the change in me. What a transformation. My whole life had turned around. All my worries were gone. No more awkwardness, no more frustration, no more embarrassment.

Just a sudden awareness - it was great to be alive.

I can't say exactly when this change in me took place. There was no special moment. No sudden revelation. Change came on gradually, bit by bit. Each day became less stressful, but slightly, so as not to draw my attention to it. I suppose I grew more confident as I moved from job to job. Meeting new people was less of a strain. Not that I realised at the time. I remained unaware of the progress I was making.

Something that helped me a great deal was a line in story written by Katherine Mansfield. In describing a character, she wrote:

'The boy blushed furiously as if he had just got out of jail.'

That line astonished me. I boggled at it. How did Katherine Mansfield know about things like that? I thought it was only me who reacted in that way. I had no idea that others had suffered the same as me. I was not alone. Others had been afflicted. For all I knew it could be a common phenomenon. I wondered who the author knew that allowed her to write that line. I would have liked to ask, but Katherine Mansfield had been dead for almost forty years.

Nothing changed overnight after I read that story. I carried on being unsure of myself. But I knew I was not cracking up. Others had been through the same thing. I still struggled, though without a doubt that line helped me regain normality.

Now everything was dandy. I leapt out of bed each morning to welcome a brand-new day. I was living in Black Rock, a hundred yards from the beach. The family moved when my grandfather's house was sold. My current job was an order picker in a paint warehouse. Each morning I drove to work by skirting Port Phillip Bay. Elbow out of the window, salt air coming in as waves tumbled onto the beach all the way into town. My parents loaned me money so I could buy a car. I paid them back week by week, interest free. I had given notice at my job and was due to start the following week with G J Coles. My first white collar job since getting out of jail.

I was making progress in the gym. Charlie schooled me on counterpunching. He said an orthodox fighter had to have two things, a good left hand and the ability to counter a lead. He drilled me on three different counters. One thing he emphasized.

'They say to counterpunch, you need fast reflexes. That's rubbish. Nobody's reflexes are that fast. When you look into your opponent's eyes you know what he's going to do. Don't ask me how you know, but you do, and you can launch your counter at the same time as his lead.'

I regularly sparred with a top middleweight and also with professionals in other city gyms. Even a Mexican brought out to fight the middleweight champion, Peter Reid.

If not taking out a girl, I drove to Echuca on weekends with Ron and my brother. Once over the border of New South Wales, we passed through Jerilderie to a wide-open space called Steam Plains. Suicidal kangaroos leapt across the road at dusk. A hazard that we risked, not having roo bars. We had some near misses. On the plains we set up camp and slept beneath a luminous sky. In the morning there were emus, swinging their necks like periscopes while tip-toeing through the grass. They humped their heavy plumage around for the rest of the day. Richard tied a wire to a stick and threw it over a branch, then attached the wire's other end to the radio's aerial. We tuned into radio stations for miles around. Though out on the plains, we were in touch with so many towns.

Thursday nights were the highlight of my week. I went directly from the gym to the Hawthorn Town Hall. The best dance in town. A new adventure every week. Who knew what might develop from taking a girl home. On arranging a future date, I made a rule for myself - three dates was the limit with any girl no matter what happened or didn't. I did not want to get involved. A girlfriend could come later. My freedom was important to me. I needed to catch up on everything I had missed. And I was catching up. This was the life I dreamed of and I was living it.

85. SUNSHINE STATE

My brother returned home from working on a farm up north. With a pocketful of money, he was in no rush to find a job. I deserve a break, he said. His arrival came at an opportune time for me. My car had blown a gasket. Capable and willing, he said he would take off the head and fit a replacement. I watched him twirl a spanner around as he removed another bolt and laid it on the path.

'We should take a trip to Queensland. Go in the car. It's different up there. You'd like it.'

'It's somewhere I always meant to go.'

'Nothing stopping you, is there?'

'Not really.'

My arm was in plaster. I had fallen off a fence and cracked a bone in my wrist. It would be weeks before I could resume full training.

'Things happen up there that you never see down here. On the way out to Longreach, the train stopped in the middle of nowhere. A guy looked out of the window and said the train driver was talking to a man on a horse. Another bloke in the carriage said it happened all the time. The train driver and the cocky went to school together.'

'Okay, let's do it. I'll give a week's notice and I'll ask Ron if he wants to come.'

I thought Ron would jump at the chance and we would get to Queensland at last. But Ron declined the offer.

'Is it the job?'

'It's not the job. Couldn't care less about the job.'

'Is it money? We won't need much. We can work when we get there. Or on the way if we need to.'

'It's not the money.'

'Well, what is it?'

'Elsie.'

'She'll wait for you, won't she?'

'Yeah, she'd wait, but I don't want to go.'

In having to choose between Queensland and Elsie, Queensland didn't stand a chance.

Nine days later we set off. Extra petrol and water were stored in the car's trunk, together with rifles, sleeping bags, extra clothes and tins of food. We planted spare cash under a mat on the driver's side. On driving due east, we soon passed Western Port Bay, an odd name for the bay considering its position. I later learned the bay was discovered and named from Sydney, not Melbourne. Once past the bay, we entered country new to us, but eager to press on, we drove straight through the early Gippsland towns. I recall Yallourn and Traralgon and we didn't stay long in Bairnsdale after we ate and topped up the tank. Then onto Orbost and beyond where thick trunked gums thrust their branches up into the sky. Without any warning the tarmac stopped and we weaved through the bush on a dirt track, riding corrugations and skittering round bends. Mile after mile of it. My brother on the wheel took a bend too fast and the car juddering over rough ground, whanged into a post, leaving a dent at its rear end the size of a dustbin lid. We pressed on, me driving, and that was the end of broadsides on rounding hairpin bends.

This was a road that nobody used. We had it to ourselves. No more towns, no more houses, only thick bush. The dirt track threw up clouds of dust. Dust that got into the car despite all windows being closed. Dust that got up your nose. Dust you could taste at the back of your throat. It lasted all the way to Cape Howe, a landmark hidden in the bush that we didn't see.

At last we were on a blue metal road courtesy of New South Wales. The Holden's tyres began to hum as we charged into the premier state as natives like to call it. With windows down we drew in wafts of South Pacific air. Heading north, from here on north, always north as we headed for our destination.

We stopped at Eden, the halfway point to Sydney and decided to stay the night. We booked into an old inn and wandered around the town and its bay which was very deep. Orcas were encouraged here to trap whales in the bay where they were harpooned. The orcas were rewarded by being given the whales' tongues. As Eden was equidistant from Tasmania, Melbourne and Sydney, it was considered as a site for the federal capital. Canberra was chosen instead.

Setting off next morning, we cruised through lush countryside and pleasant rustic towns. Each town bore the indigenous name given to its area - Pambula, Merimbula, Bega and Tilba Tilba. From one town into the bush before reaching the next town lying further on. Cruising along the south east coast and enjoying its ambience. No longer in a rush. Soaking in the atmosphere. Mentally ticking off each town as we passed through it. On the road, free as a breeze, going places and getting there.

At Narooma we stopped for a beer. Trawlermen in the pub were celebrating. They had poled nine tons of tuna. We heard them talk of one huge fish that needed double poling. Their haul exceeded their quota but they had manged to do a deal with Italians from Ulladulla. They earned more money in a few hours than during the last two weeks. A barmaid tending to them filled glass after glass. We left the trawlermen to it.

On we drove to Bodalla, to Coila, Moruya and Batemen's Bay - a big town with an access road to the Capital Territory. So glad we came this way instead of taking the Hume Highway. Lovely country and pleasant towns. So good to be on the road again, taking our time and choosing our stops, doing what we wanted to do, not having to answer to anyone. It's a shame that Ron decided not to come with us.

At Kiama we stopped to watch the waves spurt up through its blowhole. Then onto Woolongong and beyond, where towns came thick and fast. And onto Sydney, where we spent too much time and far too much money. Up and down The Corso at night and days we spent on South Steyne beach by the Norfolk pines, catching waves in the surf and lazing in the sun. I arranged to see the girl I wrote to when I was in jail. Nothing happened with her in the past and nothing happened still.

On leaving Sydney, we sliced through the central coast to reach the city of Newcastle. Going north, further north, the weather getting warmer as we put the miles behind us. We stopped the night at Nambucca Heads and stayed in a motel. Our sleeping bags remained in the trunk. In the morning to Coffs harbour (no big banana there yet) and onto the Clarence. We bypassed Ballina and far-flung Byron Bay. At Murwillumbar we knew we were close to the Sunshine State and rolling into Tweed Heads we parked the car and walked across Twin Town's Boundary Street, arriving on foot in Queensland at Coolangatta. To celebrate we had a beer. No Reishes, Tooheys or Tooths were available at the bar. No Victoria bitter, Carlton Ale or Fosters lager. No Coopers or Swan larger. Only Castlemaine XXXX. There was nothing wrong with it and we had another glass. Rum drinkers were at the bar. Understandable. In this state sugar cane was king.

We strolled back over Boundary Street and in the car drove on, crossing the border for the third time. Now we were on The Gold Coast. Tropical trees and palms adorned the towns we travelled through. Poinciana's painted the sky with exotic scarlet blooms. Bird life here was different too. Rosellas and other parrots that I couldn't identify. Not just the odd bird but great flocks of them, flapping around in disarray. One red and purple mob made an almighty din, screeching as it crashed through leaves and branches of a flowering gum.

From one town and its modest dwellings onto the next. With the map in hand, I mentally ticked off towns as we passed through them. Broadbeach was exactly that, a beach. A few houses and then a school, propped amongst sand dunes that were as white as salt. Further on, we reached a scattering of houses, a pair of flats and a pub. And then another barren patch before we came upon a sign for Main Beach.

'What happened to Surfers?'

'Dunno, must be further on.'

'No. It comes before Main Beach. Let's go back.'

He swung the Holden around and we slowly backtracked, looking for a turnoff as we thought we had bypassed the town. Railway sleepers beside the road prevented sand from crossing it. There was no turnoff. What we previously saw was the heart of Surfers Paradise. No people. This was it, this tiny place, put on the map by choosing for itself a flamboyant name. We expected to see bars, clubs and lots of life, razzmatazz and surfing bums living in tents. There was none of that.

Only the capital now to reach. We pressed on through Nerang, even though its old pub bristled with character. At Beenleigh, a rum town, we passed its distillery, standing proud amongst cane fields, its chimney like a big pea shooter pointing at the clouds. Black flakes from the cane burn off lying everywhere. Beenleigh snow, as locals like to call it. Further on were houses on stilts, built this way to encourage a breeze to run underneath. Further still, we reached the outer suburbs and as the city came into view we dropped to the level of its river and crossed the Storey Bridge. We missed a turn for the city and found ourselves going south over the river again. Next time over the Storey, we found our way into the heart of the state's capital. Streets were laid out in a grid similar to Melbourne. Lots of colonial buildings, from federation and earlier. Veranda roofs covered the paths running along Queen Street, not one long common stretch but individual coverings that merged where each store met. Elsewhere, pretty cast-iron lace adorned the balconies of pubs, on their front railings too and also on balustrades rising from the railings. Gorgeous - spectacular. Wide brimmed hats on the locals, who strolled the paths like country folk. But Brisbane being a city meant there were trams, and conductors' caps had flaps at the back to protect their necks from the sun. Humidity hung in the air. Heat shimmered. This was thirsty weather.

We booked into a public house, dumped out belongings in a room and ventured out to walk the streets.

'Don'tcha love it,' my brother said, 'the air's got something in it.'

We stopped for a beer and carpet-bag steak before returning to our room. Next morning we trawled the city again. We saw the sights and the river, which was underutilised. Too few bridges spanning it. No boats moored or sailing on it. No attractions on its banks, only mud flats. Brisbane in the sixties had lots of room for development.

My brother was keen to try out the rums, Beenleigh and Bunderberg. He bought a bottle of overproof to share with friends back home. I drank more beer on this trip than during the rest of the year.

I was keen to get home, get the plaster taken off and resume training. We spent three nights in Brisbane and returned by the New England Highway. At Tamworth we considered going west, going further inland, but decided to leave that journey for another time. On the return trip we camped, shot and ate rabbits and spent nights in our sleeping bags under a starlit sky. It's a pity Ron decided not to come with us. He missed a chance to reach Queensland. To see it at last.

86. SEISMIC CHANGE

Janet was saving herself. Saving herself for the one. Whenever we were alone she prised away my roaming hands with a strength not evident in her slender frame. All she wanted to do was kiss. One night at the drive-in movie, my attempts and her resistance turned into a wrestling match. I stopped short of committing assault and tried to watch the movie while suffering from the painful throb of unfulfilled desire. That date should have ended our relationship. But I liked her. I kept taking her out. I could tell she was fond of me and she was easy to be with. We stayed together for months and during that time I didn't go off with any other girl. No more wrestling. No more attempts to seduce her. When we kissed I kept my hands to myself. Crazy, really. Here I was, celibate - not getting any, when all I wanted to do in jail was lie down with a girl. I never expected to be in a situation like this. Our relationship continued to drift. Though not getting what I wanted, we got on well together. We had similar tastes and enjoyed our time together.

Sometimes we ventured out in a group, Janet and I with my friends and their girlfriends. Ron and John were both involved in serious relationships while Ian rolled up every time with a different girl. Not Johnny. We saw less of Johnny these days. Johnny had other commitments. The baby was a boy. My friends and their girlfriends thought Janet and I were an item. So did Janet.

We never argued. A cross word never passed between us. If I wanted to go somewhere that didn't appeal to her, she would agree providing she chose our next venue. Which seemed fair. I didn't mind.

Though she had a mind of her own Janet was eager to please, except for the one area that was out of bounds. I didn't expect her to change, not in that regard. She assumed we were a permanent couple. It wasn't what I wanted. I had let things go too far. Rather than get further involved I knew I should end our relationship. I kept putting it off as it never seemed to be the right time. The opportune moment never came. Rather than come as a surprise, I tried to give her a hint by being more subdued. I talked less than usual when we were together. I no longer enthused, and I cancelled one of our dates with a lame excuse. She must have noticed a change in me but didn't comment on it.

One night we were alone at my house. My parents were out, and my brother had gone to work on a farm in the Monara region. We were standing in the hall, ready to leave, when she asked me to turn and face the wall. Which I did. She untucked my shirt, slipped her hands under it and began caressing my back. She glided her hands in circular strokes, then slid her hands around my waist to encircle me and drawing herself closer, she pressed her body against mine. I could feel the crush of her breasts on my back. When resting her face against me, her warm breath reached up to my ears as she gently sighed.

This is what I had waited for. She was relenting, offering herself without any pressure from me. She pressed her legs and all of her body firmly against me. I didn't turn around and remained facing the wall, enjoying the feel of her. Her sighs became louder. As expectancy rose in me a nagging instinct held me back. I shouldn't do this. It didn't seem right. I wasn't the one. Not for her I wasn't. I didn't want to take from her what she had saved for someone else.

That wasn't the only reason.

I knew if we went to bed together that would be the start of it. We would go on from there. I would probably grow fonder of her and wouldn't want to leave. I couldn't let that happen. I didn't want to get tied down. Captured. Not for a long time yet. First, I had some living to do. I needed to catch up on the life I had missed.

Taking hold of her wrists, I unwrapped her arms and turning around said it was time to take her home. We hardly spoke in the car. Sitting quietly and withdrawn Janet knew that a seismic change had taken place. I didn't like to see her unhappy. It's not what I intended. I had tickets for a show on the following week. I decided to take her to the show. Now that she knew how things were she had time to accept we were not meant for each other. It did not have to end badly. Our relationship could just peter out.

87. YACHT CLUB

My father was drunk. He often came home drunk but never as drunk as this before. He was bleary-eyed drunk. Reeling drunk. Drunk with a stupid smile on his face. His speech was slurred. This was the last day of the job that I thought ruled his life. He had quit, handed in his notice after buying a boatshed on the south coast of New South Wales. You could have bowled me over when I learned of it. I thought he was married to the job. I thought he loved it. But he had chucked it. Quit. This was his last day.

He staggered into the kitchen clutching a farewell card signed by his colleagues - ex-colleagues now. My mother was furious. She pushed him with both hands and sent him stumbling across the room. He crashed into the table and managing not to fall, swivelled around on one leg and stared at the floor to see where his farewell card had gone.

'Liz . . . Liz . . .' he was saying.

That is when she slapped him. A full-blooded blow on the side of his face. One of her rings had twisted around and left a long diagonal scratch across his right cheek.

'It's all right for you. You'll spend the whole day drinking. What's in it for me? Eh, what's in it for me? What will I have in common with fishermen's wives?' Fury in her eyes. Anger in her voice. 'Will there be a tennis club? Will they have coffee mornings?'

My father had located the card, lying on the floor not far in front of him. He was steeling himself to stoop and try to pick it up. That's when she pushed him again.

'Get out,' she yelled. 'Go on, get out.'

Another push and he lurched across the room towards the back door. On reaching it he grabbed its handle and yanked the door open. On untangling his feet, one awkward high step took him out of the room.

'Mum, it's his last day. He was bound to get a send-off.'

'I'm sick of the whole business,' and slamming the back door shut, she flounced across the kitchen and stormed into the hall.

I went into the backyard. My father was slumped on the lawn, leaning against the kitchen wall beside the hydrangea. He was crying. The long scratch across his cheek ugly and conspicuous. I had never seen him look so desolate.

'She doesn't understand,' he slurred, 'she doesn't understand.'

'I know,' I said because I knew.

She had complained from the start. She was not happy about the move. The fishermen's wives were not the problem. She was a good mixer. Her friends were drawn from a wide circle. It was not the tennis club either, nor the coffee mornings. He had put their future at risk. That was the nub of it. Put an end to the regular money coming in. Good money too. She feared for the loss of her life style. Or worse, tumbling into debt. He had thrown away their security. That's what frightened her.

She hated his job. Hated him coming home drunk after spending his day entertaining clients. She should be pleased he was out of it. He would lead a healthier life. He will be in the open air all day tending to his boats. But she refused to see that far ahead.

'She doesn't understand, she doesn't understand,' and looking up at me, he said, 'but I love her.'

He looked broken. I felt embarrassed for him. On this what should have been a night of celebration. The first time I pitied him. I never expected to see him in such a woeful state. He surprised me in more ways than one. Throwing away his job to hire out little boats. I knew he liked boats. He'd always had a boat. In Sydney he kept one at the Spit. In Melbourne his boat was moored in a Port Phillip marina. But little boats, I didn't know he liked little boats.

Now I understood his attitude to money. He had always been tight, always mean, as if his wallet was permanently stitched inside a pocket. Extravagance was a sin to him. Some of the things my mother bought made him visibly wince. He used to rush around the house switching off lights. In winter he wouldn't light the fire until it was really cold. Economy, economy. Nothing was too much trouble to save a few pence. He looked for bargains and never bought expensive goods. In his opinion, the top brands preyed on mugs. Suckers, that's what they are. Who are they trying to impress by paying too much for something that's no better than the rest.

My father saved his money. And now he had bought his dream.

He had done well, my father. A country boy who came to the city and showed them how it should be done. In and out of the rat race at the age of forty-seven. He was good at what he did. Once I saw him in action. One hot day I called into a city pub for a lemon squash. My father was standing at the bar with three potential clients. They had enjoyed a liquid lunch and were still at it. I stood just inside the door with my eye on them. Their loud voices carried through an almost empty bar. They hooted and bellowed in feeling the need to laugh out loud. They were having a fine old time. My father leaned between two men and slammed his empty glass on the bar. He then loudly declared:

'Right! Let's get to the guts of the matter.'

A man in his element. Playing the role though three parts drunk. Taking control. Leading them on. Bringing the deal to a close. I had seen enough and left the pub to get a drink at some other place.

Now he looked pitiful. Sprawled on the grass against the wall, his crumpled face stained with tears. The scratch on his cheek, an angry red mark.

'Will you take me to the yacht club?' he said, peering at me through red rimmed eyes.

'Sure, I'll take you.'

Once there he sat at a table, his back against the wall while I went to the bar. There were a few members in. I don't know if they knew my father. They would see the state he was in. Drunk and upset, a scratch on his face. I brought the beers to the table and sat opposite him. Silence now between us as we sipped our beer.

He didn't let me into his life but fed me scraps. As a boy he rode a horse to school, bareback. When his father sold the farm, the family moved to the foot of Billy Goat Hill, where now over the top of it two hundred Japanese soldiers lie in a war cemetery. He could have told me more. I wanted to know.

He was looking at his glass when he spoke.

'I've bought the whole caboodle. The boatshed and a house on the hill overlooking it. It's a good business. I've seen the books. It's a cash business too, a lot of the takings aren't declared. That's the cream on top.'

He took a sip of his beer. 'I'm sure your mother will like it.'

'I'm sure she will too. She just needs to get used to it.'

'There are twenty-three different kinds of fish you can catch in the bay. There are oyster farms. It's a lovely town. I'm sure she'll be happy there.'

'Yep, I reckon she will.'

'There are three clubs – bowling club, golf club and RSL. The golf course is something. On one par three, you tee off over a cove to reach a green on the other side. Kids from the town dive for balls and sell them cheap. Your mother can take up golf. Or bowling . . . or both.'

His voice now perfectly clear. He stared at his glass without lifting it to take another sip.

'She can have a great life there. I'm sure she'll like it.'

'I'm sure she will.'

I felt like the parent, consoling one of my offsprings after the siblings had quarrelled.

'Tourists come in the summer, thousands of them, from Canberra and Sydney mainly. There are guest houses and motels. A camp site. The season goes right through to Easter. We can lock up the business in winter and take trips. Go anywhere we like.'

He talked. I listened.

'I'll set up my short-wave radio. When it's quiet I'll be able to talk to people all over the world. Peace and quiet, an easy life. Doing what I want to do. I can't wait.'

'How many boats are there?'

He looked up from his glass. And blinked as if surprised to see me sitting there.

'Umm, five skiffs - seven motor boats. They're two strokes, one has a cabin.'

'Sounds good,' I said. 'Sounds really good.'

'You betcha. It's going to be great.'

And then for the first time he looked at me properly.

'I don't know what you'll do.'

'I'm coming with you,' I said.

'Good. Alright. You can work in the boatshed during the season. After that, I don't know what work there is. There are trawlers, a tuna canning factory too. I don't know what else.'

'I'm not bothered about work. If there's nothing local in winter I'll go to Canberra to work. Canberra or Sydney, it doesn't matter which.'

I'd been thinking about the move since he broke the news. I was good and ready for it. My early fights had not gone well. All were close affairs. Nerves got the better of me. I was too tense and didn't relax. I waded in throwing leather and didn't punch correctly. I got hit as often as landing a blow. Even dropped a decision. I could do with a fresh start. There was nothing to keep me in Melbourne.

I drank my beer, he stared at his.

An arrangement had been made. A settlement agreed. Things moved quickly after that. The house was sold, furniture shipped.

My father's boat fetched a good price. I didn't tell Janet I was leaving. She deserved better. I should have told her face to face.

My father had gone quiet. My glass was empty, his hardly touched. His eyes had taken on a far-away look.

'Do you want to go?'

He came back from where he had been.

'Yes, let's go home.'

He was pensive in the car. I drove at cruising speed, home just over a mile away. Traffic was light on the Beach Road. We didn't speak. I left him to mull with his thoughts.

My father never took to me. There was something about me he didn't like. Even as a little kid. He was always at me for no good reason. Later I gave him reason. But we were close that night. That night at the yacht club. The night I drove him to Sandringham. That was as close as we ever got.

Once home I went to my room and stayed in there. I don't know what my father did.

88. CANBERRA

Plenty of work in Canberra. So much happening. The city was going ahead at a frenetic rate. Prior to World War Two, Canberra was no bigger than a large country town. In 1961 the National Gallery and National Museum were projects for the future. The High Court did not exist and the basin of Lake Burley Griffin had not yet been dug. No National Carillon. The theatre centre a far off dream and nine years would pass before the James Cook Memorial was installed.

But money was being shovelled into the Capital Territory. Construction was evident everywhere. Houses were being built, offices, government departments and embassies too. People were moving in – politicians and diplomats. Spies took up residence. Menzies was pushing to get Canberra built and though he was its driving force people still called him Pig Iron Bob. The pig iron he sold to Japan was made into bombs and dropped on us.

I shared a room in a boarding house with an older bloke. His feet stank. You need to wash them I said. It makes no difference he replied. I kept the window open and tried to get to sleep before he came into the room. I was working as a brickies' labourer on a construction site.

The gym in Canberra had less facilities than the one in Melbourne. Fewer people were using it. After my first session, the trainer said a troupe from Sydney was due to visit in three weeks' time. He could put me on the bill if I liked.

'Do that,' I said.

I thought of little else for the next three weeks. I was determined to get it right this time. Stay relaxed. Fight like I sparred in the gym or during an exhibition. Show my real potential. When the night arrived, I felt no nerves in the dressing room. I had never been so confident prior to a fight. When gloved up and dancing around the weight of my gloves tugged at muscle on my chest and arms. It felt as if rocks were in in my gloves.

My opponent stood in the ring with his back to me. Looking at his physique brought on the butterflies. His broad shoulders tapered down to a narrow waist. He had travelled almost two hundred miles for this fight. I guessed he must fancy himself.

At the bell my calmness returned and the butterflies stopped fluttering. We circled each other and traded lefts. I knew from the start that my jabs carried more power than his. Our eyes were locked. More lefts, and I jolted back his head. He retreated as I advanced. He was pawing. I crossed over the top of his lead and landed a solid right. Though the punch landed high on his head I knew he felt its impact. We continued feeling each other out, keeping distance between us. Then he took the initiative and came at me, spearing out left jabs. I let him come. I drew him in, backtracking and blocking his leads. On he came, determined now, I could see it in his eyes. I sensed he was about to lead, and as he lunged I slid inside the jab on my left foot, then dragging my right foot forward, I clipped him with a short right hand. The punch was effortless. It travelled merely inches, but all my body weight was behind it plus a turn of the shoulder. His chin and my fist met in a head on collision. He went down like a sack of potatoes. I watched the count being applied from a distant corner. The ref's arm pumped up and down on every number that he called. I wanted him to get up, to get up onto his feet. I was desperate for him to get up. Get up, get up, I urged him. I wanted him to get up so I could knock him down again. My dominance had been short lived. I wanted more of it. He lay motionless. It was clear he wouldn't beat the count. On reaching ten, the ref drew his arms apart and a corner-man rushed into the ring to tend to his fighter.

A wave of exhilaration swept through my body. A mighty surge of emotion. I had never felt anything like it before. Beating your opponent is the aim of every sport and the most emphatic way to win is by a knock out. No other type of victory compares. I raised my arms in triumph and basked in self-earned glory. I always knew it would be like this. I knew it in the brickyard when slamming the rammer down. I knew in the gym when thumping the heavy bag. I knew it when sparring or in an exhibition. I knew it when lying in bed, visualising my moves. There had been doubts and false starts, times when it wasn't happening, but I knew. I always knew.

I continued to fight out of Canberra and surrounding country towns. I put my opponents down. They didn't always stay down. Some got up again. Some stayed on their feet for the entire bout. But I was never at risk and controlled every fight. I could knock men down and knock men out with big cushioned gloves. I imagined what I could do as a pro with gloves almost half the weight. But I never did get to fight as a professional.

My next opponent was known as the Wild Man. I had seen him in action when we fought on the same bill. A real street fighter. Crude and awkward, he waded in throwing punches from all angles. He overwhelmed his opponent. Chased him down and battered him and gave him no respite. I could not wait to meet him. I loved these fighters who rush in. We would see how wild the Wild Man is after he rushes in to meet a short right hand.

The fight was in Canberra. At the bell he raced from his corner just as I knew he would. I threw a left to stop him, to halt him in his tracks. It sailed over his shoulder which surprised me. Then two of his blows thudded home. I tried to get my left hand going. It wasn't working. My timing was out. No zing in my punches. He was all over me, punches landing everywhere. My co-ordination was out of synch. I felt sluggish. Nothing was working properly. The Wild Man was bossing the fight. I couldn't understand why I felt so drained. I was glad to hear the bell at the end of the round.

The next round started like the first. And desperate now I stood my ground and swung away at him. We slugged it out, toe to toe. Neither of us took a backward step. We swung and clubbed and grappled and locked in the centre of the ring. He had succeeded in dragging me down to his level. The fight became an ugly brawl, crude and amateurish. The crowd loved it. I could hear its roar. It went on like that round after round. I swung my gloves like pillows, while all the time the wild man was chucking bombs at me. Haymakers I threw failed to connect. Nothing tires a fighter as much as punching thin air. My arms and legs were heavy. Brain dulled. My lungs were on fire. Between rounds my trainer's words fell on deaf ears. Never at any stage of the fight did I feel in control. At the final bell and standing mid-ring, the ref raised my arm. All I felt was unexpected relief. I didn't celebrate. The wild man's trainer suggested we have a rematch. You bet we should. Next time he would meet the real me and not the imposter he met that night.

Our next fight was at his home town - Binalong. My trainer said this time I would knock him out. That's what he always said. Tactics were not his strong point. I knew what Charlie would have said – keep your left hand in his face and once you've drawn his sting, then go to work on him. That was my plan.

At the bell the wild man danced from his corner and flicked out a left hand. Not what I expected. We exchanged jabs, feinted, circled around and jabbed again. This fight was going to be easier than I originally thought. The wild man could not hope to outbox me. It was too easy, a stroll. I piled on the points round after round. At least that's what I thought. I sleep walked through that fight. I thought I had breezed it, but at the end he got the decision. My trainer was not happy with me and I was annoyed with myself. I should've taken the fight to him when he kept standing off.

At the dressing room door a young boxer stood blocking my way. A kid of twelve or thirteen. He didn't move to let me pass and looking up at me he said:

'I saw you fight in Goulburn. You looked really good.'

Then disappointment in his eyes turned to undisguised disgust and he stepped aside to let me pass. The look from that kid and what he said cut me to the core. I realised I had blown it. Thrown the fight away. I hadn't performed and let myself down. I sat alone in the dressing room feeling really low. My trainer did not come in. We paid each other too much respect, the wild man and me. That was the truth of it. I realised that our first fight was just as hard for him as it had been for me. I wished I had known that before. I would've gone at him from the start. Would've, should've, could've - but didn't. That was the point, I didn't. I underperformed. Didn't turn up. Let myself down. Blew it.

I didn't want to be just another boxer. I wanted to be a champion. A champion would never do what I had just done. I didn't exert myself. Didn't commit. Champions apply themselves. They never slacken. Ron Clarke at high school won every cross-country race with ridiculous ease. Now every time he pulled on his spikes he broke another world record. And I had seen Sid Patterson ride at the Essendon velodrome. World champion at both sprint and pursuit – two conflicting disciplines. A sporting freak, he could produce explosive speed as well as maintaining long term endurance. Champions never underperform. They excel. I no longer considered myself as championship material.

I quit that night. I quit while sitting alone in the dressing room. Threw in the towel. I decided to do what other young men of my age were doing - drink beer and party. It's not against the law to enjoy yourself. And I did enjoy myself.

Years later, a nasty thought occurred to me. Did I quit because deep down I knew I was a coward. I pushed that thought away, but it came back from time to time and niggled me.

89. PARTY NIGHT

During winter, I went to work in Canberra. Rose took a job in Sydney. We didn't keep in touch. It was not that kind of relationship. When back in town at the same time we picked up where we left off. As if we had never been apart. An arrangement that suited both of us. There were no ties or demands - no jealousies. We were free to come and go as we pleased. That was the understanding between us. Perfect, really. We were just having fun.

Rose was not at the party that night and though it was late, I decided to go and fetch her. On pulling up at her house, I saw her bedroom light was on. The rest of the house in darkness. I let myself in through the screen door and padded down the hall. She was sitting up in bed as pretty as a picture, reading a book propped against a tent made by her legs.

'Come on, get up, there's a party down on the surf beach.'

That's when she turned weird.

'Are you mad? You can't just walk into the house and come into my bedroom. My mother is home.'

An angry tone in her voice, a mean look on her face. Which shocked me. There had never been a cross word between us. We had never argued. Never fallen out. I stared at her, open mouthed. I had no idea what brought her outburst on. Then she yelled at me in a fit of rage.

'Get out. Go on get out. Get out, get out - get out.'

I gaped at her, stupefied, as she beat the bed with her hands on either side of her legs.

'Get out. Go on, get out.'

The book she was reading slid off the bed and landed on the floor, closed. It was a thick book. It would take a long time to find the right page. Then she started to grow like a dog – 'grrr, grrr.' Her face all twisted and strained. Not so pretty now. She would die if she could see herself. If only I had a mirror, that's what I was thinking, to let her see how unattractive she looked. Her shouting became louder. I couldn't understand it. I stood there, dumbfounded.

'Get out. Will you do as I say? Go on, get out.'

I wanted to tell her there was a fire. Kingfish were getting barbequed. Prawns were cooking in metal hub caps. There was plenty to drink. It was a good party.

Her shouting might have woken her mother. A consequence lost to her. Her temper overruling her common sense. I stared at her, stunned, rooted to the spot. Her face all distorted. Eyes full of venom. Mouth twisted out of shape, and not only shouting now but flinging her hands at me in trying to shoo me out of the room.

'Get out. Get out. Leave. Will you just leave.'

I left, got out of her room and stomped up the hall. Stopping at her mother's door I put an ear to it. Not a sound from inside. No band of light beneath the door. Onwards I stomped up the hall and on leaving the house, I gave the screen door a good hard slam. Once in my car I revved its engine and spun the back wheels on taking off. I roared towards the camp site, shot past tents and caravans and flew uphill to the main drag. The town was dead. No one about. At the second pub I hung a left to the squeal of rubber. The next bend I took too fast. I was on two wheels then no wheels, flying through the air with the car lying on its side. It surprised me the length of time that I remained airborne. The road ahead looked strange when seen from this perspective. Lamp posts at odd angles, lying across my eye line. The sky off to one side. The car landed on the road with a sickening clash and skidded along to the sound of grinding metal. I imagine it left behind a decent shower of sparks. Then all was quiet. The engine had cut out. I was lying on top of the door. I felt no pain and twisting my body around, I flexed as best as I could. Ran a hand over my head. No blood. I rose from a curled position, stood on the steering column and clambered out of the passenger door. On jumping down to the road, I checked myself for injury. I was fine, not a scratch.

I couldn't say the same for the car. I knew the driver's side would be totally wrecked. The uppermost back wheel was spinning at a furious rate. Still doing forty I reckon.

The porch light of a house came on and a man wearing pyjamas rushed from his front door. A hurricane lamp in one of his hands. As he neared he asked if I was alright. I said I was fine.

'I've rung Bill Dudley,' he said.

'Why did you do that? There was no need. No one is hurt. I wish you hadn't done that.'

'Bill would want to know.'

I told the man he should have checked before he made the call.

'Too late now. Bill is on his way.'

Bill Dudley was the local cop. The only cop. Bill ran a clean town and he had his own way of keeping it clean. I had never heard of anyone having to go to court. I didn't know where the nearest court was - Batemans Bay probably. Anyone who played up spent the night in a lock-up at the back of Bill's house. Next day they worked in his garden. Bill had the prettiest garden in town. All kinds of flowers and shrubs flourished. That was at the front. At the back he grew vegetables. You name it and Bill grew it. Veggies sprouted in neat rows, some propped by stakes, others protected by nets. Jimmy Slater did most of the work. Green fingered Jimmy could not handle drink. Sober he was a lovely man. Drunk, he got obstreperous. Bill and Jimmy gave the gardens quite a lot of thought. Midmorning they discussed their plans while sipping mugs of tea. Jimmy used to get upset at what the other guests had done. Especially the younger guys. Jimmy told Bill to keep them locked up. Don't give them any tools, he said. Look what they've done. Look at the mess.

Other men arrived on the road, all in night attire. The first man informed them that Bill was on his way. They wandered around and looked at my car. Men kept coming. I must have woken half the street. Standing apart from their gaggle, I could hear their comments drifting across to me. None were complimentary. The men lingered. No one returned to their house. They were waiting for Bill.

It was a beautiful night, the sky glittering with stars. I considered a night in the lockup and spending the next day working in Bill's garden. At the back I hoped, amongst the vegetables. Bill duly arrived. He surveyed the scene from inside his car and on getting out, eased the door shut so that it closed with a dull clunk. Then he ambled towards me.

'Hello Bill.' – 'Night Bill.' – 'Get you out of bed, Bill?'

Bill gave the men a wave as he passed. He walked beyond me and hooked a finger. I came to him as beckoned. He watched me approach, giving me the once over.

'You're new in town, aren't you?'

'Pretty new.'

I stood facing him, allowing his eyes to scrutinise me.

'Been drinking?'

'I've had a few.'

He continued to study me. Thumbs stuck in a belt from which a holster and gun hung A big man, Bill Dudley, placid nature, features composed. Happy in his own skin. His voice calm when he spoke.

'I give everybody one chance,' he said in an easy drawl. He didn't have to raise his voice to know that you should listen. 'This is yours. You've had it. Step out of line again and I'll come down on you like a ton of bricks. Understood?'

'Understood.'

'If we get your car back on its wheels, think you can drive it?'

'If it'll drive I can drive it.'

His eyes were fixed on my face. I relaxed and let him read me. He was taking his time about it.

'Right then. Let's see to your car.'

Bill got the men organised. They worked as a team. Pleased to do it. Happy to work for Bill. I wondered if any of them had worked in Bill's garden. They bounced my car back onto its wheels. The driver's side was caved in. An oil slick on the front wheel arch had run from under the bonnet. The driver's door wouldn't open. Jammed solid. I got in through the other door and turned the engine over. It fired, it ran. One headlight was cross eyed, its beam shining across to the opposite side of the road. Bill leaned in through the passenger door.

'Drive real slow. I'll follow you,' and he shut the door.

Slow was the only way it would go. One front wheel was wonky and rubbed against the inside of its wheel arch. Bill crept along behind me as we drove through town. He pulled up beside me at the front of our house and on leaving his car he left its engine running. He approached me and stood very close.

'Now go to bed.'

I will I said and I did.

90. THE ASSESSOR

An insurance assessor called to check the damage to my car. He travelled down from Woolongong. It didn't take him long to reach a conclusion. It's a write off, he said, more or less at first glance. He didn't take the trouble to walk around the car. Nice fella. He and his wife had just taken in their second adopted daughter. He was tickled pink.

'Now we're a proper family,' he said.

As it was time for lunch, he said he would take out a boat and do a bit of fishing. He insisted on paying for boat and bait though he accepted the loan of a hand line. He was not dressed for fishing, but took off his tie and rolled up his sleeves. I told him about a spot up river where flathead like to lie in the mud. He caught one too, a beauty. He also caught two tailor and asked if they were good eating. I said they were oily but I liked them.

'They should be gutted as soon as possible. Here, I'll do it for you.'

I showed him how to clean blood off the fishes' backbone, and I scaled and cleaned the flathead too. I wrapped the fish in pages of the Sydney Morning Herald. He had eaten his sandwiches in the boat and now asked for a bottle of coke. I refused to let him pay for it.

'A cheque will be in the post,' he said.

I intended to buy a car in Sydney when the cheque arrived. There were plenty of car lots in Sydney. Car lots everywhere. So much choice available, and I should get a good deal up there.

Up at the house while eating my lunch I read the morning paper. I spotted an advert for a ship due to sail to Europe later in the year. The S.S. Roma. Tickets were on sale now. I scanned its itinerary - Sydney, Brisbane, Singapore, Bombay, Aden, Suez, Port Said, Valetta, Messina, Naples, and Genoa. It set me thinking. Instead of buying a car, I could buy a ticket on that ship. Worth considering. Why not? When I finished my lunch, I reached for the telephone and dialled. The agent reserved a berth for me and said I could pay when my cheque arrived. Done, that was it, a decision made and acted on. I fetched an atlas from the lounge and traced the route. Searched for the port where the Roma would dock. It lay in the north of the country at the top of Italy's leg, by its left hip. Genoa, where Christopher Columbus was born. A perfect place for me to start my European adventure. Monte Carlo just down the road and further on the French Riviera stretched towards the Spanish border.

After lunch I walked along the jetty with a pump in my hand. Molly Dukes flew overhead while smaller gulls pecked at fish guts I had cleaned earlier. The tuna canning factory lay across the bay to the left. Now rusting and desolate. These days the tuna were frozen there before being hauled to Sydney. No more canning. Local workers proved to be unreliable. Even after their pay was increased. Off to the right of the jetty, our dog raced between the stakes of an oyster farm. He was trying to catch a seagull. The gulls timed his run and flapped their wings and took off as the dog closed in on them. After circling in the sky they settled again on the sand. The dog thought the gulls were teasing him, while all the gulls wanted to do was scratch around in in the wet sand for something to eat.

Further to the right, the bay curved past mangroves and merged with the river that went on to flow beneath the highway bridge, where it crossed a shallow sand bar and ran into the ocean. The mouth of the river lay to the right on the other side of the bay. Behind it a two humped hill dominated the sky line. Just as the Alligator River is full of crocodiles, the early settlers also misnamed Mount Dromedary.

Tourists returned to this resort year after year. They considered it idyllic. I reflected on the scene stretching out before me. Pretty, really pretty. But a decision had been made.

My urge to leave was stronger than an inclination to stay.

Two skiffs and three motor boats were tied to the jetty. They had not been taken out all day. The season was drawing to a close. I wasn't needed here. The old man could manage it by himself. I should leave for Canberra and build a kitty for my trip. Work all the hours I could get. I hopped into a skiff with the pump, and drawing its plunger up and then pushing it down, I named the Roma's ports of call with every gush of water - Sydney ... Brisbane ... Singapore ... Bombay ... Aden ... Suez . . .

I decided to take a bus to Canberra on the very next day. Get a job and start to save. Build a kitty for my trip.

91. TEN DAYS

Ten days before the Roma sailed. Ten days before she slipped her ropes and steamed out of Sydney Cove bound for Genoa. I could hardly bear to wait. Ten days. And then six weeks at sea, crossing the equator to the northern hemisphere and calling on exotic ports, each having its own brand of foreignness. Should I take the tour from Suez to see the pyramids, or sail on through the canal to reach Port Said. No need to decide yet. I can do that later. Then into the Med and Malta, to Sicily and Naples before docking at Genoa where my big adventure would begin. The countries of Europe are interlinked by hundreds of different routes and the tip of Spain to Africa is a stone's throw on the map. I would have to get shipping papers to see the rest of the world. Dutchy had been a sailor. I saw no reason why I couldn't be a sailor too. Ten days. The time couldn't pass quick enough.

Two and half years had passed since my release from jail. The same term as my sentence. What a contrast there was between those two periods. In jail I did nothing, went nowhere. Since being free I had lived in Melbourne, Kalgoorlie, Narooma, Canberra and Sydney. I had boxed in three states plus the Capital Territory. I had had blue collar and white collar jobs, worked on boats and done several stints of manual labour. I had travelled north to Queensland. I went to Western Australia too which was a story all in itself. At Kalgoorlie I worked a shaft by myself in the Great Boulder Gold Mine. Me and my small locomotive, we shifted tons of mullock, from the top of the stoke to the grizzly, where I broke the rocks by swinging a heavy and long handled hammer. I had seen the sun rise from the Pacific and set in the

317

Indian Ocean. All of this a mere prelude to my big adventure. Only ten more days to go.

We were sitting that Saturday morning, Mike and I, on the front veranda of our boarding house. Sited in Bondi Junction, it catered only for male guests. Breakfast and evening meals were served in a dining hall, and a cut lunch could be provided at extra cost. These lodgings were a better standard than other places where I had stayed. I had my own bedroom here.

We were trying to decide what to do that night. Where we might go. We often went to Bondi, or jazz pubs in the Rocks, or sometimes took a ferry across to Manly. We'd have a few beers before going on a hunt for girls. Tom-catting, Mike called it. We were in the mood for something different, though not one of our suggestions appealed to both of us. Ten pin bowling came up as a possibility. That was it, that's what we would do. It was agreed.

I don't know where Mike came from, but he didn't know the eastern suburbs any better than me. We had no idea where the nearest alley might be. I said the only one I knew was at St. Leonards. Mike said that was miles away.

'I know, I know, I'm just saying, it's the only one I know.'

Mike said there must be a closer one at which point Doug piped up. Doug was an older guy, sitting on the veranda steps further along from us. He was sipping beer from a bottle that he swilled around in his hand.

'I'm going past that alley tonight. I can drop you off if you like. I'm going to see a lady friend out at Coal and Candle Creek. If it comes to that, I could pick you up on the way back.'

If we waited by the Speedo sign, Doug would pick us up. Eleven fifteen he said, eleven fifteen to half past. We agreed on the spot. That's what we would do. We would leave with Doug at half past seven.

It suited me to knock round with Mike, living on the cheap. He was always short of cash if not completely broke. Mike had a problem with horses. He also had a problem with dogs, cards, one armed bandits, two-up and pool. When it came to throwing away his money Mike was spoilt for choice. Paid on a Thursday, he settled a few debts on Friday and by Sunday he would be cadging again. He put the bite on me a few times. I told him straight. No good asking me for money, I had debts to pay. The debt was to myself. I owed myself some living after wasting part of my life in jail. The money I saved was for my trip and not to finance his gambling. At Canberra I worked all the hours I could get and banked a decent sum. I came to Sydney to tie loose ends before shipping out, and I took a job behind a counter in Anthony Hordens store. Mike knew I had been in jail but he didn't know I was going abroad. When the time came to leave, I would say I was going down the coast. Which was true. I had to pick up my passport, my ticket and the rest of my stuff.

We left with Doug at half seven. On reaching the alley we found we were evenly matched. Mike wanted to play for a tenner. No way, I said. Okay, a fiver. He'd had a bad day on the horses, I now realised. We'll play for a round of drinks, I said. A pub was next to the alley - a pub on one side and Speedo sign on the other. After the bowling, Mike got in the beers and I bought the next two rounds even though I won the match.

'Mate, I'm flat broke,' he said.

We were under the big Speedo sign at ten past eleven. A quarter past came and went. So did half eleven. At a quarter to twelve we knew that Doug had let us down.

'I'll kick his skinny arse,' Mike said.

Every passing car ignored our attempts to hitch. Wearing only shirts, we were starting to feel the chill on a cool September night.

'We'll have to walk. I haven't got enough for a taxi.'

'To hell with that, it's miles. I'm not walking. We'll hail a cab and do a runner at the other end.'

No, I wouldn't be in that. Mike said I could please myself but that's what he was going to do. Every passing cab he hailed already had a fare. We kept trying to hitch while walking up the slope, hoping someone would give a lift to two young guys at midnight.

On noticing a used car lot on the other side of the road, we ran across to it. A chain running through metal stanchions secured the cars in the lot. All the cars were unlocked. Keys were in their ignitions. We hopped into a Holden for a bit of warmth. I fired its engine and revved it. Mike flipped open the glove box, took out a pair of pliers and slipped them into his pocket. After a few minutes, I cut the engine and we got out of the car. Above us, a window in the wall flew open and a man wearing a singlet leaned out of it.

'What the hell do you think you're doing?'

'Having a look at the FJ,' I shouted back at him, 'I might come on Monday and buy it.'

And laughing we hurdled the chain and walked further up the slope beneath a row of veranda roofs. A stretch of vacant land lay on the other side of the road. Beside it a car had parked with its headlights still switched on. And there in the paddock we saw a woman being chased by a man. She tripped and fell to her knees. The man stood over her and rained punches onto her head. We raced across the road. I got there first, wrapped an arm around his neck and threw him aside. He was a lightweight. I stooped to help the woman get up to her feet, but before I laid a hand on her, she leapt up like a jack in the box and raced away through the grass, waving her hands above her head and screaming hysterically. I chased after her without gaining any ground. If she ran as fast as this before the man would not have caught her.

'Stop,' I yelled, 'you don't have to run. He can't hurt you now. You're safe.'

She was oblivious to my shouts and of me even being there. Racing like a top sprinter, she ran in a line that took her closer to the road. On reaching the road she didn't slow down and ran out onto it. I stopped to watch, fearing for her life. A car coming from the city, braked heavily and skidded. It stopped before reaching her and its rear door flew open. As soon as she leapt into the car, the door slammed shut and the car roared off, heading in the direction that she originally came from. People in the car would assume I was her attacker. Mike and the real culprit were deeper in the paddock and not likely seen from the road. I watched the car round a bend, heading towards Lane Cove.

Tramping back through the grass, I wondered what kind of shoes she wore. Certainly not high heels. Over by a high brick wall only Mike was standing. The abuser still lay on the ground. I could hear Mike's voice carrying across to me.

'Like beating up women do ya? Is that what you like? Eh, eh. Do ya? Is that what ya like? How do you like it, you piece of shit. How do you like it?'

When closer I saw that Mike was giving him short and sharp toes pokes. Technically you would have to say the man on the ground was getting kicked.

'Mike, that's enough.'

The man lay curled on his side, an elbow over his head.

'And you, get up. I've got an idea.'

'You heard what he said. Get up,' and Mike leaned down and hauled the man onto his feet. When upright and swung around, I saw his nose was gripped between Mike's pair of pliers.

'Jesus, Mike.'

When released from the pliers, red abrasions could be seen on either side of his nose. A nick above one eye had wept a drop of blood. His head wobbled around on his neck. His eyes were out of focus. He was drunk, hopelessly drunk. Almost falling over drunk.

'You're lucky we came along. You might've really hurt that lady and then you'd be in trouble. So you can do us a favour and take us across the bridge. Where do you live?'

'Roash Bay.'

'Perfect. You can drop us at Centennial Park,' and looking at his squiffy eyes and how he teetered on his feet, I added, 'but you're too drunk to drive. I'll drive while you try to sober up. That okay with you?'

'I'm driving,' Mike said, and he was off on the toe, heading for the car. I overtook him and claimed the driver's seat. Mike waited for the drunk, and when he arrived, pushed him into the car got in beside him. The drunk squashed between us. I fired the ignition, and ran my hand under the dash and underneath the seat.

'Where's the handbrake on this thing?'

Leaning over me, the drunk pointed down between the edge of the seat and the door. His breath reeked of alcohol.

'Dopey place for a handbrake. What kind of car is this, anyway?'

'A Vash . . . a Vashall,' came out of his mouth, together with a waft of fumes.

'Pommy car,' Mike said.

I released the handbrake, flattened my foot and took it to maximum revs in first before whanging through the gears. We shot up the slope past Falcon Street and roared along the flat before dipping towards North Sydney and the harbour beyond.

'What's your name, pal?' Mike said.

'John . . . my name's John . . . I'm a doctor.' His diction now clear, no sign of a lisp or any trouble finding his words.

'Hear that? He's a doctor.'

John leaned closer to me and muttered, 'your friend is a very rough fellow.'

'You're no pussy cat yourself. Why were you bashing that woman?'

He turned to face the windscreen and gave my question some thought before answering it.

'She's my seck . . . secretary . . . and my fiancé.'

'No kidding? Do you reckon on Monday morning she'll turn in for work?'

No answer this time from Doctor John.

Luna Park came into view. On the far side of the harbour, Darling Island's woolsheds were hidden in the dark. Then on a sweeping left curve we mounted the bridge's approach, and once on it we cruised beneath its majestic arch without having to stop. No toll to pay when travelling south. And taking the Cahill Expressway, we sliced through Woolloomooloo and on Crown Street shot across the junction at William Street. At Oxford I hung a left. Doctor John sat mute as he stared at the road ahead. Mike had gone quiet as well. On reaching Centennial Park, I pulled into the curb.

'You know where we are, John?'

'Yes.'

'You can find Rose Bay from here?'

Yes, the Doctor said. I slid out from behind the wheel while Mike got out from the other side. He came around beside me and said to John through the open door.

'Take it easy, John. Keep this side of the white line and you'll be apples.'

The doctor didn't answer as he shuffled across the seat and grasped the steering wheel.

'Thanks for the ride,' I said.

We watched him drive away, slowly gathering speed and holding a line straight and true. He disappeared going towards the Old South Head Road.

'That worked out pretty good,' I said, after we crossed the road.

'Better that you think.'

The hand Mike extended to me had something clutched in it.

'What's this?'

'Twelve quid, your sharc. I lifted his wallet while you were driving.'

I slapped his hand away. 'You clown, you fucking clown. You know I've been inside for Robbery with Violence. You've bruised his nose with the pliers, nicked his eye with your boot. You've taken money off him.' I was shouting into his face. 'My prints are all over that car.'

I thumped his chest with the flat of my hands and pushed him back a step.

Mike was making a series of err, errr, noises.

'If he goes to the cops, it's five to seven years for me - minimum,' and I thumped his chest again.

Fear now in his eyes. He thought I was going to whack him.

'He won't go to the cops. No way will he go to the cops.'

I couldn't stand to look at his stupid face, and spinning around I walked away. Stunned at how the night turned out.

'Don't be like that. He won't go to the cops.'

I'd heard that before. The exact same words. I'd fallen for it once. Not again, please. I couldn't do jail again. I couldn't. Mike called out to me as I walked away.

'He won't go to the cops. No way will he go to the cops.'

I knew by the distance of his voice that he hadn't moved. Why wouldn't he go to the cops. In the morning he would be sober. He would know he had been robbed. There were marks of assault on his face. Why would he let anyone get away with that. The soles of my feet were slapping the path. Arms swinging like a soldier. Plans were running through my head. I would have to jack in the job. Hitch down the coast in the morning. Couldn't stay there though. Too easy to trace. Get my passport, ticket and stuff and come back up to Sydney. Book into a boarding house under a bodgie name. Pull in my head, lie low - sweat it out. Ten days I was thinking. Ten days were all I needed. Now really alarmed, I began to mutter what was going through my mind.

'Ten days, please . . . that's all I need . . . just give me ten days, please . . . that's all I ask, nothing else . . . all I want is ten days.'

I didn't know who I was talking to but I needed help from someone. My fate was completely out of my hands.

'Ten days, please . . . surely you can give me that . . . It's all I will ever ask . . . I've paid for what I did in the past. Do I have to keep on paying? . . . ten days is all I need . . . please . . . ten days. That's all.'

Later, much later, I used to wonder where and how Doctor John's fiancé ended up that night.

ACKNOWLEDGEMENTS

To Katherine Nelson and Simon Graham Findlay for their collaboration, who were aided by Steve Brady, Margaret Tynan, Stephen Lord, Mark Lowrey, Margaret Craig, Chris Plummer, Lisa Capstick and Gabrielle Hall. Also to Andy Welsh for his creative suggestions.

www.ingramcontent.com/pod-product-compliance
Lightning Source LLC
Chambersburg PA
CBHW052108030426
42335CB00025B/2892